Inequality in the Promised Land

Inequality in the Promised Land

RACE, RESOURCES, AND
SUBURBAN SCHOOLING

R. L'Heureux Lewis-McCoy

STANFORD UNIVERSITY PRESS
STANFORD, CALIFORNIA

Stanford University Press
Stanford, California

Printed in the United States of America on acid-free, archival-quality paper

Library of Congress Cataloging-in-Publication Data

Lewis-McCoy, R. L'Heureux, author.
  Inequality in the promised land : race, resources, and suburban schooling / R. L'Heureux Lewis-McCoy.
     pages   cm
  Includes bibliographical references and index.
  ISBN 978-0-8047-9070-3 (cloth : alk. paper)
  ISBN 978-0-8047-9213-4 (pbk. : alk. paper)
     1. Educational equalization—United States—Case studies. 2. Suburban schools—United States—Case studies. 3. African Americans—Education—Case studies. 4. Minorities—Education—United States—Case studies. 5. Social classes—United States—Case studies. 6. Education—Social aspects—United States—Case studies. I. Title.
  LC213.2.L48 2014
  379.2'6—dc23

                                                          2013047783

ISBN 978-0-8047-9245-5 (electronic)

This book is dedicated to the beautiful families of Rolling Acres
and to the ones who are yet to come.

Contents

Preface

The Promised Land metaphor has a long lineage in narratives about group struggle and hope. Originally a biblical reference to the land of Canaan promised to the descendants of Jacob, the Promised Land represented a new physical space where the old social order would be dissolved and from which opportunity would spring. The Promised Land was geographic, political, and simultaneously corporeal and non-corporeal.

Among black communities, the metaphor of the Promised Land has long signaled a place where the perils of racism were circumscribed and opportunities abounded. For many African-Americans,[1] the Great Migration from the South to the North and Midwest was the pursuit of a dream of a better life for themselves and their children. In 1965, Claude Brown wrote the iconic *Manchild in the Promised Land*, which traced the lives of black youth in New York City who descended from Southern migrants.[2] In Brown's gripping text we learn that hope that was envisioned seldom panned out in the concrete jungles of the North, leaving broken dreams and lives among the shards of glass that littered the urban landscape. The unfulfilled hopes of the urban North soon gave way to dreams of a better life on the suburban frontier. While a number of scholars have explored the suburban experience of black adults, too little scholarship has examined the worlds co-inhabited by adults and children, in and outside of school, and by blacks and whites. This book helps address that lacuna.

The passage of the Civil Rights Act of 1964, greater economic prosperity, and shifts in social policy allowed the African-American middle class to expand. These "new black middle class," as Bart Landry would call them, benefited from comparatively better housing and occupational and educational opportunities than members of the black poor. Still these relative advantages over the black poor did not mean that the black middle class enjoyed the same freedom as the white middle class. Although white suburbanization began in middle of the twentieth century following the end of World War II, black suburbanization began considerably later, with a boom occurring in the late 1960s.[3] Middle-class black families that relocated to the suburbs often landed in predominantly black suburban enclaves, which featured better amenities than central-city neighborhoods; yet middle-class blacks remain segregated from their white middle-class counterparts.[4] In addition, for black families that managed to move into predominantly white suburbs, white out-migration meant these suburbs often "browned" over time, changing their demographics, property values, and amenities.[5] Despite these challenges, many middle-class blacks remained hopeful that suburbia would serve as a buffer for issues of racial discrimination and limited social opportunities. For many families, moving to the suburbs meant starting a better life—particularly when it came to educational and social opportunities for their children. This book explores the outcome of these hopes and the realities faced in a Midwestern suburban school district, which I call Rolling Acres.

Erica Frankenberg identifies six types of suburban school districts: exclusive enclaves, countywide districts, stable mixed-income, inner-ring transitioning, satellite cities, and developing immigration meccas.[6] In her typology, Rolling Acres would be a stable mixed-income suburb because of its increasing student enrollment yet slow racial demographic change. In Rolling Acres Public Schools (RAPS), between 2000 and 2010, the white student population declined approximately 6.5 percent.[7] Over this same period, the black student population remained relatively stable at about 15 percent, and the Latino and Asian population increased by 1.5 percent. Rolling Acres is not a suburb that is only recently experiencing racial/ethnic diversity; like many other suburbs, it simply has not found a way to successfully address educational inequalities. Each year, white students passed state standardized exams at a rate of approximately 25 percent higher than that of their black schoolmates. This gap has both narrowed and widened in the past twenty years.

In this book I concentrate on black and white families because they constituted the largest racial/ethnic groups at the time I began my field research in 2006. The study is designed to capture a range of familial residential and socioeconomic statuses. Some families were new to the district when I began my study, while others had intergenerational roots in the city. Although it is often assumed that suburbs are economically homogeneous, if not simply skewed toward affluence, the families in my study vary greatly along the socioeconomic spectrum. My goal is to give validity to their range of voices, which create a chorus of both advantage and disadvantage.

My goal in this study is to make sense of a suburban educational terrain and illuminate processes and patterns that may prove fruitful for other studies of suburban schools. When I began the study, I was interested in the "peculiar" achievement gap in Rolling Acres Public Schools, but soon learned that most suburban school districts had serious race and social-class-related gaps in educational achievement, and most important (in my opinion), gaps in everyday schooling experiences. Rolling Acres is simply one example in a larger field of suburban education. In this analysis of meaning-making, narratives, and policy, patterns of power and exclusion are brought to the surface that reflect why Rolling Acres, and many districts like it, are still struggling to make education great for all children.

The families of Rolling Acres often shared sensitive information that helped explain their experiences in schools and the city, but did so with the assurance that their privacy would not be compromised. The names of the schools, the district, and the people in this study have been changed, as maintaining a high ethical research standard requires.[8] For some, this anonymity may be a reason to challenge to the validity of some of my claims. And even I sometimes questioned the decision to anonymize my data as I began the study. However, when I began to present my preliminary research findings around the United States, that concern was quelled. In making presentations to audiences I often received responses like, "That's just like this city!" or "That's like where I grew up." These spontaneous comments reminded me that for decades people have been living with suburban school inequality, but seldom has it been studied or richly captured. There are many assumptions about suburban schools (e.g., they are good, have strong teachers, and are bastions of opportunity), but these assumptions cannot substitute for rigorous research. My hope is that this book creates space for more intersectional and nuanced conversations about race, social class, and educational opportunity in non-high-poverty schools.

Acknowledgments

This book may have a single name on its cover, but it is the product of collective labor. First, thank you to the staff at Stanford University Press. Careful reviews and editorial guidance by Frances Malcolm and Kate Wahl immensely improved the final product. In addition, the comments of the anonymous reviewers were both insightful and tremendously edifying. The press's work with this book was smooth, professional, and refreshing.

Second, I would like to thank the families of Rolling Acres for sharing their stories, their time, and parts of their lives with me. Over the course of years, they allowed me to spend hours in their homes, obliged last-minute requests for interviews and follow-ups, and shared honestly their experiences. Although this book provides only a snapshot of individual and collective lives, I hope it serves the project's original intentions and helps pave a more equitable path for future generations of Rolling Acres families.

My desire to write this book came, in part, from my upbringing and school attendance in West Haven and New Haven, Connecticut. The divergent lived experiences of families in a state known for gross affluence are seldom discussed in mainstream media or in everyday conversations. The full cast of "isms"—racism, classism, sexism, and others—operate there but most remain hidden from plain sight. Connecticut is a small state whose population is often perceived as overwhelmingly white. The blue license plates of Connecticut are lined with the words, "The Constitution State." One day as I sat to speak with a reporter from the *Hartford Courant* he noted, "I almost feel like Connecticut's license plates should be changed to say, 'The Apartheid State.'" His interpretation of social distance in Connecticut may have been hyperbolic, but it struck a chord as it encapsulated many of the feelings I had coming of age in the state. Connecticut's inequalities showed me that even in environments with great means, inattention to inequality can lead to pernicious outcomes for those who are unheard and overlooked.

I attended an elite private high school whose student body included only a few students of color and few low-income students. In the first class period of my freshman year, one of my teachers, Bill Ray Johnson González, taught me that questioning the world was not only a right I had, but also necessary for knowledge creation. His unflinching spirit and willingness to speak back to systems of oppression set me on a path to study the world, particularly "the Negro Problem." At Morehouse College I was fortunate to have a set of mentors, Professors Ida Rousseau Mukenge, Obie Clayton, and John Stanfield, who shaped my sociological and Africana imaginations. It was through Professor Daniel Omotosho Black that I encountered the Nation of Ndugu and Nzinga. From the Adebayo to the Chukwuemeka, I have found myself blessed by a community that spans time and place. Words fail to capture my gratitude to this community, which has pressed me to go fast and to travel far, yet remain accountable.

At the University of Michigan, I was surrounded by a bounty of scholars and was introduced to schools of thought that run throughout the pages of this text. At Michigan in the Department of Sociology, Alford Young served and continues to serve as an intellectual mentor. His willingness to entertain absurd questions, half-conceptualized research proposals, and pedagogical mistakes was priceless. His public policy counterpart, David Cohen, repeatedly stressed the need for deeper introspection in my work and pressed me to reconsider the role of resources in the policy process. Whether we met in person or via Skype, he gave my work serious consideration and offered valuable guidance. Carla O'Connor opened her intellectual and personal space for my own scholarly and personal growth. Her steadfast commitment to high-quality research taught me what it means to think creatively about a question, rather than rely on dominant tropes or simply test shallow theory. Tony Chen is a rare breed of scholar who understands the big and small pictures simultaneously. His challenging questions still resonate with me and remind me that a project is never done, but at some point we must just leave the field.

A community of people at Michigan sustained me, and I thank them all (there is no way this list can be exhaustive; for any omissions please charge my head, not my heart). SCOR, SOC, GEO, SSAA, and HEADS all offered me communities that supported activism, reflection, and love of

justice. A few key individuals carried me through the gauntlet and were my brothers in the struggle: Rodney Andrews, Andy Clarno, Alfred DeFreece, Lumas Helaire, Odis Johnson, Jeffrey Page, Thomas Parker, Julio Perez, Fouad Pervez, Mark Kamimura. My sisters in the struggle included Fatima Ashraf, Claire Decouteau, Saida Grundy, Sarah Janel Jackson, Maria Johnson, Janeen Lee, Rosa Peralta, Monica Sosa, Tanya Saunders, Amber Taylor, Salamishah Tillet, Maria Tucker, and Naima Wong. The American Sociological Association Minority Fellowship Program, the Rackham Merit Fellowship Program, the National Poverty Center, and the Ford Foundation Diversity Dissertation Fellowship provided generous financial support for this research in its earlier incarnations. Later support from the PSC CUNY and the CUNY Faculty Fellowship Publication Program was invaluable. There was an army of talented young research assistants who saw this book in many stages to whom I owe tremendous gratitude: Jacob Faber, Ashley Aijeba Hollingshead, Rakim Amalu Jenkins, Evangeleen Pattison, Joslyn Pettway, Reuben Ombeni Quansah, Kate Schuster, Maureen Smith, and Janelle Viera.

The City College of New York and CUNY in general have been great spaces for scholarly and pedagogical growth. The Department of Sociology and the Black Studies Program offer collegial support, warmth, and feedback; in particular, I am grateful to: Gwen Dordick, Gabriel Haslip-Viera, William Helmreich, Jack Levinson, Iris Lopez, Maritsa Poros, and Keith Thompson. Thank you to the staff of the Colin Powell School for Civic and Global Leadership! My New York City scholar/author circle has helped to sharpen and uplift me: Juan Battle, Jessie Daniels, Tara Conley, Jonathan Gray, Christina Greer, Charon Darris, Alondra Nelson, Samuel K. Roberts, Jessica Rodriguez, Carla Shedd, Josef Sorett, Alia Tyner-Mullings, Blanca Vega, and Alex Welcome.

There are few people who spent more time on this text than Leslie Paik and Marc Lamont Hill. To both of you I owe an unquantifiable debt. Leslie, you are an exemplary colleague and an even better friend. Marc, your intellectual honesty and commitment are an inspiration not just to me, but to the world.

My family, both born into and chosen, has wrapped me in love and support as I completed this project and far beyond. To my partner Aisha/Thandiwe, your championing of me is unparalleled. I only pray that I am able to return the support and sacrifice to you in our quest to create a more just world. To my mother and father, you are shining examples of what it means to fight for educational and familial excellence. Words fail to express my eternal debt for your stewardship of the past, present, and future. To my sister Felicia/Nsanzya, 99.95 percent genetic similarity is just the beginning. You have read, talked about, edited, and corrected my book, my life, and my outlook—they do not make big sisters better than you. Last, I am thankful for the ancestors and the Creator who order my steps.

Inequality in the Promised Land

ONE

Welcome to Rolling Acres

Rolling Acres is a promised land.[1] It is a manicured suburb nestled in the midwestern United States that features a well-run and -resourced school district. Rolling Acres is the type of school district that families move to because of its strong reputation for nurturing student learners. In any given year the district receives national academic accolades by graduating National Merit Scholars and extracurricular praise when its bands are invited to perform on the national stage; its schools showcase their ethnic diversity by hosting "International Nights" to which families bring foods from their ancestral homelands. To most eyes, Rolling Acres and its public schools are what many U.S. schools—both urban and suburban—desire to be. However, this is not the full reality of Rolling Acres and its schools.

In the early 2000s, I attended the commencement ceremony at one of the high schools in the Rolling Acres Public Schools (RAPS) district. During the ceremony I heard white families cheering loudly as the college destinations of the graduates were announced from the dais: they ranged from Harvard to Bates to the University of Michigan. These cheers for white graduating seniors at times drowned out the announcements of their black classmates' next steps. Those included local community colleges, work plans, military service, and less-selective colleges. Just as the cheers served to cover up the divergent lives of black and white youth, many of the mechanisms that breed inequality in Rolling Acres remain concealed. Although considerable attention has been paid to gross inequalities between inner-city and suburban schools, too little research has interrogated inequality in suburban areas.[2] As suburban school districts become more racially and economically diverse, understanding how they respond to diverse families is essential to understanding future paths to equality.

Districts like Rolling Acres are consistently confronted with questions such as: How can we provide a quality education to racially and economically diverse families? If we have ample financial resources, why do we still see educational disparities? What programmatic or policy changes will reduce observable disparities in our students' educational experiences? How do differences in family background relate to observed disparities? And how can we respond to demographic changes in ways that accommodate long-time residents and new arrivals? These questions remain inadequately addressed both by current discussions in education policy and by sociological theorizing about educational inequality. With this book I offer some answers based on a careful ethnography of education in a desegregated suburban setting.

Although Rolling Acres contains many of the resources that are typically associated with positive student achievement, these resources seldom trickle down to the district's economic and racial minorities. Through multiple mechanisms (e.g., social networks, school-to-home communication, teacher beliefs, and others) the resources of Rolling Acres are not only funneled away from minorities; they are leveraged by affluent white families to gain greater educational advantages for their children. By building on and challenging past work on educational inequality, I hope to clarify why the presence or availability of resources does not necessarily mean that those resources are accessible to everyone, and why we must look beyond individual or group orientations and instead look at the relations *between* groups and within schools. I explore the micro-level interactions between school staff, teachers, parents, and students and link them to broader macro issues such as racial ideologies and the formation of contemporary equal opportunity policies. The result is an intricate web of relations and dynamics that weaves together race and social class and reproduces disparities in student educational experiences in both subtle and overt ways.

SUBURBAN SCHOOL INEQUALITY

While researchers debate whether resources matter and to what extent they influence school achievement, laypeople are at near consensus that resources matter.[3] Over the past forty years, many African-Americans have migrated to suburban locations with the hope of sending their children to higher-quality schools. Historically, suburban schools have been better resourced than their inner-city peers and have become known for their diverse offerings and college preparatory curriculums. All of these features have made districts like Rolling Acres highly desirable among families who want to give their children an early life advantage. Despite these opportunities, gaining access to the educational resources of a district is not always straightforward, particularly for black families.

In Rolling Acres, different social worlds collide, and the puzzle of educational equality remains unsolved. For decades, Rolling Acres has spent increasing amounts of money in the hope of reducing educational inequality and improving the educational experiences of all families; but there remain seemingly intransigent race and social-class gaps. Although RAPS is a land of plenty, Rolling Acres residents engage in stiff competition to get their children the best teachers, sign them up for extracurricular activities, and glean insider information with the goal of creating an idyllic educational experience for them. On its face, the same resources are readily available to all students, but upon closer examination one sees that access to these resources is not equal, particularly for racial and economic minorities. These differences in resource access are not based simply on disparities in provision; access is influenced by differences in family backgrounds, institutional reception (how schools receive families and their requests), and interactions between families.

To illustrate, imagine that a school's science scores on the state standardized test arrive and the scores of black students are lower than those of white students. While the gap in average scores might not be not surprising, the district notes that the gap between black and white students had declined for nearly ten years, but for the past three years that progress has stalled. There are mounting pressures from local, state, and federal authorities to "close the gap." In response, some proactive school district members propose creating a "Saturday Science Academy" that will target both black and white students, with the goal of raising science scores. It will be an extracurricular program designed to increase access to science and technology and provide hands-on instruction in a small-classroom environment. An announcement about the creation of the Saturday Science Academy is then sent to all families in the target school. Parents are invited to sign up online or to mail program attendance requests back to the school. After the final enrollment is tallied, it is discovered that the enrollees come disproportionately from white families, particularly middle-class and affluent families. This is a common dilemma among schools and districts that have attempted to close achievement gaps, particularly in racially and economically diverse settings. District staffs are often left wondering why and how some families take advantage of the available resources and other families do not.

SOCIAL-CLASS-BASED EXPLANATIONS

Researchers Annette Lareau and John Ogbu have offered two influential theories of processes that influence educational inequality in suburban districts like Rolling Acres; however, I do not believe that either approach adequately explains the processes that occur in such places.[4] Social reproduction theorists such as Lareau may explain the observed disparities in program enrollees as directly tied to social class, particularly the role of cultural capital and the alignment of norms between families and schools. Lareau suggested in *Home Advantage* that differences in parental participation were driven by differences in families' social class.[5] Based on an ethnographic analysis of white families in two predominantly white schools, Lareau applied Pierre Bourdieu's notion of cultural capital and argued that middle-class families possessed cultural repertoires that aligned with the norms of schools and thus contributed to favorable social relations and higher levels of school engagement. This middle-class cultural capital was the foil to low-income and working-class cultural capital, which did not align with school norms and led to tense social relations and low levels of parental engagement at their schools. Lareau's work importantly argues that differences in parental engagement are not based in differences in familial desire; instead they are rooted in mismatches between cultural toolkits and institutional arrangements.

Later, Lareau extended her social-class-based arguments in the now seminal book *Unequal Childhoods*. She continued to examine the role of cultural capital, not only in connection to schools but also in other formal institutions. Based on observations of twelve families—six white, five black, and one interracial—she argues that two coherent patterns of class-based child-rearing strategies were observable: "concerted cultivation" and "natural growth." These two patterns of child rearing, in her view, demonstrate the significance of social class, which she believes eclipses the power of race to explain current and future inequalities between groups. She observed these social-class-based differences at three junctures: the investment of parents in extracurricular activities for youth, parental engagement with school professionals, and communication between parents and children at home.

"Concerted cultivation" is practiced by middle-class families and is often characterized by the enrollment of children in structured extracurricular activities with adult supervision. These organized activities then assist in the development of positive experiences, dispositions, and networks with adult authority figures and formal institutions. In addition, Lareau argues that parents who practice concerted cultivation have generally positive and strong relationships with authority figures and formal institutions.[6] As a result, those parents are able to engage institutions and often achieve their desired results. These socialization experiences serve as fields of learning where their children develop cultural capital that proves to be advantageous in school, at the doctor's office, and in any number of other formal spaces, allowing those with middle-class standing to ultimately replicate or even advance their position.

In contrast, says Lareau, families that practice the "natural growth" method of child rearing are working class or poor and have children who are less engaged in formal extracurricular activities and have less favorable relationships with formal institutions and authority figures. Children reared in this way tend to engage in unstructured play after school and often do not participate in formal organized activities like sports; they thus have fewer opportunities than children reared by concerted cultivation to develop positive rapport with adult authority figures. Lareau also argues that, because parents who practice the natural growth method of child rearing also often do not have positive relations with authority figures, they are likely to socialize their children to replicate a contrarian or non-empowered engagement of authority. As a result, these children and families have fewer positive experiences engaging schools, medical facilities, and other institutions than their concerted cultivation counterparts. Lareau argues that natural growth families thus do not actualize their putative stocks of cultural capital in the form of favorable institutional returns, thus replicating their lower position in the social hierarchy.

If one applies Lareau's theory to the case of the Saturday Science Academy, one might assume those who signed up for the Academy were concerted cultivators, but this would likely not be fully accurate. First, while Lareau's concepts of concerted cultivation and natural growth are parsimonious illustrations of how cultural capital operates, they are dispositional—meaning that people's actions are based on their attitudes and orientations and not necessarily determined by the dynamics of social interaction—and thus overlook the importance of relations between groups. Charles Tilly argues, "Dispositional accounts similarly posit coherent entities—in this case more often individuals than any others—but explain the action of those entities by means of their orientations just before the point of action."[7] While dispositions toward child rearing and institutions matter, interactions with institutions, and between families, are critical to understanding why some families are oversubscribed to the Saturday Academy and others are undersubscribed.

Second, for Lareau's model to account for the observed disparities, race and social class would need to be nearly perfectly correlated. However, this is not the case nationally or in Rolling Acres. The majority of white families are middle class or above, but there are also middle-class black families and working-class white families. It is important to note that Lareau does have black middle-class families in her sample, but these families are drawn from a private school using a snowball sample—a type of sample based on families referring other families—which tends to make responses non-random and representative. As I discuss in chapter 4, this likely misrepresents the role of race and eliminates relational analysis possibilities. The overlap between social-class and racial categories problematizes a parsimonious tale of engagement based simply on social class. The inclusion in her model of black and white middle-class families who send their children to the same schools would help elucidate the tensions in—or limits of—her model in a setting like Rolling Acres.

Third, Lareau underestimates the role of race in her explanations of differences in institutional engagement. She argues that race plays a small secondary role to social class. She writes, "While race did have situational consequences for some youths, the power of social class was striking for all."[8] She categorizes race as situationally relevant and therefore meaningful only in moments of interracial conflict. In further examples in *Unequal Childhoods* and other work, she identifies these moments of situational relevance as occasions when black families perceive racial discrimination.[9] Lareau's constellation does not consider how white families' whiteness serves as an advantage, which makes her identification of race selective and misspecified. Social constructionist perspectives on race have stressed its importance not only for racial minorities but also for racial majorities.[10] Ultimately, Lareau's scholarship and model under-theorize the role of race and over-privilege the role of social class.

RACE-BASED EXPLANATIONS

John Ogbu's Cultural Ecological Model (CEM) is a widely popular explanation for differences in educational engagement and could be applied to the case of the Saturday Science Academy.[11] The CEM was developed from Ogbu's work with Signithia Fordham in a predominantly black high school in Washington, D.C.[12] Ogbu argued that black youth took on an oppositional culture characterized by academic disengagement and heightened attempts to gain peer acceptance. Ogbu would likely explain the lack of black enrollment in the Saturday Science Academy through two mechanisms: perceived barriers to mobility and racial allegiance. Ogbu argues that black children see the race-related barriers that black adults have faced and that these barriers signal to the children that the traditional opportunity system is not open to blacks. In response, youth increase their sense of racial allegiance and solidarity and disengage from school because they identify domains like schooling as a pathway for white mobility, not black mobility. He argues that this cumulatively leads to disengagement from schooling.

In the late 1990s, Ogbu was invited to the suburb of Shaker Heights, Ohio, by concerned black middle-class parents. The parents had observed disparities in their children's treatment at school and academic performance between blacks and whites and enlisted his scholarship to generate answers. The results of his research in Shaker Heights were published posthumously in the book *Black American Students in an Affluent Suburb*,

Ogbu concludes that the CEM, which he originally observed in a segregated poor school, is in operation in the wealthy diverse suburb and that academic disengagement among black students and their families is the reason for black underachievement relative to that of white families. However, in order for the CEM to hold, the black families in suburban areas must convey to their children that the opportunity structure is not open or accessible to blacks. This runs counter to the observed reality in Shaker Heights, as in most suburban areas; the children of the black middle class are, in part, the product of increased educational access.[13] The narrative that education is the domain of whites runs counter to the experience of the students' parents, their friends' parents, and other suburban residents who compose an expanding black middle class.

Black American Students in an Affluent Suburb is a phenomenological study, but it suffers from the lack of a comparison group, which is troubling given that Ogbu is interested in understanding educational disparity. He infers, but fails to demonstrate, that the white families have a greater investment in education, stronger study habits, and more positive schooling experiences than black families in Shaker Heights. Ogbu's work and that of others rely on a deficit model of race, which locates educational failure with blacks only, and does not consider race relations to be an important feature of racial inequality. In this way, he commits a similar error to Lareau, who sees race as meaningful for black families but does not consider how the contrasting relationships between black and white families and schools matter for differences in educational experience.

Neither Lareau nor Ogbu offers a model that can adequately account for the types of unequal suburban educational experiences represented by the Science Academy example. Lareau's emphasis on disposition and overemphasis on social class obscures the ways that race intersects and affects the experiences of both the black middle class and lower-income whites. Ogbu's overemphasis on race relies on phenomenological individualism, which he steeps in assumptions of black deficiency and a monolithic, inescapable group identity, giving little credence to the social-class positions and identities that members of the black middle class have achieved. In both of these scholars' works, the role of race is not portrayed *relationally* because neither one seriously investigates the influence of race on black *and* white families, or how this shapes the educational access of those families. The dilemma of suburban school inequality necessitates a consideration of the intersections of race and social class that looks carefully at the relationships of diverse families in the same space and how they jockey for, and ultimately stratify, educational resources. In the next section, I propose and describe such a model that responds to the analytic/theoretical challenge of explaining unequal outcomes among presumptively equal families.

THE MISSING LINK—RELATIONAL RESOURCE ANALYSIS

In this book I offer a relational resource analysis model for studying suburban education. My analytic framework draws heavily from Charles Tilly's work on categorical inequality. Tilly described the project of relational analysis in the following way:

> Relational analysts characteristically conceive of culture as shared understandings that intertwine closely with social relations, serving as their tools and constraints instead of constituting an autonomous sphere. Strongly relational analysis remains a minority movement in social science as a whole; individualisms and holisms continue to reign. In the choice between essences and bonds, nevertheless, I want to hold high the banner of bonds. I claim that an account of how transactions clump into social ties, social ties concatenate into networks, and existing networks constrain solutions of organizational problems clarifies the creation, maintenance, and change of categorical inequality.[14]

In my work I accept this challenge of relational analysis by using ethnographic data to look carefully at the role of bonds and how everyday processes over time lead to palpable categorical inequality. The shared meanings between black and white residents, as well as competition between them for valued educational resources, provide fertile ground for locating levers of change. It is important to note that my work not only extends Tilly's, but also challenges aspects of his arguments in several ways.

First, I argue that ideology and structural features are equally important mechanisms for perpetuating inequality between groups and over time. Tilly's commitment to explicating structural mechanisms ultimately gives short shrift to the role of ideology, particularly achievement ideology and racial ideology. Tilly argues that ideology plays a secondary role to structure: "Feelings of identity, on one side, and intergroup hostility, on the other, may well accompany, promote, or result from the use of categorical differences to solve organizational problems. But the relative prevalence of such attitudes plays a secondary part in inequality's extent and form."[15] I disagree. I believe that ideology necessarily operates in the service of categorical inequality and is not oppositional to relational analysis. Instead, when considered—often on equal terms—it only further highlights the critical need to examine the nexus between belief, policy, and praxis. For example, in chapters 2, 5, and 6, I discuss the role of colorblind racial ideology in shaping education policy, everyday (mis)understandings of the role of race in Rolling Acres, and how race talk and silence shape social and academic experiences.

Second, this book advances the method of using naturally occurring samples to conduct relational analyses within education. Influenced by ecological considerations of schooling, I draw the empirical data here mainly from three fourth-grade classrooms in two schools and examine how the actions of individuals and groups affect others in the same classroom or school. As noted previously, studies emphasizing parents' or children's dispositions and phenomenological individualism have come to dominate qualitative studies of educational inequality. With this small-scale study, my goal is not to generate grand generalizations; rather it is to capture the processes at play in Rolling Acres that can potentially shed insight on mechanisms operating in other classrooms, schools, and districts in similar predicaments.

The application of a relational resource perspective to the example of the Saturday Science Academy uncovers a more complete reckoning of how race and social class simultaneously influence the pathways of resources. To better understand these resource pathways, I employ Tilly's concept of opportunity hoarding. In *Durable Inequality*, Tilly argues that opportunity hoarding "operates when members of a categorically bounded network acquire access to a resource that is valuable, renewable, subject to monopoly, supportive of network activities, and enhanced by the network's modus operandi."[16] In Rolling Acres, the race and class categories that families belonged to were meaningful for shaping access to education-related resources like information, proposed policy changes, and influence, as evidenced by the schools' accommodation of parents' requests. I argue that, via subtle and overt processes, the educational resources that were provided in Rolling Acres were often hoarded by the privileged, and made inaccessible to the families that most needed them.

In looking at the path of resources relationally, I identify three key junctures: resource provision, resource valuation, and resource uptake. Consider again the aforementioned example of the Saturday Science Academy. Funding for this resource was provided by the district and was originally intended to reduce the racial gap in exposure to a science curriculum and ultimately in science test scores. However, it is important to note that the Academy was offered to all families in order to comply with race-neutral civil rights laws, which no longer allow race-considerate policies. Districts like Rolling Acres are often able to locate money for programming, but how those programs are implemented is subject to local, state, and national constraints. Their implementation often betrays or compromises the original intentions of the programs and provides limited traction for redressing educational inequality. In chapter 2, I explore how such equal opportunity programming emerges as a product of the national policy environment, local legacies of racial discrimination, and aggressive lobbying from select residents.

Once a resource has been provided, a critical question is, "Do all families understand the value of that resource in the same way?" I would argue that the answer is no and that considering how differing individuals and groups understand the value of resources is critically important. Resource value involves an individual or a group's perception of a resource's worth for a desired outcome. Importantly, this not a binary distinction (i.e., valued, not valued), instead one must consider how social position and past experiences shape a resource's perceived value. While attending the Academy may provide benefit to children who enroll, it does not necessarily follow that those benefits will translate to immediate educational performance returns. Because families have differing levels of interest, time to dedicate, and past educational experiences, it should not be assumed that all families view a resource in a similar fashion. In Rolling Acres, minority families, including middle-class ones, routinely expressed concern that they had too little time to read through the voluminous school mailings and often considered extracurricular activities to be optional rather than educationally supplemental. In contrast, among white middle-class and affluent families, stay-at-home mothers often scoured the mailings for extracurricular activities and placed a premium on enrolling their children. The differences in financial, cultural, and social capital when coupled with limited resources (such as the number of spaces in the Academy) shape who considers the resource meaningful and/or valuable. In chapters 3, 4, and 6, I further investigate how differences in family background, neighborhood, and the meanings of race serve to structure opportunities between groups.

The third critical juncture of resource utilization taps into an individual or group's ability to partake in the sustained use of a resource to achieve a desired outcome. Engaging a resource necessitates financial as well as cultural capital. For example, if the Science Academy is offered on Saturdays, providing transportation will often fall to individual families. Although publicly funded buses run during the school day, even after-school programming often requires individual families to transport their children between home and school. The costs of owning a car, fuel, and maintenance are significant, and while public transportation may be an option, it is also a time-consuming one: travel to and from school can take up to two hours round trip. For families with few economic resources, enrolling their children in extracurricular activities can be financially costly and time intensive, factors that often influence the uptake of these resources.[17] Middle-class and affluent families often have more financial resources, making car ownership more likely and transportation less of a barrier to participation. In chapter 4, I present a case study of how affluent and middle-class white families hoard opportunities such as critical information and how black families across class categories experience race-related barriers to parental engagement. In chapter 7, I examine the choice of black families to opt out of Rolling Acres Public Schools and send their children to schools of choice; many of them said that the uptake of resources was easier outside of RAPS.

In sum, we must look carefully at the relationships between black and white families as well as intersecting social-class positions to observe the subtle stratification of educational resources. To date, dominant theories of inequality and schooling such as the Cultural Ecological Model and Concerted Cultivation/Natural Growth have failed to deliver truly intersectional analyses that can adequately explain why districts like Rolling Acres suffer enduring educational inequality despite ample resources. Without considering how a resource is provided and valued, how people gain access to and use it, analyses will misidentify the mechanisms that lead to unequal schooling.

A relational resource perspective looks at the relations between groups, not simply dispositional orientations or phenomenological individualism, in order to form a comprehensive portrait of how individual actions and social ties aggregate to group interests and networks, ultimately leading to phenomena like the achievement gap. In the following section I explain some central concepts that undergird this book's analysis to orient the reader for later discussions.

RETHINKING RESOURCES

The bulk of contemporary work on educational inequality has been framed around disparities in the furnishing of material resources (e.g., per pupil expenditures, classroom size). These discussions, in large part, emerge from the legacy of *Brown v. Board of Education I* (1954) and *Brown v. Board of Education II* (1955). The words of Justice Earl Warren, "separate facilities are inherently unequal facilities," set in motion a national movement toward equalizing access to educational facilities. Implicit in the argument of the cases was an assumption that unequal facilities contributed greatly to the observable educational disparities between white and black citizens. This assumption was more explicitly tested by James Coleman and colleagues in a report commonly referred to as the Coleman Report and further explored by Christopher Jencks and team in the book *Inequality*.[18] Both studies found that family background was more influential on student achievement than material resources such as school size or expenditures. This finding was largely counterintuitive given that the differences in school facilities were thought to be very influential in the educational racial disparities discussed in the *Brown* decisions. As a result, interventions in schools were curtailed and more discussions of family background emerged. Coupled with resistance to desegregation efforts, schools resegregated and funding disparities reentered the policy debate about educational opportunity.[19]

Contemporary discussions of educational inequality have assumed that racially separate schools offer different access to quantifiable material resources and thus lead to educational gaps; but this is not the case for a growing number of suburban schools where, although children of fast-food workers and doctors share classroom seats, inequality persists. This book examines less easily quantified, but I would argue equally valuable, resources in an affluent school district.

Throughout the book I examine the role of less formally recognized resources that are provided by local school systems—including equity policy, extracurricular access, information, race talk, culture, and the ability to customize education—and their implications for educational inequality. Although each of these aforementioned resources may not be easily quantified, their availability and subsequent manipulation make them the object of competition and subject to monopoly. Both these difficult-to-quantify resources and the material resources documented in quantitative studies on student achievement are useful for determining the degree of disparities between districts and states; and both are critical for shaping inequality within educational settings.

It is important to note that the competition for and attempted monopolization of resources are tied to differences in family background, as well as institutional reception. Within Rolling Acres, white families routinely took on a concerted cultivation orientation and then were extended latitude by schools, which assessed their presence as more valuable than that of black residents. As a result, white families were better able to exploit social networks and institutional relationships to create educational experiences that benefited their children, but their decisions often had collateral consequences for the children of black families enrolled in the same schools.

THE STUDY

Gaining access to and understanding the lives of black and white families is a difficult task. The data in this book are compiled from over 100 in-depth interviews with parents, children, teachers, community members, and school administrators. In particular, I observed fourth-grade classrooms in two public elementary schools, River Elementary and Cherry Elementary, and observed and interviewed the families whose children were enrolled in them, as well as the schools' administrators and teachers. At River Elementary, which served approximately 350 students, the classrooms of Mr. Marks and Ms. Reno were my study sites. During the 2005–2006 academic year, the school's student body was approximately 45 percent white, 7 percent Latino, 23 percent black, 11 percent Asian, and 8 percent multiracial. At Cherry Elementary, which served nearly 500 hundred students, Ms. Jackson's classroom was my study site. During the 2005–2006 academic year, the school's student body was approximately 54 percent white, 1 percent Latino, 8 percent black, 30 percent Asian, and 7 percent multiracial. The Rolling Acres Public School system served nearly 18,000 students and expended more than $10,000 per student. White students constituted the largest racial group at 50 percent, and black students followed at 15 percent; 20 percent of students received free or reduced-price lunch. These percentages provide a cursory portrait of who attended the schools of study, but they tell us little about the lives of individual families. For this reason, I used multiple forms of qualitative inquiry—particularly in-depth interviews—to uncover the processes at play within schools and homes in Rolling Acres.

I interviewed, students, parents, teachers, support staff, principals, and educational advocates with the hope of hearing what mattered for education and social relationships in what was viewed by many as a suburban oasis. I had my own suspicions about why Rolling Acres schools remained so unequal, but as it turned out, my perspective was not always shared or right. I began by interviewing families in three classrooms—two in River Elementary and one in Cherry Elementary—but soon I realized they did not provide access to a significant portion of the Rolling Acres population in which I was also interested: affluent black families that opted to send their children to schools of choice—private, religious, and charter schools. So I added interviews with those families to my sample. In total, I interviewed and observed forty-one families in Rolling Acres over the course of four years. In addition, I hung out with and observed a subset of boys, both black and white, as they attended extracurricular activities and elsewhere in their out-of-school lives.

In talking with and observing community members, I was forced to widen my thinking and methodological approach. I delved into the city's historical and cultural archives by exploring newspapers, magazines, and websites. Each publication and opinion showed the diversity of thought and the stakes tied to schools. Each decade's records demonstrated that all Rolling Acres residents believed education was important, but few agreed on the best methods for producing an education that benefited everyone. The vigor with which differing factions fought over education demonstrated that it is one of the most politically contentious arenas both in Rolling Acres and nationally. All stakeholders believed that their actions were in the best interest of their constituents, which meant that each move by a school board or parents' group was scrutinized, rebuffed, and revisited in public debate. While the city's promotional materials painted the picture of a utopia, its archives revealed deep racial and class fault lines that were established in the past and still divided the present. This book begins to unpack the contentious yet critical issue of educational opportunity in a space that has been too long overlooked by social science scholars and offers recommendations for addressing inequities.

RACE AND SOCIAL CLASS

Both social class and race are key considerations in this discussion of educational inequality. Although there are many ways to classify race and social class in this study of Rolling Acres, I employ a relational perspective. Rolling Acres is a city where the largest racial groups are still white and black, and while the city and school district have continued to diversify ethnically, race is still thought of largely in a binary fashion. I attempt to remain sensitive to the multiple levels of racial meaning throughout this book, and in chapter 5 I further discuss the contested significance of race, not simply racial labels.

In RAPS schools, teachers spoke about students as black or white and rarely used the labels "biracial," "multiracial," or "mixed." This was particularly meaningful for multiracial families, who were often pushed across the racial line into black or white classifications. Racial assignment typically followed the one-drop rule of hypo-descent, with multiracial children who had a black parent being identified as black. However, this was not always the case. For example, when I sat down with Ms. Thomas, a white mother in my sample, she identified her son Matt as biracial, while Matt's teacher identified him as white and Matt identified himself as white. As I watched interactions in classrooms, on the playground and in neighborhoods, I came to understand that each child's racial identification deeply affected his or her schooling and social world.

For these reasons I have analyzed the data predominantly along black-white racial lines, paying particular attention to when the experiences of multiracial students or families diverged from those of families that identified as black or white. The ability to draw distinct racial lines was less difficult than drawing social-class categories within the text. While I do not necessarily think the category of race is less socially meaningful or complex than social class, there are few agreed upon measures of social class, and because income and wealth distributions are unequal along racial lines, the definition of middle class is not the same for white and black populations.

In the suburb of Rolling Acres, the most contested category was "middle class." In 2007, white households had a median income of $53,714; black households had a median income of $31,100.[20] Income disparities are only the tip of the iceberg. Scholars have found that there are even greater disparities in wealth than in income, and this is particularly important if it is true that wealth is a better predictor of educational achievement than income, as some have argued.[21] For purposes of parsimony, here I have followed the approach of scholars of the (black) middle class like Mary Pattillo, who uses two times the poverty line as the lower bound for middle-class status.[22] When I collected my data, this meant that families whose annual income exceeded $40,000 were considered middle class. In addition, I considered families in which at least one parent had a college education or above and worked in a white-collar profession to be middle class.[23]

However, none of these individual indicators can truly capture social class. I agree with John Jackson's assessment that "It is not just education or occupation, income or wealth but lifestyles—skills and cultural practices—that distinguish and determine classes."[24] The complexity of social class and its influence are seen in the divergent experience, desires, and reception within the schools of Rolling Acres. Race and class were entangled and often conflated in troubling ways. For example, black middle-class families often found their middle-class status under challenge, both subtly and explicitly. Ms. Towles, an African-American mother, recounted a story to me about her son Jeffrey and how peculiar she found it that he had suddenly stopped eating breakfast at home. When she prepared him breakfast he refused it. Perplexed, Ms. Towles asked him why, and Jeffrey replied, "I got it at school." Ms. Towles was surprised because she had not given Jeffrey money to buy breakfast. When she asked him how he received breakfast, he responded, "Well, they tell all the black kids to go down to the cafeteria to get it before school starts." Both astonished and concerned, Ms. Towles instructed her son to stop accepting the free breakfast and took the opportunity to talk to him about social class and perceptions of black wealth. In this case Jeffrey was casually "misidentified" as a student who should receive a free or reduced-price meal, which may appear benign (because he received a good, in this case, and was not barred from receiving a good), but it signals a deeper set of issues and troubled relationships between school staff and families and demonstrates the permanence of race and class in structuring everyday life.

CONCLUSION

Within Rolling Acres, black families' experiences were significantly different from those of their white counterparts. While black families were often saddled with disadvantage on the opposite side of a racial line, white families enjoyed great levels of privilege. Past scholarship has suggested that race is not at the root of disparities or proffered social-class differences or black cultural dysfunction; but none of these explanations adequately explains what happens in Rolling Acres schools. A relational exploration and understanding of the mechanisms and processes that embed inequality is necessary in order to devise viable solutions.

This book analyzes relationships between families and those families' relationships to schools, because in these bonds inequalities are bred. Through a careful ethnography of suburban school inequality, I offer some conclusions about the importance of considering how groups are defined, how resources are hoarded, and whose voices animate policy. This book is not simply about what it means to be black or white in suburban schools; rather it is about how being white provides unearned and pervasive advantages that, in implicit and explicit ways, constrain the ability of black families to harvest the fruits of the suburban frontier. It is also about the voiced and unvoiced needs of black families that go untended and that have left the promises of the Promised Land unfulfilled. Until these relationships are disentangled, traction on the path to equity will remain difficult to achieve.

TWO

From Concerted Cultivation to Opportunity Hoarding

> Yeah you know, a couple of years ago the [achieve-
> ment] gap was all the rage. What are we going to do
> about the gap? The Gap Initiative, blah, blah, blah,
> nothing happened. Nothing has changed! There was
> a lot of talk. I believe there [was] money thrown here
> and there, but nothing substantial happened. I feel like
> we are right where we started. I don't think they have
> done anything different to try to close the gap.
>
> —MS. TOWLES, *AFRICAN-AMERICAN*
> *PARENT, RIVER ELEMENTARY*

Ms. Towles was not alone in her cynicism about progress on closing the achievement gap between black and white students. Ms. Towles was used to rhetoric about the achievement gap, and she was not convinced that Rolling Acres Public Schools or its residents were ready to deal with racial inequality.

Discussion of educational inequality and proposed policies for elimi-nating unequal treatment of students had spanned nearly four decades by the time I arrived in Rolling Acres. Over those years, the conversations between residents and elected officials were constant and took multiple forms. In the 1970s the conversation was about educational access for poor black students; in the 1980s the conversation shifted to school desegrega-tion; and in the 1990s the district proposed programs to deal directly with the academic plight of African-American students. In the early 2000s the discourse shifted to discussions of the achievement gap. Districts instituted policies that were no longer race-based; instead they embraced a race-neu-tral policy frame. These changes in policy and underlying shifts in ideology did not occur in a vacuum; instead they were strongly influenced by local residents, particularly middle-class and affluent white families.

In this chapter I explore this process with the goal of elucidating how unequal access to the policymaking process has impeded progress toward educational inequality. I respond to three overarching questions: How do districts decide what policies will help achieve equity? How do national discourse and racial ideologies influence policy construction? What roles can families play in setting formal policies? I address these questions by analyzing four policy interventions: the redistricting plans of 1985 and 1997 and the achievement gap initiatives of 1997 and 2004. By revisiting these policy moments we will obtain a greater understanding of Ms. Towles's and others residents' cynicism about rectifying the gap and greater clarity about how local lobbying can bias educational opportunities in favor of white residents.

EARLY HISTORY OF RACE CONSIDERATION

Rolling Acres' racial diversity is not new. Archival evidence shows that black and white residents attended the same schools throughout the 1950s until a neighborhood school system was implemented. Because black and white families were residentially segregated, the district's move from open enrollment to neighborhood schools concentrated black families in a handful of schools.[1] Since the 1970s, black students in Rolling Acres Public Schools have constituted 13 to 17 percent of the student body.[2] This sizable black population means that Rolling Acres Public Schools are not strangers to the challenges of demographic diversity. While such a large minority population is uncharacteristic of many suburban areas, it is important to note that schools and residents have not managed to educate all students equally. In the 1960s a district-wide commission found that black students who attended schools with majority-black student bodies performed less well than black students who attended schools with majority-white student bodies. The commission's findings set in motion a limited conversation about racial inequality and school segregation, but actions to remedy these inequalities were few and limited in reach. By the early 1970s at the elementary school level, black students were concentrated in three of the district's more than twenty-five schools.

The segregation that was observed at the school level was directly tied to residential segregation patterns. African-Americans had greater access to Rolling Acres than other blacks did in comparable suburbs in the state, but their ability to locate freely within the city was curtailed. Because the bulk of black families lived in the western and southern sections of the city—where public housing was also sited—the three elementary schools there were more than 40 percent black. This racial imbalance led to multiple public debates about how to remedy de facto racial segregation in schools.

These tensions came to a head in the mid-1970s, when African-American residents in a local public housing development sued the district for providing inadequate educational programming. Although the district maintained that it was nondiscriminatory and provided an equal education to all children, a court found that the programming was inadequate for children from racially and economically disadvantaged backgrounds. But that decision did little to disrupt segregation between residents and schools; instead the court demanded that the district increase its efforts to provide greater educational access to poor black students. This case book-ended ongoing local conversations about school racial (im)balance and what roles RAPS should play in fighting inequality between students and between schools.

As the district moved into the 1980s, it continued to observe quantitative and qualitative differences in the experiences between black and white student across primary and secondary schooling, and there was increasing pressure from national and local advocacy groups demanding change. This pressure resulted in tensions that played out in a series of citywide public conversations, policy recommendations, and contestation by residents that reshaped policy.

CONCERTED CULTIVATION
AND OPPORTUNITY HOARDING

In Rolling Acres, public schools function with relative autonomy, unlike in larger urban areas where the city often has majority control over school governance. Because of the size of the city and the school district, the wills and concerns of community members dynamically refashioned academic policies to correspond to local desires. Local control is often idealized in discussions of education policy, but it can create considerable hazards when there are inequities embedded in stakeholders' influence and desires.

To examine disparities in the stakeholder policy, I draw from and extend Annette Lareau's notion of concerted cultivation, with particular attention to its "dark side." Lareau argues that concerted cultivation enhances institutional relationships between children and adults, as well as between formal institutions and the home front. However, Lareau identifies a number of drawbacks to concerted cultivations. For example, she writes:

> The latter [middle class concerted cultivation users] routinely intervene in schooling, requesting that teachers "round up" their children's grades or demanding that their children, despite failing to meet the qualifying criteria, be placed in a gifted program, or threatening legal action if educators appear hesitant to comply with these or other demands.[3]

Although Lareau accurately captures how the concerted cultivators make unreasonable demands on local teachers, she fails to see the potential larger consequences of such actions. Changing grades and moving children into classes they have not qualified for exacerbates disparities and potentially sends a message to other families to act similarly. The practice of concerted cultivation also does not simply influence a family or group's own children; it has collateral effects on resources that are finite.

Within Rolling Acres, some middle-class and affluent white families practiced a form of concerted cultivation that did not stop at structuring their children's lives, but extended to cultivating district staff and policymakers. At the school level, teachers were encouraged to change decisions and policies for the benefit of individual children, and at the district level parents attempted to shift district-wide policies; they were often successful in doing so on a range of issues, from impeding desegregation plans to blocking financial resources targeted at poor and black families. Not all white families practiced this form of concerted cultivation; however, I argue all white families benefited from it as their children received more resources or non-white families were deprived of them.

In all policymaking environments stakeholders hold different levels of influence and use diverse tactics to shape policy formation. Among parents in Rolling Acres, one group of parents was particularly successful at intervening in the policy process. These stakeholders received the most attention from city and district staff, and for this reason I refer to them as "squeaky wheels" (drawn, of course, from the adage that says the wheel that makes the most noise will receive the most attention). Squeaky-wheel families were not simply influential because of their disposition (e.g., concerted cultivation); they carried sway because the school district viewed them as desirable. As the white population declined over time and the district diversified, the premium on retaining middle-class and affluent whites increased.

It was the intersection of their vocal activism and the district administrators' perception that their presence was essential for district success that placed them in an ideal position to be heard. When the concerns of the squeaky wheels were listened to, other communities, particularly low-income African-American residents, were denied access to the decision-makers' ears. The district's decision to listen to a vocal minority of affluent white residents shaped the policies that were prescribed and ultimately implemented, thus allowing the white families to hoard the best education-related resources.

THE POLITICAL LANDSCAPE OF RAPS

Policies related to educational equity are not conceived, implemented, or evaluated in a vacuum. How policies come about is as important as the policies themselves. As a policy is conceived, it must be matched to economic demands and travel a gauntlet of interested actors who routinely attempt to refashion it according to their own preferences.

We should remember that the Rolling Acres school system is regarded as a successful one. The underperformance of black students is thus viewed as anomalous by many white residents. When I interviewed families about the educational inequality in their schools, parents often expressed bewilderment about race-related disparities and sometimes referred to a single African-American family or student that they knew who was achieving well to provide a counter-narrative. By pointing to these exceptional students and families, individuals played down the role of racism, but these counter-examples did not reflect the larger achievement trends in the district.

Families were often unaware of the degree of inequality that persisted in RAPS or were unwilling to advocate for school-related race-targeted interventions to combat the achievement gap. For example, Ms. Cooper, a white parent at River Elementary, blamed the gap on the home lives of black children, not on structural matters (i.e., segregation, teacher attitudes, or differential treatment). The attention being given to the achievement gap—study of the gap, policy debates, and the like—did not sit well with her. She stated:

> It is great all the studies [on the achievement gap] and everything, but go to the Rolling Acres Public Library at story time when your kids are little, it's free. Totally free! It's wonderful, [they have] music, stories, and there are no black kids there. The housing project is within walking distance. It is a shame. It's free. You know what I mean. But [it is] something in their background, and I totally understand it.

Ms. Cooper voiced a common view among white families in Rolling Acres: racial educational inequality was not the fault of anyone other than the black families themselves, whose family backgrounds and practices were barriers to educational success. Public discourse on the gap was seen as pervasive, but unnecessary for resolving educational issues. Ms. Cooper informed me that a number of families she knew were also concerned about actions the district might take to abate educational inequality and had written letters to the school board and local paper.

I believe that the small size of Rolling Acres allowed some families—affluent and middle-class whites and middle-class blacks—to have immediate and often the most significant influence on the policy formation process. Figure I shows the formal and informal political landscape of public schooling in Rolling Acres as a hierarchy of influence.[4] While there are district guidelines on the flow of power, I found that informal lobbying by ad hoc organizations and families under the right conditions could become formal lobbying, which then altered policies and their influence. The informal-turned-formal lobbying reflexively affected equity efforts in all four of the case studies discussed in this chapter. Organizations and individuals towards the top of the diagram hold more power, and those next to each other have relatively equal influence. At the bottom, students were the target of equity policies but had little influence on the policies adopted by the district. Even within larger groups, such as parents, there were varying degrees of influence. Middle-class black parents had greater influence on equity policies than low-income white families did. While black middle-class influence on policy was greater than that of poor whites, the collateral benefits of policies accrued more easily to poor whites.

The school board is the body responsible for representing the interests of the Rolling Acres residents and the implementation of policy. School board elections occur annually, and each elected member serves a four-year term.

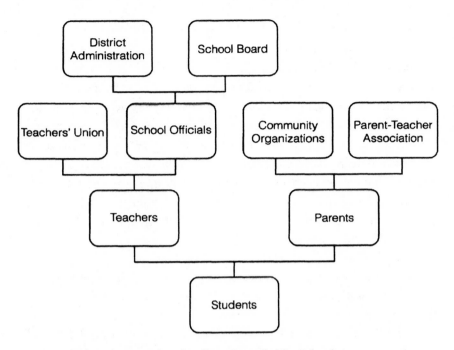

Figure 1. Political Hierarchy of Rolling Acres Public Schools

Unlike in large urban districts, there are no smaller local school councils. The district administration includes the superintendent, deputy superintendent, and at times an appointed Achievement Gap Administrator (AGA). Collectively they are responsible for operating in the interest of the school system and are held accountable by the school board. The school board and the superintendent's priorities may align, but they do not always, so they sometimes operate in a "checks and balances" fashion.

One level down, the teachers' union is the formal body responsible for representing the voices of teachers collectively. School officials represent the interests of groups such as building administrators and committees created by the district to address special sets of issues. Community organizations both ad hoc and established (e.g., grassroots parental advocacy groups, the NAACP) have a similar influence on policies as the teachers' union. The Parent-Teacher Association (PTA) is the formal organization that is designed to represent the interests of parents to the local school administration.

Just below the union, community organizations, and the PTA, teachers are the street-level bureaucrats of the RAPS system. The interests of individual teachers often differ from those of the union, though they are responsible for implementing policies established at higher levels of governance. Teachers have a great deal of autonomy in making classroom-level decisions. In Rolling Acres, teachers and parents respond individually and collectively to policy changes. Parents remain powerful because they have the freedom to voice their concerns to administrators or exit the school system when they are dissatisfied and enroll their children in schools that better meet their children's needs.[5] Students occupy the lowest level because they have little influence on policy as it is defined within the district, though they are the subjects of most policies. Figure 1 shows the relations between these groups as a hierarchy, but they are dynamic and do not always operate in a top-down fashion. Policies may be drafted at the top; but they are then challenged, rearticulated, and influenced by those on the lower levels.

Because school district decisions are widely covered by the local media, families, with and without children enrolled in RAPS, are engaged in school system debates around policies. On equity issues in RAPS, individual groups leveraged their power uniquely. For example, affluent white parents who disliked a policy dangled the option of leaving RAPS and enrolling in private schools or moving to other school districts to encourage building administrators to yield to their desires (discussed at greater length in chapter 4). The district and school staff often responded to those threats of exit by acquiescing to their demands. However, school staff only acquiesced if they perceived that the family threatening to exit actually had the resources to leave and they perceived the exiting family to have desirable demographics.[6] In contrast, low-income and African-American parents often did not have the financial resources to move away from Rolling Acres or to send their children to private schools; thus their voices and concerns were given less consideration than those of their white counterparts.

Although many policies targeted the black and the poor, these policies were often conceived and administered without a comprehensive needs-based assessment of low-income and black populations. Instead, people who were perceived to be experts, who rarely took the time to study the local issues facing these communities, articulated the issues facing these populations. Also, since Rolling Acres is composed of a highly active citizenry, one might assume that the democratic possibilities would also be high; however, these possibilities were often crushed by inequities in lobbying power, which allowed resources to be further stratified in favor of affluent white residents.

The success of a policy is often measured by its influence on a targeted outcome. The set of policies presented in this chapter were intended to reduce racial segregation between schools and to increase African-American students' scores in order to narrow the achievement gap. Although these were the goals of the school district, all RAPS stakeholders did not share them. Each group had its own definition of what a "successful policy" was. The alignment of political and social power allowed the voices of affluent whites to be the most audible in debates over the district's policy direction.[7] Pressure from them and the district's response led to the eventual adoption of a colorblind approach to equity-targeted policies.[8]

IDEOLOGY AND POLICY

Colorblind attitudes and policies have gained popularity as racial attitudes have shifted in the post–Civil Rights era. With the shift in attitudes, abstract support for policies such as busing have increased, but not everyone is willing to support said policies locally. Instead, when faced with choices, many districts have opted for colorblind "achievement for all" policies that do not target programming or resources toward minority groups.[9] Multiple theorists have tried to figure out how the dissonance between abstract endorsement of race-considerate equity policy and ground-level implementation of colorblind policies comes about. Eduardo Bonilla-Silva has labeled this dissonance "colorblind racism," while Lawrence Bobo and colleagues have labeled it "laissez-faire racism."[10] Endorsers of both approaches stress that equality is the goal and that equality must be achieved immediately by not giving "preferential" treatment to any group. These approaches ignore historically rooted disparities and instead highlight even-handed approaches in the present.

Another way of looking at these attitudes among whites is offered by Amy Stuart Wells in her book *Both Sides Now*.[11] In discussing the dissonance between abstract endorsement and on-the-ground support among white residents who grew up in desegregating schools, she suggests that some whites exhibit "white double consciousness." She explains:

> Though they frequently buy into the color-blind argument and insist that neighborhoods are racially segregated mostly because blacks and Latinos want to be with their "own kind," *they are also more likely than whites with*

a racially segregated upbringing to at least explore complex questions and
explanations of the current state of our racially divided society.[12] [italics mine]

Wells argues that whites who grew up during desegregation are more willing
to question racial dynamics in complex ways. Despite this intellectual consideration, their on-the-ground support of race-considerate policies seems hardly
different from that of whites who grew up in predominantly white areas. If
the white parents who experienced desegregation in Rolling Acres thought
with increased complexity about racial issues, it was not readily apparent.
Many who were strongly against race-considerate policies drew from a belief
that schools and classrooms were already desegregated and that the achievement gap resulted from the inability of blacks to take advantage of opportunities. One of my interviewees offered this: "Our [Rolling Acres'] children
are in the same classrooms. Children in the same classroom have the same
opportunity to learn. If some [black students] choose to not take advantage
of opportunities, we can't make them." This person gave voice to two important underlying assumptions that were shared by "squeaky wheels" and most
of the white residents I interviewed. Because Rolling Acres Public Schools
were racially diverse, white adults often assumed that children in the same
classrooms had the same opportunities and that some children/families opted
not to take advantage of these opportunities.[13] These assumptions allowed
the responsibility for rectifying the gap to lie with black families and served
to raise concern that the school district's investments in African-American
students were unnecessary and unfair to whites.

ENGINEERING THE RACIAL UTOPIA

The extreme racial turmoil that surrounded desegregation in large cities like
Boston was not the only type of response that desegregating cities provided.
Since desegregation occurred on a city-by-city basis, Rolling Acres' unique
history played a role in plans to racially balance the schools. Among residents
in Rolling Acres, there was a common narrative that the city was already
desegregated and more liberal than its neighboring cities, which featured
entrenched racial and economic segregation. Though residents commonly
voiced this narrative, the city's history portrayed a different reality.

Like its neighbors, Rolling Acres featured both de jure and de facto segregation. De jure segregation (segregation imposed by law) was enforced

by selectively excluding blacks from areas occupied by whites. Restrictive covenants included in housing deeds prohibited the passing of property to blacks. De facto (in practice) segregation remains because the remnants of de jure segregation were largely unaffected by school busing, which simply shuffled a small number of students from different racial backgrounds and neighborhoods to the same school, thus leaving the housing stock unaffected. Housing costs, selective loan provision, and residential preferences perpetuate the racial and economic segregation of black and white families. Segregation along both race and class lines remains to this day.

These divisions came to a head in the 1970s when black families whose children attended a local elementary school named RAPS in a class-action suit. The suit claimed that a local RAPS school underserved African-American students from a low-income housing development. The district was found guilty of not providing sufficient instruction to, and engagement of, black students who came from disadvantaged family backgrounds. A court decision mandated that the school district alter its instructional treatment of African-American students, who were overwhelmingly poor, and ensure that students received appropriate instructional accommodation regardless of their background. This landmark decision marked Rolling Acres' first legislative battle with racial inequality in a city that claimed few racial issues. As a result of this court mandate, individual schools began to seriously grapple with the education of all students, but a larger set of racial issues affecting the system still did not immediately get taken up.

The racial fault lines of Rolling Acres were exposed by the legal decision, but the path to addressing these fault lines remained unclear. The fear of another legal challenge against the public school system motivated school district administrators and the school board to take proactive steps in dealing with educational inequality. In 1985, 1997, and 2004 this resulted in "voluntary" redistricting and achievement-related initiatives. "Voluntary" is the word commonly used to refer to desegregation plans that districts choose to implement without being mandated to do so by the court. However, the clear objections of some residents suggests that labeling these plans voluntary glosses over the mixed sentiments that often characterize school desegregation. While the word "voluntary" is bandied about in legal and policy discussions of schools, this chapter demonstrates that very few of these changes are ushered in via goodwill; and the interests of the district often conflicted with both vocal and non-vocal residents. In the case of

Rolling Acres, the tensions between public desires and policy demands were clear.

VOLUNTARY DESEGREGATION, 1985

In the 1980s, both the enrollment in RAPS and the test scores of black students were declining. In 1985, the board of education responded to these two phenomena by commissioning a committee of twenty-one community members to examine the contemporary and future needs of the district with the goal of providing a high-quality education for all children. The committee presented a final equity report with over 100 recommendations to the school board for achieving greater equity within RAPS. The recommendation that drew the most attention and controversy was the need to redraw district lines to reduce segregation between schools. While previous conversations about race had been about individual schools' failures or the push to integrate black students from a few schools into the surrounding largely white schools, a redrawing of district lines was a more radical change.

Redistricting was seen as necessary because some of the local elementary schools had African-American student concentrations of over 70 percent, while others had student of bodies with less than 2 percent African-American students. In response to the committee report, the school board adopted many of the suggestions and attempted to develop a formal school redistricting plan that would increase racial balance and ease financial burdens. Racial balance was to be addressed by busing students so that all elementary schools would have 12 to 27 percent black students, thus bringing the district's schools closer to the citywide average in representation of African-Americans. The commission argued that the closing of several schools and busing children to other schools would ease the financial burden on the district.

The redistricting plan of 1985 was not met with open arms. Most parents accepted the idea that equitable schools and more efficient ones were desirable, however they rebuffed the idea to close some schools and bus students. Immediately after the plan was announced, a group of predominantly middle-income and affluent white parents began to mobilize against it through letters to the editor and, eventually, protests. I call these parents and their supporters anti-redistricting advocates.[14] Anti-redistricting advocates had three main objections to the redistricting plan. First, they did not

believe busing children from their local "neighborhood" school was necessary. Second, they argued that RAPS was not in a financial crisis, so closing
schools was a preference, not a necessity. And third, few believed that racial
segregation was a "problem" in Rolling Acres and that busing was thus
another matter of preference, not a necessity.

These anti-redistricting advocates pounced on the consulting company
that had been commissioned to design the proposed redistricting plan,
for two reasons: first, because the company was not local, anti-redistricting advocates suggested that it did not fully understand the local schools
beyond crude demographics. They argued that these "outsiders" had overlooked important local social and cultural factors. Second, they said the
data provided to analysts were dated and inaccurate, so the portraits of
RAPS as segregated and financially burdened were false.[15] These data issues
were exploited by anti-redistricting advocates who provided an unscientific,
yet compelling counter-narrative that if the outsiders' plans were adopted
the city's schools would lose a "community feel." It is common for school
desegregation plans to be resisted by white families who argue that desegregation destroys "neighborhood schools."[16] In their responses they often rely
on coded racial language which suggests that "community" (maintaining
predominantly white schools) is more important than "disruption for diversity" (introducing a small number of students of color to predominantly
white schools). In Rolling Acres, anti-redistricting advocates in their letters
and public comments said that redistricting today would impose a toll on
Rolling Acres for generations to come.

In addition to the loss of community schools, anti-redistricting advocates consistently questioned why race needed to be a factor in redistricting
and the redistribution of students. In local papers, parents were quoted as
saying that Rolling Acres schools were accepting of students from a wide
range of backgrounds and that using race as a tool for redistricting was
unnecessary. Because segregation is often understood asymmetrically—
those who are the subject of limited residential options are more aware of
them than those who are not limited—whites advanced a narrative that
race should not matter. The board of RAPS provided extensive data that
schools were racially segregated and that the problem needed attention, but
this evidence was largely ignored and overshadowed by the idea that Rolling Acres was a racial democracy where diversity was a point of celebration,
not to be contested. The suggestion that schools were on a path to heavy

segregation seemed illogical to many white residents. White residents had little understanding of the degree of segregation within the schools and little political will to support desegregation practices.

After public outcry over the redistricting plan was expressed formally and informally, the plan was revised. As noted earlier, an out-of-state consultant had developed the first redistricting plan. This became a battering ram with which anti-redistricting advocates increased doubt about the school board's ability to govern RAPS and to serve residents' needs. As a result, the plans was quickly dispensed with; in response, the school board formed a committee that developed two more plans, which were also met with resistance from the same families who resisted the first one. The school board, in closed-door meetings without public influence, developed one more plan that was eventually accepted. Over the course of the school year, the school board held five public hearings and multiple private meetings on the redistricting plan and its subsequent revisions.

Over the plan's five incarnations, the voices of anti-redistricting advocates rang loud in local media, but had limited support on the school board. The final breaking point in resistance to the district's adoption of the redistricting plans was an electoral cycle in which anti-redistricting school board members, who were already in the minority, lost their reelection bids. The result was the adoption of a modified redistricting plan that affected nearly twenty elementary schools and relied on the busing of a few African-American students to majority-white schools. The implementation of the redistricting plan was set to occur over two years, and there were few incidents of resistance to its implementation.[17]

Spearheaded by affluent white parents, the vocal dissent of anti-redistricting advocates stood in contrast to the silence of residents whom redistricting was intended to benefit. The local newspaper archives revealed few comments from families that identified as black and/or as potential busing subjects. I do not have evidence to suggest that the voices and needs of these communities were intentionally ignored, but there is little in the historical record to suggest that their needs were advocated for beyond the initial 1985 report on equity and the school board's attempt to redistrict. While it could inferred that the school board was altruistic in its motion to redistrict, in reality the threat of legally violating desegregation mandates loomed in the background of the district's haste to implement a program to avoid further segregation. The political pressures that produced the redistricting plans, however, were not sufficient to gain support among the most vocal in Rolling Acres. The inability to gain the support of the most vocal, and by some accounts the most powerful, residents of Rolling Acres would continue to shape the direction that the city took to address educational inequality for more than twenty years.

REDISTRICTING, 1997–1998

As Rolling Acres grew over the next twelve years, its demographics shifted, and once again RAPS was faced with the need to redistrict in order to optimize building use, relieve crowding, and improve racial balance. New housing stock located on the periphery of the city had been developed with little attention to how it concentrated low-income and racial minorities in certain schools. Schools located on the outskirts of Rolling Acres became overcrowded as developers gobbled up farmland to build subdivisions. These newly constructed neighborhoods remained largely economically and racially homogeneous: predominantly white and affluent.

In 1997 the RAPS School Board commissioned a consultant to propose a redistricting strategy. The introduction of the 1997 redistricting plan eerily resembled the struggle over redistricting in 1985: redistricting plans drafted by outsiders were criticized, and the destruction of community schools was a central concern of anti-redistricting advocates. There was at least one significant difference between the 1985 and 1997 plans. In 1985, the superintendent was a white man named Richard Stephens. In 1997, the superintendent was an African-American man named Henry Patterson. Patterson's advocacy for redistricting was read as a personal agenda item, rather than a district need.

The emphasis on race was ironic given that, in the 1997 redistricting plan, racial balance was expressed as the tertiary concern, not the primary one. This was a more colorblind approach to redistricting, but public conversations in newspapers and other venues elevated the role of race, which riled affluent white residents and created an opportunity for them to reshape the direction of the policy more successfully than they had in 1985.

During the middle of the campaign for redistricting, at a school board meeting during a discussion of future plans, Superintendent Patterson inquired if anyone had consulted the state guidelines on racial balance.

He was not suggesting that racial balance was the issue, merely asking the question to ensure that all bases were covered to achieve compliance. Following his question he added, in his estimation, that in redrawing district lines the consideration of racial balance likely would not be required. After hearing these statements, a local newspaper highlighted his question and suggested that Patterson had implied that racial balance was legally mandated by the state. In the following weeks, the local *Rolling Acres Courier* carried quotes from state representatives and legal scholars questioning the need for redistricting with racial balance in mind. The consensus was that the district could potentially face legal issues related to race, but that its current standing called for no immediate action. The newspaper's reporting of the redistricting process painted the superintendent and his deputy as adding race to the redistricting equation under the guise of a legal mandate. No matter how Patterson denied this claim, this image remained attached to his leadership.

SILENT AGENDAS AND SILENCED VOICES

A partial view of the public's mixed reaction to the 1997 plan can be seen in editorials and letters that appeared in the *Rolling Acres Courier*. The editorials tended to be highly ideological and fell into two camps. One camp advocated race-blind redistricting and said that considering race when making redistricting decisions about attendance boundaries was discriminatory. The other camp were race-conscious advocates of redistricting who said that race needed to be a central consideration in the future of Rolling Acres Public Schools. The majority of the letters to the editor advocated the race-blind approach. This is probably because those who were most likely to write in to voice their opinions were those who were both most invested in blocking the changes and felt the most empowered in the political process of Rolling Acres.

A few days before the vote on the redistricting plan, a group that called itself Residents for Neighborhood Schools purchased an advertisement in the *Rolling Acres Courier* that was written as an "open letter to the RAPS School Board." The letter asked the board to reconsider its plan to "destroy neighborhood schools" for the purpose of fixing a few overcrowded and underused schools. The letter strategically referred to the 1985 redistricting:

Like you, we want efficiency in our schools. But we want efficiency with the least disruption, not the most. Eleven years ago, Rolling Acres suffered through a painful redistricting. The community lost a generation of schoolchildren with a sense of belonging, and a generation of parents with a commitment to the schools. Only in the last few years have that belonging and commitment returned.

The authors of the letter never directly invoked discussions of racial balance; instead they alluded to past redistricting and its troubled history. The authors opted to discuss the redistricting exclusively in terms of efficiency and the associated costs to residents who would be removed from their "nurturing" neighborhood schools. Between the lines of this colorblind letter, the racial and economic relations of Rolling Acres were an important subtext. This type of rhetorical writing activated racial memory; although race was never explicitly invoked, it served to shape perceptions that redistricting came with a secret racial agenda.

The voices of low-income and African-American families were largely silent and made invisible by the cacophonous clashes between the school board, the superintendent, and anti-redistricting advocates. The images of black families were used to add color to articles about the segregation that existed within Rolling Acres schools, but their voices and perspectives were seldom quoted in-depth or elevated to any level of importance. African-American voices were not entirely absent, however; the African-Americans who were often quoted were school board members or other professionals in the Rolling Acres school system who were squarely middle class or affluent. It is important that those African-American voices were present in the public discussion, but the interests and realities of these middle-class and affluent blacks did not mirror the experiences of low-income and working-class blacks. Middle-class black families were often located in more socially desirable neighborhoods (e.g., single-family houses and neighborhoods with high incomes), which contrasted with the circumstances of poor African-American families, who were typically located in rental properties and neighborhoods with low incomes.

The parental lobbying and public response was so great that Superintendent Patterson asked groups of concerned parents affected by redistricting to draft their own potential redistricting plan. The plan they came up with did little to change the distribution of schools and ultimately was rejected because it maintained the status quo of racial imbalance.

Although their plan was not accepted, the superintendent's response to the vocal citizenry marked an important moment in the political history of Rolling Acres schools. The formal inclusion of the voices of citizens not affiliated with established organizations was unprecedented and emboldened squeaky-wheel parents to expect a response and greater consideration in the policymaking process. The final desegregation plan that was approved affected 20 percent of students in the primary grades, a far smaller percentage than initially targeted.

The responses to advocacy in the 1985 and 1997 redistricting plans served to bolster affluent white residents' power, whether they were anti-redistricting advocates or not. It sent a message to the RAPS district that "hidden agendas," or more accurately race-consciousness, would be challenged.

ACHIEVEMENT GAP INITIATIVES, 1997

Around the time of redistricting, RAPS again became concerned about the low academic performance of black children and established the Committee on Black Academic Excellence (BAE) to explore the issue and make recommendations. The BAE suggested ten initiatives: (1) increasing access to all-day kindergarten, (2) improving home-school linkages at the elementary level, (3) increasing mentorship and tutoring, (4) creating support groups for African-American parents, (5) adding cultural sensitivity training for staff and teachers at three schools, (6) creating programs that publicly acknowledged African-American student achievement, (7) monitoring disparities in school suspension rates by race, (8) increasing communication between the district and the teachers' union on their efforts to reduce the achievement gap, (9) increasing communication with the African-American population about their needs, and (10) identifying structural areas in RAPS schools that affected African-American achievement. The RAPS school board agreed to undertake the BAE's set of ten initiatives, which had a price tag of nearly half a million dollars.

These ten initiatives marked the first time that Rolling Acres had agreed to undertake a set of district-wide sustained policy actions *and evaluations* focusing on educational equity, particularly the issues facing the black community, which was the largest minority community in RAPS. Past responses to educational inequality were based at the school level and small in scale or did not include evaluations of the interventions. One of the most significant elements of these initiatives was the creation, recruitment, and hiring of an Achievement Gap Administrator (AGA). This individual occupied a full-time position with the RAPS and was responsible for overseeing the implementation and evaluation of the outlined ten initiatives.

During the fall of 1997, a set of parents from the Rolling Acres school system filed a complaint with the Department of Education's Civil Rights Office to block implementation of the program. The complaint argued that the singling out of African-Americans as targets of the plan discriminated against non-African-American students. One of the complaint's authors was quoted in the *Rolling Acres Courier* as saying, "When you start excluding students based on race, to me, that's racism."

The legal response and editorials in local media agreed that the achievement gap needed to be fixed, but that using race as the central factor in the repair was discriminatory. At the time that the first complaint was filed, nationally targeted programs for communities of color were common, but they soon came under legal attack en masse.[18] Rolling Acres was not alone in its concern about the gap, but its choice to dedicate services by race was a political lightning rod. Ultimately, the Civil Rights Office issued a resolution agreement that required all programs be open to all residents, regardless of race. The agreement suggested that use of race-based language was also discriminatory, so any language referring to a particular racial group needed to be removed. The district was then responsible for producing annual reports evaluating the application and utilization of programs, which clearly outlined racial demographics. The decision and other national conversations served to raise concern about race-considerate policies.

CENTRALIZATION AND DIFFUSION

Rolling Acres Public Schools, like many districts across the nation, attempted to deal with inequalities by centralizing resources and adding personnel. The hiring of Karyn Tolliver, an African-American woman, as the Achievement Gap Administrator, embodied this centralization. In my communications with past and current Rolling Acres personnel, numerous staff suggested that the hiring of a new full-time employee to deal with the achievement gap left district staff such as teachers and principals feeling little responsibility for individually contributing to the adoption of initiatives. This attitude ran counter to the intent of the hire, but with the labor demands on district staff increasing and no additional staff hired to do the work, the staff looked for places to "lighten their load." The addition of the AGA position gave Tolliver resources but few staff eager to assist in implementing the requisite changes.

The timeline for evaluating the new initiatives was also problematic. The school-based initiatives (all-day kindergarten, diversity training, elementary school relations, and others) were designed with a short implementation window of just two years before being evaluated and scaled up to the district level. A year after the initiatives' adoption, internal district correspondence indicated that only five of the ten were on track to meet the two-year goal of full implementation and evaluation. The initiatives were ambitious, but too little attention was paid to how the centralization of the task would influence their implementation.

From 1997 to 2000, AGA Karyn Tolliver attempted to corral the resources of the RAPS to address the black-white achievement gap. She was unable to garner much support from within the district or from non-African–American community members. When interviewed by a local news source about the interest of non-African-American parents in supporting the initiatives and reducing the gap, she responded:

> If there is disruption or there is not a climate conducive to learning in
> the classroom, that's going to affect students who are high achievers and
> students who are low achievers. If a teacher is spending an inordinate
> amount of time in class going over material, having to provide remedial
> skill building, then those students who are on the higher fringe are really
> not as engaged in the education process as they could be. And they're not
> given the opportunity to learn more. What we've got to do is make sure
> the learning environment is positive for all students.

Tolliver framed her answer in colorblind language, despite having been asked specifically about the interests of non-African–Americans in supporting the initiatives. In her description of the interests of families with students "on the upper fringe" this category becomes synonymous with white, while readers are left to imply that students who provide a "disruption" in the classroom are African-American. Even if this was only a rhetorical strategy, it is still troubling because of its implicit assumptions about race, behavior, and student performance. Her attitude was not unlike that of multiple African-American staff that I spoke with who viewed black children as a "problem" within RAPS. As AGA, Tolliver was responsible for rallying public support for the initiatives in a contentious environment. Her choice to frame black children as "problem children" played into a deficit model in which the deficiencies of black youth held them back and, according to her statement, also held back whites. Her comment reinforced stereotypes that black students were underachieving and white students were excelling. Derrick Bell's theory of interest convergence suggests that, for equity-based policies to be adopted, both blacks and whites must hold a vested interest and both groups must stand to gain.[19] Tolliver's estimation of the benefits for whites was considered small in comparison with spending a half-million dollars in resources primarily on black students. Thus Tolliver and the district's approach to "selling" the initiatives fell short on all sides, making the program susceptible to co-opting and to arguments to eliminate it.

LEADERSHIP TRANSITION

An additional challenge to the implementation of the initiatives was the transition in leadership in the school district. When the district personnel changed, the implementation, evaluation, and revision of the 1997 initiatives became piecemeal and inconsistent. Each superintendent between 1997 and 2004 took a different approach to addressing the gap between black and white students. Patterson's successor, Michelle Henderson, an African-American woman, was brought from a larger urban district to lead Rolling Acres. At a PTA meeting in 2000 Henderson commented, "The achievement gap is not only Karyn's [Tolliver's] problem." Her plea was aimed at garnering greater support from her staff, parents, and the community at large so that work on the achievement gap would be a shared effort. Her call for greater community engagement was met, but not in the way she expected.

Parents at the meeting began organizing around issues of equality of opportunity, rather than equality of outcome. These affluent white parents stressed the need for all students to receive equal educational supports; their goal was to undermine the provision of different resources to black and white students and to deemphasize the achievement gap. Their organizing effort centered on improving education for "all children" and suggested that concentrating on a specific minority was a disservice to all children in RAPS. Later in the year, Henderson made another call for collective engagement in addressing the gap at a district-wide PTA meeting. The PTA produced the following statement:

> The gap arises from complex interactions of many variables, not all of which are under the control of RAPS or its staff. However, we are tired of hearing these used as excuses and believe that RAPS can take actions which it is not now taking that will raise achievement generally in our school system. The district should change its focus from one of "closing the gap" to one of promoting high academic achievement for all children. Not only do we have an achievement gap, but we note that overall, achievement is lower in RAPS than we think it should and could be in a system with our resources. Undue focus on race-based gap has many counterproductive side effects that perpetuate the problem.

The PTA's use of the term "undue focus" challenged the priority of race-conscious policies. This challenge inverted the district's priority to align with families who had questioned the utility of race-considerate approaches. The statement codified the backlash that had been brewing for years over the district's concentration on the achievement gap. Despite parental dissatisfaction with this focus, the district's leadership maintained its attention on the achievement gap. The resulting tension eventually came to a head when the superintendent, a black woman, was dismissed.

With the turnover of multiple superintendents, the AGA position and the monitoring of the initiatives were discontinued and subsumed by the traditional RAPS bureaucratic structure. Quickly the 1997 initiatives faded from the policy spotlight but remained a part of the district's collective memory. The next superintendent selected was a white male, and under his leadership the language around student performance officially transitioned from a focus on the achievement gap to achievement for all.[20]

NEW INITIATIVES, 2004

Changes in local education policy do not occur in a vacuum. The schools' 2004 initiatives on educational equity reflected both local and national pressures. The district approved a set of seven new initiatives that focused on improving all student achievement. Unlike the initiatives of 1997 that were generated from outside the ranks of RAPS staff, in 2004 the instructional services office generated the initiatives internally. I discuss two of the seven initiatives here: academic achievement and special education. I chose this subset because they were closely tied to race and the achievement gap, but there was no race-considerate language used in their articulation. Instead words like "equity," "equality," and "subgroups" became the core lexicon. This shift in language could be attributed in part to the passage of the No Child Left Behind Act (NCLB), but it also partly reflects the backlash from the 1997 initiatives.

The first initiative was designed "to improve achievement for all students" and featured thirty-two points to address achievement issues in the district. One initiative centered on meeting adequate yearly progress (AYP) for all subgroups on the state standards test. The language about raising the performance of African-American students from 1997 was nixed, and equality of outcome became the focus. This initiative closely matched the language of federal policy. While the achievement gap was implicated, it was not the central outcome of concern; instead AYP stressed proficiency for all students. Unlike the 1997 initiatives, these achievement goals were clear and tied closely to current local and national mandates for student performance.

A second initiative focused on special education placement and programming. The goals for this plank included getting all students who needed one on an Individualized Education Plan (IEP) and reducing the special education caseload by 10 percent. Within Rolling Acres, black students were disproportionately classified as in need of special education. In one of the fourth-grade classrooms I studied, 50 percent of the black children were classified as needing some type of special education. This overrepresentation was commonly mentioned in local newspapers and was a source of discussion among district personnel, but the initiative did not mention race as a factor of concern. If race was not a consideration in special education placement, the reduction in caseload could occur unevenly, with affluent white parents being better positioned than poor and working-class black families to lobby for removing their children from special education. If this were to occur, African-American students would remain outside of mainstream classrooms and continue to be marginalized within RAPS.

The 2004 initiatives were much more aligned with the national discussion of equality for all children, and because they left race out of the conversation public concern was kept at bay. Given that NCLB was ushered in by a colorblind policy advocate, President George W. Bush, the lack of race-considerate language and programming is not surprising. Some may suspect that the language of the 2004 initiatives had trickled down from the federal level and thus limited discussions of race. However, federal policy called for states and municipalities to develop their own programs and paths that complied with federal outcomes; alignment of language was left to their discretion. The adoption of federal language allowed the district to downplay the role of race and allay concerns of white residents who sued the district for programming in 1997 and 2001 while boasting alignment with national policy trends.

COMMUNITY INFLUENCE
AND POLICY CHANGE

Community influence in 1985, 1997, and 2004 animated local policies in powerful ways that demonstrate the contentious and difficult job of developing and maintaining equity policy in the post–Civil Rights era. In Rolling Acres, community influence was directly tied to stocks of information and the ability to get those in power to respond to concerns. Ostensibly, both economic and racial minority families had the same information as more affluent white families about the changes that were proposed. However, minority families could not and did not act in a coordinated fashion to make their support for desegregation and achievement-related policy interventions a reality. Instead, they were edged out of the opportunity to shift educational inputs (local policies around access to school and educational resources) and watched past programming aimed at equity whittled away. Because the voices of the black poor, in particular, were absent from public discourse, it is difficult to assess the degree to which they understood how these resources could benefit them.

During the time of controversy around the 1997 initiatives, one local newspaper carried an article titled, "Black Families Join Fight to End the Achievement Gap." The article reported on black families that had attended a training session on developing black family support groups. It is ironic and telling that the article suggested that black families "join[ed] the fight" only after the initiatives had been approved. Still, the article quoted heavily from program organizers and school board members who were part of the African-American middle class.

Given the absence of working-class and poor blacks and the limited number of middle-class black families who were actively engaged in setting the policy agenda, building coalitions with power-holding whites was necessary. But coalitions between middle-class blacks and whites took precedence over making coalitions with the black poor. Ultimately, the black poor were not engaged in the fight to retain race-conscious policies; nor were their voices represented at citywide meetings on educational equity.

Advocates for a race-considerate policy tended to be those in the African-American middle class, and they were small in number. Their advocacy did not carry much weight, even when it came from black families that had lived in Rolling Acres for multiple generations. In part, this was due to a more subtle class divide within the black community, which I explore in chapter 7. Middle-class and affluent blacks tended to live in Rolling Acres for multiple generations or moved there for work or educational opportunities. Working-class and poor black families tended to be recent arrivals or embedded members of the Rolling Acres poor and working classes. The division was most clear when the BAE committee drafted a set of policy recommendations that were largely based on research conducted in large, high-poverty urban districts such as Chicago. Though Rolling Acres did include a sizable number of black and poor residents, the concentrated poverty of a large city was not the poverty of Rolling Acres. Both types of poverty carry hazards, but equating the two demonstrated the disconnect between district-developed advocacy for black residents and a more ground-up approach that started with needs-based advocacy. The NAACP and other organizations were often charged with conveying the issues facing Rolling Acres' black population, but they were largely unable to connect with lower-income black families. Black advocacy was thus largely driven by middle-class and affluent residents, with the voices of low-income residents silent and/or absent from policy discussions.

CONCLUSION

For a mid-sized school district like Rolling Acres, the adage "the squeaky wheel gets the oil" certainly applies. The concerted cultivation that affluent white residents exercised, whether in anti-redistricting or anti-achievement initiatives, shifted the policy approach of the district from race-considerate to race-blind and resulted in the hoarding of resources for their children. All families had the basic opportunity to agitate for change in local educational policies, but poor and black families faced a number of barriers to doing so; affluent and white families had multiple conduits for making sure that their agitation mattered. The ownership that affluent white residents felt over the district was based on longstanding relationships in the system and strong social ties to local media outlets. Letters to the editor, local stories, and advocacy with school board members amplified the voices of a few to affect the fate of many. In reality, the bulk of Rolling Acres residents did not express their disdain or support for the race-considerate policies; however, their silence was interpreted as compliance with the move toward race-blind policies and a colorblind ideology.

By late 2005, advocacy by the squeaky wheels had succeeded in fashioning the district's approach to increasing achievement for all students using race-blind policies. While on its face this appears to be the most equitable approach to addressing educational inequality, in fact it reflects a caving in to the pressures from local and federal stakeholders. The district's concentration on student achievement obscured the everyday, unequal realities that informed the educational inequality that they sought to reduce.

In this sense, Rolling Acres is like most school districts that have focused on a narrow slice of schooling—school achievement—to the detriment of other important dimensions of schooling. While reducing differences in average student performance and raising all student test scores remain the national mandates under NCLB, the processes that contribute to this inequality remain hidden and missed by many of Rolling Acres' past interventions. The move to a colorblind policy and the lack of consideration for the poor and black undermined the success of equity interventions, yet it pacified the concerns of affluent white residents.

THREE

Segmented Suburbia

> I think the diversity is the number one thing. There's
> not a group, not only in race, but there's not a group
> that's not represented here. I think it opens our eyes to
> different ways of thinking, different ways of living. I
> think you realize the world is a much bigger place than
> your own little world.
>
> —MS. MORRIS, WHITE PARENT, RIVER
> ELEMENTARY

> It used to be you would rather your kids go to Rolling
> Acres [schools] because you think they get taught bet-
> ter or more, but that is not true. I see a lot more black
> people moving from Rolling Acres, kids [are] going
> back to city schools.
>
> —MS. DOWNING, BLACK PARENT, RIVER
> ELEMENTARY

Ms. Morris and Ms. Downing have very different views of Rolling Acres,
its virtues and its vices. Ms. Morris is compelled by the diversity of Rolling Acres; Ms. Downing is dismayed that expectations of better schooling
have not panned out for black families. Their sons attend the fourth grade
together at River Elementary School, yet in other ways they are worlds
apart.

This chapter examines how the social distances between black and white
lives lead to divergent opportunities by highlighting the roles of family,
residential location, and social networks. Although Rolling Acres is commonly referred to as integrated, this is a misnomer because it was never fully
desegregated. Residents share schools, but they rarely share neighborhoods,

friendship circles, or the same paths toward opportunity. Here I document the distance between the white middle class and black middle class; this is not new within the sociological literature, but little scholarship has interrogated how black middle-class families (adults and children) make sense of their position and how their communities influence their children's education and potential future pathways. In this chapter I introduce you to a white family, the Morrises, and a black family, the Downings, to illustrate the subtle yet deep inequality that exists but is often overlooked.

To grapple with the outlooks that emerge from being a part of the black middle class in a suburban area, I draw from the theory of segmented assimilation. Portes and Zhou suggested that the new second generation—children of immigrants after 1965—had three possible assimilatory trajectories: (1) straight-line assimilation (upward), (2) acculturation and assimilation to native minority populations (downward), and (3) selective acculturation (mixed).[1] I am most interested in the third path, selective acculturation, in large part because it allows for a more complex consideration of mobility, citizenship, and ethnic/racial group membership.

The suburban black middle class occupy a precarious location because they are considered successful relative to other black families located in cities; still, their measured successes (e.g., educational attainment, median income) do not eclipse or even equal those of the suburban white middle class. This position of relative advantage and deprivation is important because it is in some respects analogous to the condition of contemporary immigrant communities. An emerging literature on transnational frames of reference has begun to articulate the dynamic ways that children of immigrants understand their position and how these positions shape their worldviews.[2] Vivian Louie, in a study of Chinese and Dominican second-generation college-educated youth, found that they described their social position using three frames of reference: (1) their parents' homeland, (2) peer co-ethnics, and (3) mainstream representations of their ethnic group. These frames were used by youth to reference their own achievements and express what sometimes read as contradictory sentiments of success and failure.[3] The Downing family and other black middle-class families expressed similarly complex views of success in discussing Rolling Acres Public Schools, their children's mobility, and living in Rolling Acres.

I observed and interviewed Danny Morris and LeBron Downing, who are classmates at River Elementary. I selected Danny and LeBron because their personalities, academic orientations, and goals were similar, and both came from families that represented the middle class of their respective racial groups. They lived only a few miles apart and sat near each other in Mr. Marks's fourth-grade classroom. The boys figured sports would play a major role in their futures, with Danny dreaming of a career in hockey and LeBron dreaming of a career in basketball. They were identical in so many ways, yet divided by color and class. In 1903, W.E.B. Du Bois opined, "The problem of the 20th century is the problem of the color line";[4] today, when one understands Danny's and LeBron's lives, one sees how Du Bois's forecast has endured in material and psychological forms.

ENVISIONED FUTURES

Sociological research on education has long been concerned with social reproduction and how the outlooks of youths and adults influence where they end up in a given society. School is often seen as "the great equalizer," but social reproductionists regard schools as inequality reproducing, not inequality abating.[5] Social reproduction theorists have carefully analyzed how varying forms of capital—social, cultural, economic, and human—shape access to schooling and shape later life trajectories. While early social reproductionists concentrated on the role of social class,[6] in recent years a more intersectional analysis has emerged, with race and ethnicity figuring into methodological and theoretical considerations.[7] These theories have given us a vocabulary with which to understand how biography, family background, and institutional arrangement intersect to shape adults' and children's outlooks and futures.

Jay MacLeod's study of Boston youth examined the outlooks of adolescents and identified the differences between aspirations and expectations, along class lines.[8] He wrote, "Aspirations are one's preferences relatively unsullied by anticipated constraints, expectations take these constraints squarely into account."[9] In his analysis, MacLeod found that idyllic aspirations are common among youth from low-income backgrounds, but as they grow older and begin navigating the world, these aspirations are altered by the realities they face. Ultimately, many youth with high aspirations and high social hurdles to overcome are led to low social opportunities. MacLeod's distinction between aspirations and expectations helps clarify youths' youth-centric understandings of their current social position and future opportunities. However, a significant omission in MacLeod's work is the voices of adults, which prohibits the exploration of messages that shape awareness and the negotiation of pathways to opportunity. Youth rarely heed all of the messages sent by their elders; still, the messages that penetrate undoubtedly affect how youth understand and navigate the world.

Before adults pass messages about opportunity on to youth, they must develop and make sense of their own views on mobility and opportunity. Alford Young, in a study of black men, argued for the distinction between projective and constructive realms, which are adult constellations of MacLeod's aspirations and expectations.[10] The constructive realm refers to an adult's general understanding of the operation of the world and the openness of the opportunity structure. In contrast, the projective realm captures an adult's understanding of his or her ability to navigate through the world. Adults' worldviews are shaped by how open they perceive the opportunity structure to be and whether they are able to take advantage of opportunities. These worldviews are the result of cumulative experiences that have been shaped by race, class, and gender.

In my extension of MacLeod's and Young's work, I introduce envisioned futures, which is a concept that melds aspirations and expectations (of youth) with the projective and constructive realms (of adults). Youth and adults are constantly (re)fashioning their worldviews as they try to grasp opportunities. By looking at what both adults and youth present, believe, and how they map onto the racialized educational terrain of Rolling Acres, a composite of future pathways becomes clear.[11] The tracks on these pathways lead to opportunities and inequalities that will play out for years to come. Although not always easily observed, mechanisms such as differences in social location (e.g., neighborhood amenities and social networks) guide the direction of future pathways. While discussion of the future often centers on the possible, envisioned futures center on the probable.

In this chapter I concentrate on the domains of education and employment, which are two central vehicles for mobility in the United States. Through my analysis of parental and youth narratives and observations, I demonstrate that the distance between the Downings (a black family) and the Morrises (a white family) are far from benign and have implications for when or if equality between races can occur.

THE MORRIS FAMILY

Danny Morris's family lives in the Stone Hinge subdivision, which is located in a census tract where the median household income was approximately $130,000. Nearly 75 percent of the adult residents held a bachelor's degree. In their community, 85 percent of the residents were white, 4 percent black, and 9 percent Asian. The Stone Hinge subdivision was a desirable place to live, not the type of space that residents "settled for."

Danny was the Morrises' only son and one of two children. At the time of the study, Danny was 10 and had an older sister who was also still in primary school. Like many white residents of Rolling Acres, the Morris family viewed Rolling Acres as a great place to raise children. Most white families in the city believed that diversity, particularly racial diversity, was an important and desirable quality. In the past, racial diversity had been frowned upon by communities that desired white exclusivity, but this was not the dominant sentiment of most of the white Rolling Acres families I interviewed and observed. Mr. Morris told me:

> Look at the friends that they [Danny and his sister] bring home . . . I look at their class pictures from their school and they look like the United Nations to me. And that is just so dramatically different from the world that I was brought up in, and so I think from that standpoint, what they get out of it is they get the world that they will live in.

Other Rolling Acres parents echoed Mr. Morris's belief that his children were part of a racial tapestry. But Mr. Morris's observation that his children's school picture resembled the United Nations overstated the true degree of diversity at his children's school. At River Elementary, the auditorium flew twenty-three different flags that represented the countries of origin of its students. The flags represented the nationalities of both current students and those who had attended the school in the past. Given this display and events like "International Night," where each family was charged with bringing a dish that represented their ethnic background, many white parents suggested that River Elementary was a cultural melting pot. However, among the more than 350 students who attended the school, most countries had just one student representative. Local businesses and universities drew an international population, and some children were enrolled in local public schools for only a short time. Rolling Acres' schools were thus more diverse than many in the Midwest, but this diversity was seldom felt in the classroom; most classrooms remained majority-white with a few students of color sprinkled throughout the school.

DANNY

On most days at River Elementary, I found Danny in a hooded sweatshirt emblazoned with a college athletic insignia. Danny loved hockey, baseball, and any other sport he could get his hands on. Though shorter than most of his classmates, Danny was a fierce competitor and enjoyed friendly battles on the playground during recess and on the hockey rink on weekends. For Danny and his parents, sports were central in preparing him for the future, whether he became an athlete or a businessman. He played on multiple sports teams; sometimes his teams traveled to neighboring parts of the state to compete.[12] Scheduling an interview with Danny and his family was difficult, given the many extracurricular activities that they juggled.

Danny's family looked and behaved like many others in the Stone Hinge neighborhood. His father worked in finance and spent long hours away from home, while Danny's mother worked as a medical assistant and handled most of the day-to-day homefront needs. Afternoons, evenings, and weekends were often spent away from the neighborhood doing extracurricular activities. The Morris family fell neatly into Annette Lareau's conception of concerted cultivators.[13] The Morris house was always abuzz whenever I visited, with Ms. Morris running in and out from errands and other obligations, phones ringing for Mr. Morris's business, and Danny and his sister entertaining friends. One of the centers of the family's life was sports, whether playing, watching, or traveling to and from events, the Morrises lived and died by them.

SPORTS AND SCHOOLING

In Rolling Acres, maintaining a child in extracurricular athletics was a costly undertaking. Depending on the sport, the annual cost could quickly top $1,000, given fees like registration, equipment, training, and travel. For the Morris household, whose income exceeded $125,000, these annual fees were manageable. Mr. Morris complained about the costs, but the family was able to cover them and other services, such as childcare, with little strain.

Danny, at the age of 10, saw his participation in sports as central to his academic and future endeavors. When I asked him what helped him with his schoolwork, he replied:

> Well. hockey a little. It doesn't sound like it would, but it sort of says you have to focus, because our coach says, since they play travel [team] and stuff he says, "You guys have to get [good] grades" or I might have to miss a game or something, cause there has been people who had to miss a game because they didn't finish their science project.

The link between academic performance and sports eligibility is an important one for Danny to see at such a young age. Though this link is well understood by college athletes, Danny too understands the two as interdependent, which sets a precedent for maintaining both sports and academics rather than privileging one over the other. Restrictions on playing time are much more common on competitive teams, in this case travel teams, than on citywide recreation league teams. City teams typically operate with the model "everyone who can pay shall play," and do not demand any academic reporting. For Danny, playing sports and doing well in school were inextricably linked. For his parents, the teams he had access to were important for social and academic reasons. At the age of 10, Danny saw sports and academics as mutually tied and beneficial, not as opposing forces.

In addition to organized sports, on some summer nights Danny played in a community-wide hockey game on his cul-de-sac. Local fathers would block off roads in the subdivision to create a space for their sons to play in the street. These hockey games demonstrate a number of things. First, residents of Stone Hinge felt a strong sense of ownership of their space. By closing off streets, they took public space—roads—and made them private. Second, gender operated as a unifying force for residents in these social interactions. Sons often initiated and requested the hockey games, but they were organized by their fathers. These gathering were public displays of male-centered parenting where lessons around sportsmanship, community, and physical prowess were front and center. Third, race and class played a role, even within the exclusive subdivision. Hockey is a predominantly white sport with prohibitive equipment costs. Street hockey was more affordable but still required each participant to have his own equipment. The teams were overwhelmingly white and all male. Although the Stone Hinge subdivision had a sizable population of Asian descent (the subdivision's largest minority group), they were not represented in the street hockey games.

WORLD OF WORK

During the hockey games and community barbeques, Danny was able to talk to his neighbors about his schoolwork and his possible future pathways. At one such neighborhood gathering, Danny discussed jobs with his neighbor, a law enforcement officer. Danny told me about their discussion, "He was a county sheriff and a detective, and he told me one time when I asked him, 'How is it? Is it hard to become a police officer?' He said if you work hard in school and you pay attention you can mostly go to college and become what you want to be." Though Danny did not receive specific advice, he was able to talk to people beyond his immediate family about career options and paths. In all likelihood, he will not end up being a police officer, since his exposures and interests will evolve as he grows up; but he has access to and will likely retain a rich network of employed professionals. Danny's household and his neighbors aligned to pass along consistent messages about his potential future opportunities. In Danny's milieu, professional occupations and college were not only an option; they were the expectation. In addition to his neighbors, Danny's parents stressed the importance of education to opening up future pathways for him. When I asked Ms. Morris to describe her role in Danny and his sister's education, she said:

> We'll guide them when they tell us some of their interests. He describes some of his interests, and so [we say,] "you might want to think about this kind of education" or "you might want to look at this kind of subject," you know, guiding them maybe with some of their class work. Guiding them with maybe extracurriculars that may make a difference with what they want to pursue.

Danny's mother, like most other white middle-class parents, suggested their role was to steward their children through formal education but allow them to determine their own path. Her parenting strategy was one of facilitation with the goal of maximizing her child's options, rather than directing him toward a particular career path of high prestige or one with large earning potential.

The liberalness with which the Morrises approached Danny's education reflects a degree of privilege. Having both attended college and holding jobs with high salaries, they emphasized exploration, and they were willing to support Danny and his sister's exploration of a range of possible futures. By the age of 10, children were keenly aware of their parents' intentions and desires for their schooling, with most youth feeling that school was a necessary part of their future.

Danny's family did not stress education as much as other affluent white families in my sample. Other families enrolled their children in supplementary programs such as Sylvan Learning Centers, but the Morrises focused on Danny's completion of his homework and "doing his best." The community that surrounded Danny provided support and enrichment through social and cultural capital. Every day Danny learned more about his future options, and they were plentiful. The bounty of economic, cultural, and social resources from which Danny drew were not available to LeBron Downing, who lived just a short drive away.

THE DOWNING FAMILY

The Downing family was part of the black middle-class core. Both of LeBron's parents were raised in Rolling Acres; they owned their home, but neither attended college. Their annual income did not top $75,000 and fluctuated from year to year. LeBron was the younger of the family's two children and his high-school-aged sister also lived in their home. When I first sat down with LeBron's parents, Mr. Downing was employed as a manager of transportation and his mother was wading through a spate of unemployment. They were happy to talk to me about Rolling Acres and its schools because of their familiarity with its virtues and vices. Rolling Acres was a land of many possibilities, but these possibilities, when accessible, often came at a cost. Mr. Downing, LeBron's father, told me:

> But you know, Rolling Acres is more structured. There are more opportunities, but you got to dig hard to get the opportunities here. In [the big city], they got YMCAs. They have numerous programs that run there that

your kids can get into. Here we have YMCA, but can you afford to send your kid to the YMCA? You can send your kid there if you got enough money to keep them in the program.

Mr. Downing and many other black families were concerned about the financial and social costs of Rolling Acres. Although Mr. Downing was raised in the city and owned a home, he still found the area financially and socially demanding. Because the financial costs of living in Rolling Acres posed a challenge to black families, they tended to participate in fewer extracurricular offerings and were thus less likely to benefit from the potential advantages of concerted cultivation. However, financial obstacles were not the sole or the primary barrier to black families in pursuit of opportunities.

EXTRACURRICULAR ACTIVITIES

Once children were enrolled in expensive extracurricular activities, the social barriers of race remained. One black family told me of their son's experience at a local summer camp. Their son was one of few black students and came home telling his parents he was mistreated by the camp counselors. The parents inquired and found that counselors routinely referred to the camp's black children as "scholarship kids" and treated them differently than the white and Asian students who attended. The counselors perceived that anyone who was black and attending the camp could not afford it without a scholarship and thus felt less inclined to provide them with equal services and treatment.

The parents of the mistreated campers quickly insisted that the staff be reprimanded. This was easy to accomplish because, much to the chagrin of the staff that had discriminated against the boy, the offended parents were major donors to the camp and sat on its governing board. This type of quick response is ideal but uncommon, given that black parents were rarely in positions of power in Rolling Acres. One counselor was reprimanded for his treatment of the black students, and the entire staff received training on issues of diversity. These parents could have simply advocated against their children's mistreatment, but instead they made it an issue for all black students at the camp. Unfortunately, this type of intervention was rare, and class lines often divided the benefits of advocacy between the black middle class, the black working class, and the black poor. Even if addressed at the camp, black students—both poor and non-poor—were commonly lumped together in the eyes of many in schools, extracurricular activities, and other social spaces.

Black residents of Rolling Acres were not only unequal in material resources (income, wealth, neighborhood location) but also received treatment that marked them as "outsiders." In Rolling Acres, whites were treated as citizens with full rights, responsibilities, and privileges. Contrastingly, blacks were treated like resident aliens; their right to be in Rolling Acres was constantly questioned, and their access to institutions such as camps and schools was often controlled by whites. In the above example of the summer camp, although counselor was reprimanded, issues of racial exclusion were much larger than individual prejudices. The idea that all black families were poor and were not entitled to occupy spaces that have been historically and predominantly white was pervasive. In an ideal world, all who lived in Rolling Acres would be treated as fully incorporated citizens, but this was far from the case. The everyday prejudices and discriminatory acts that black families, across the class spectrum, encountered cast them as outsiders, regardless of their length of residence and fights against such ostracism.

LEBRON

On most days I found LeBron wearing a baggy T-shirt with slightly saggy jeans or jogging pants. LeBron, at 10 years old, was a little taller than most of his classmates and was athletic. His complexion was a deep espresso that contrasted with his white fitted hat, which he liked to toggle between his head and his hand throughout the school day. LeBron loved sports: basketball, professional wrestling, and football. If you began a conversation about sports, he was sure to finish it with the latest on his favorite players. When I informed him that I allow people participating in my research to choose their own pseudonym, he quickly informed me that he wanted to be called LeBron, after his favorite basketball player, LeBron James.

I first talked to LeBron at length on a field trip to a dance performance. As I sat next to him, he seemed uninterested in the performance and uninterested in talking to me. I looked for an entry to conversation and then noticed LeBron playing with a few folded dollar bills. I motioned to the money in his hand and he said, "They call me money man!" Perplexed, I inquired why, and he responded, "I don't know I just be having money." When I asked him where the money came from, he informed me that he "made it" playing basketball. I inquired further and he said, "I make money playing basketball and I have a team, so they make money." He went on to explain that he "set up" other kids in his neighborhood to play pick-up games for money and that was how he got his money. Much of LeBron's time was spent at a basketball hoop that faced his cul-de-sac. The hoop served as a sort of community hoop, where LeBron and other neighborhood youth shot around. While I do not believe LeBron actually made money by "hustling hoops," I do believe he saw basketball as a legitimate route to getting ahead, particularly by making money. Like most boys his age, he held big dreams of being a professional athlete but was willing to consider other paths when pushed.

LeBron was often eager to tell me about his desire to play basketball in the near future. But unlike Danny, he was not involved in multiple sports teams locally or regionally. He told me about his cousin who participated in a local basketball league that was for "good players," and in a few years he planned to enter that league. He played local pick-up games but did not participate in adult-organized sporting activities. LeBron, like a number of black boys in my sample, participated in child-organized activities where rules were set and maintained by youth.

While Danny's saw his participation in athletics as tied to his academic performance, there was no such connection between sports and school for LeBron. For many black families and lower-income white families, the financial cost and opportunity costs of enrolling children in formal extracurricular activities were significant barriers to participation.

Annette Lareau and others have argued that parents who practiced concerted cultivation enrolled their children in extracurriculars to support their development, but this style of parenting is closely tied to socioeconomic resources, not simply disposition.[14] Repeatedly, I found that black and poor families had orientations that stressed nurturing children's development intentionally, but their limited economic, social, and cultural capital kept them from enrolling their children in activities similar to those the more capital-affluent families participated in.

EDUCATION AND OCCUPATION

Unlike Danny and his parents, the Dowings did not see a consistent link between sports, everyday study habits, and his future opportunities. When I asked LeBron's parents about the role of education in their lives, they told me that they had not attended college but that LeBron would. When I asked his father about LeBron's future career options and education, he said:

> For his life, he has aspirations of going into the entertainment type stuff [sports]. But he must realize . . . I am trying to relay to him that education is [the] number one key that he has got to have. Man if you can't count money, then how much money do you know you have? That is the thing, the basics is the first thing that you got to grasp. After the basics everything else moves along pretty smooth.

Mr. Downing emphasized the basics of education and the need to have the basics to manage money. I call this approach a *utility-focused approach* to education, where the value of education is defined by its ability to achieve a desired end. Utility-focused approaches might in turn deemphasize the process of educational exploration and/or overemphasize the return to investment.

The majority of black families with children in Rolling Acres Public Schools said that a central rationale for pushing their children's pursuit of education was to get a job that was better than their own and to accumulate wealth.[15] This attitude is not grossly different from that expressed by immigrant parents who champion education as the engine of social mobility and wealth accumulation; but those parents do so by focusing on a narrow set of majors and occupational choices that they project to be tied to social and material success.[16]

In contrast, in middle-class and affluent families, of which the majority were white, discussions about the value of education centered on intellectual exploration and more abstract concepts of social good. I call this an *abstract approach* to education. The abstract approach is tied closely to family background, such as higher educational attainment, income, and wealth. Families that had multiple generations of college graduates and financial stability, like the Morrises, tended to employ an abstract approach to education. The utility-focused approach of the Downings is quite logical given the instability of the black middle class. At the same time, this approach can serve to maintain the gaps in educational and economic accumulation between the two groups.[17]

The Downings pledged allegiance to high expectations for LeBron, and Mr. Downing described some potential careers for their son:

> Oh, a doctor, teacher . . . I would like to see him in any kind of a profession [where] he could help to serve other people. I would like to see that. I really would, 'cause I think that is what I have done a lot of my life is you try to help and service other people. As far as my knowledge, I have a lot of good hand skills: carpentry, automotive, electrical, plumbing, and heating. Those types of things. And I have always tried to help other people out, you know, as far as them needing that type of service. Once I started being involved with the neighborhood center I started doing more things with service as far as drug intervention, teen counseling, and it's nothing I learned at school or anything.

Mr. Downing's desire to have his son in a service-related job meant there were many different options. Although he suggested potential jobs ranging from those with high prestige to more working class, in all likelihood the jobs closer to his own occupational experiences were most accessible to LeBron.[18] Jobs like doctor and lawyer represent an ideal, but the pathways to those occupations are not easily negotiated. Despite Mr. Downing's lack of formal education, his job as the shuttle driver for a local community center exposed him to social service–oriented jobs.

When time and space permitted, he shuttled LeBron to a community center where his child could join in on activities. This was one of the few times that LeBron got to play sports or take part in other activities offered for youth in his age range led by adults. Unfortunately, this happened less often than the Downings desired. As I followed LeBron and the Downings, Mr. Downing let me know that he had a nephew who had recently graduated from a Southern university with a master's degree in social work. He was confident that he could call on his nephew for assistance with LeBron and career exploration when the time came.

Access to people with expertise or knowledge is critical in assisting with the steps between school and a desired career path. Odis Johnson has argued that "proximal capital" is one of the advantages of being located in an area of concentrated affluence; but the ability to actualize this capital is mediated by relationship quality and reach.[19] From his connections, Mr.

Downing had access to information about social services jobs, but other job sectors were not equally accessible to him. When asked, Mr. Downing and Ms. Downing could not identify any close connections to doctors or lawyers in their social network. Ms. Towles was an African-American lawyer who lived near them, but the relationship between the Towles and Downing families was strained. There were few occasions when these families interacted, and the Downings were not likely to reach out to the other family for assistance. The few highly educated or white-collar neighbors the Downings had paled in comparison with the Morrises' neighbors and networks.

Erin McNamara Horvat, Eliot Weininger, and Annette Lareau have argued that the black middle class and the white middle class have similar social networks;[20] however, they simply count the number of connections, not the quality of those connections. From this type of estimation, networks may look similar, but their social capital may not be equal. James Coleman importantly advanced the idea that social capital was not defined simply by the number of associations one had, but by the ability to use those connections to achieve a desired end.[21]

The Downings could list a number of people with high-prestige occupations, but it was not clear that they had any kind of access to those people. Their network was centered on their local neighbors, their family, and their workplaces, all of which were heavily influenced by their race and class. Their highly localized networks offered only weak ties; the people in those networks were more like passing acquaintances than associates that they could contact for advice or assistance with achieving goals, such as career path information. While studying Rolling Acres, I seldom saw weak ties provide a net benefit for black and or lower-income families. Viewed in an idealized sense, the Downings and their children were immersed in networks with little overlap and had access to people in a wide variety of careers, but in reality their networks were more circumscribed than they seemed.

At school, LeBron sat next to the children of lawyers, doctors, and a multitude of other professionals, but this did not mean he had access to their social or material assets. For many, the chance to attend school in Rolling Acres would cause them to brim with hope, but the Downings approached LeBron's schooling with less grand expectations. Their approach was partially grounded in their own experiences in Rolling Acres. As children, Mr.

Downing and Ms. Downing were a part of what he called "the first desegregation." Mr. Downing said:

> Remember I told you I was [part] of the desegregation in the schools.
> Didn't really know that [then], really didn't know what people were call-
> ing me, but I knew it wasn't what I should have been called. I didn't think
> my name was nigger 'cause Mommy and Daddy never called me nigger.
> But you know, going to those schools and having these parents outside this
> building saying, "niggers get back on the bus," you know. We had no idea.
> You know we were pretty much sheltered. Not really . . . yeah I guess you
> could say we were sheltered, because we [black families] were throughout
> one portion of town and that was it. We never had a chance to fan out,
> you know, to different portions of the town.

Although Rolling Acres' busing project was less violent and tumultuous
than that in other cities, such as Boston, Mr. Downing still carried remnants of the hatred that marked his childhood schooling. He recalled that
his white classmates treated him well enough, but that their parents rejected
the busing of black students into predominantly white schools.

When I brought up the value of desegregation in his life, he said that
he was able to build interracial friendships early on in his schooling, but
also acknowledged these friendships dissolved as they progressed through
high school. After high school, he remained more closely tied to his black
classmates than his white ones. When I asked Mr. Downing about the
trajectory of his white school friends, he said that some had continued on
to higher-prestige jobs; he was unclear about the paths of others because
he did not have much contact with them as adults. After our interview, he
confessed that he had not consciously thought about the divergent pathways between himself and his white classmates until our interview.

To Mr. Downing the "first desegregation" had been a success, particularly because his son was able to sit in a multiethnic classroom and
had never experienced the outward racial animus he experienced. For Mr.
Downing, this marked clear progress. While things were certainly not
equal between black and white families, he knew some of the outward
fights of old had dissolved and given way to more amicable race relations,
at least publicly.

Ms. Downing did not wholly share Mr. Downing's optimism. Ms.
Downing was born outside of Rolling Acres but moved to Rolling Acres
at a young age and went to school in the district. As a former attendee and

the mother of multiple children in the system, she watched Rolling Acres Public Schools carefully. She told me:

> I like Rolling Acres. The qualities you can get out of Rolling Acres, some places you just can't get. It ain't that I like it because of fairness, the reason why I really like Rolling Acres is because just say if your kid played football good or basketball good, they would get recognized in Rolling Acres schools [more] than they would get in other schools.

Ms. Downing was certain that while the schools of RAPS had a positive reputation, this did not necessarily mean that it was good for all families. Neither academic prestige nor diversity gave RAPS its value, she said; instead RAPS was noteworthy because students who performed athletically received national attention. Ms. Downing's rejection of the RAPS educational system was not based on naïveté but on her own experiences with the system. Although she never mentioned it in our multiple interviews, I learned that Ms. Downing was one of the child plaintiffs in the 1970s case over educational services to black families discussed in chapter 2. It is not hard to imagine that the district's ultimate inability to provide a better education for herself and other black students left her with some bitter sentiments.

In the epigraph that opens this chapter, Ms. Downing notes the perception of Rolling Acres as a desirable school system, but also that there was some out-migration of black families after they experienced Rolling Acres Public Schools. The in-migration and out-migration that Ms. Downing mentioned reflected both the rigor and the rigidity of the RAPS system. Black parents who enrolled their children in RAPS were often informed that they were academically behind. These parents often had little recourse but to try to adjust their children's educational program when confronted with the school's assessment of their skills. But both newly arrived black families and longstanding black families dealt with RAPS reluctance to accommodate black parents' attempts at educational customization.

While families like the Morrises saw Rolling Acres as diverse and well-intentioned, and its schools as high-performing, the Downing family knew a different Rolling Acres. The Downings' Rolling Acres still represented a step forward from high-poverty, high-minority school systems, despite the racially segmented school experience their son received. In the next section, I discuss the two families' views on mobility, which are rooted in their relative deprivation and segmented experiences.

GETTING AHEAD, NOT CATCHING UP

The Downing family was very strategic about finding the best educational opportunities for LeBron and his older sister. Mr. Downing confided that RAPS was not easy to negotiate for black families, and having sent one child through they would do whatever it took to ensure LeBron's success. One potential strategy he identified was sending his son to a local alternative high school led by an African-American principal.[22] The school was for students with behavioral issues and also featured the greatest concentration of black students in a RAPS high school. In conversations with the principal and other residents, Mr. Downing deduced that the principal was responsive to the needs of black families, unlike other building administrators. For the Downings, the gamble of having their son attend a special-needs school was balanced by the prospect of increasing LeBron's chances of attending college, a goal they often articulated to him.

The Downings were excited that LeBron's older sister was in the midst of preparing to attend college. When I inquired about her college selection process, her parents beamed that she had been accepted to a local community college and would matriculate there next fall. They told me that she did not complete a national college search and did not do a comprehensive local search. Instead their daughter qualified for scholarship money at a local two-year college and chose the school based on scholarships funds. This created a perfect storm of conditions for her attendance. Some would look at her decision as a failure to seize greater opportunity, but when considering their family's educational history her choice represented meaningful progress in the family's cumulative educational attainment.

For the Downings, and for most black families I interviewed, catching up to other families (particularly white families) in Rolling Acres was not necessarily the litmus test for success. Mr. and Ms. Downing used their own educational experiences as a frame of reference. It was common to hear black residents say that they wanted their children "to do better than me." Black families considered their position relative to other family members whose children did not attend suburban schools. The Downings had family throughout the Midwest and the South, and they routinely referred to family members who had fewer opportunities or greater hazards because of where they lived. Relative to other black families, they were doing well, but in comparison with local white families their experiences and accomplishments lagged behind. In this way, black national frames of reference were important for understanding how they invested in education and measured success. When one compares the Downing family with the national images of blackness that centered on poverty, violence, and hyper-racial segregation, they were doing very well.

The Morris family had high educational attainment. Mr. Morris held an advanced degree and Ms. Morris held a college degree. Both Danny and his sister had visited their parents' collegiate alma maters and were looking forward to college. Danny and his sister said that they would follow in their parents' footsteps and attend one of their alma maters, but Mr. and Ms. Morris informed me that both children would have to conduct a national search for schools. The Morris family stressed college attendance, but also reassured their children that its cost would not prevent them from attending their dream school, even if it strained the financial resources of the family.

There are many steps between elementary school and college, but the mechanisms that led to the disparities that I observed at a district high school graduation were well under way by the fourth grade. From family background to networks and messages, LeBron's and Danny's pathways diverged early and often. Attending the same school did little to offset the fault lines that ran beneath the surface of their lives and fragmented their futures.

CONCLUSION

Predicting the future is impossible, of course, but the probability that LeBron's and Danny's lives would have different outcomes was clear from the communities, networks, and other resources that surrounded them. My analysis runs counter to the claim of other scholars who have suggested that middle-class standing confers similar benefits to black and white families. For example, McNamara Horvat, Weininger, and Lareau wrote, "aspects of everyday life such as time use, social networks, and strategies for interacting with institutions that were exhibited by middle-class black families were extremely similar, and in many ways indistinguishable, from those of their white counterparts."[23] This was far from the story that my data uncovered. Even for locally grounded and savvy black families like the Downings, getting the most out of networks, schools, and the city was difficult.

The Downing family's children represented Rolling Acres' second generation, yet the fruits of the Promised Land had not fully ripened. As multigeneration residents of Rolling Acres, the Downings arguably had more claim to the city than the Morrises, who had arrived more recently, but by virtue of their skin color and their social position they were deprived of the suburban spoils. The Downings did not suffer from the lack of opportunities that would be typical for a black family living in a poor urban area. However, they did suffer from an unequal ability to gain access to opportunities in Rolling Acres. From sports to schooling, black families remained behind white families.

While black families in Rolling Acres likely had richer networks than black families elsewhere, they did not compare with the networks available to white Rolling Acres residents. Black families' less rich networks meant they were less likely to attend the same schools as whites or hold the same view on the utility of education. In residential location, family background, and messages passed to children, the lives of black and white middle-class children were unequal. Unequal histories often manifest in unequal futures.

Both Danny and LeBron viewed their pathways as open, but they had already begun to take shape. For Danny, rich out-of-school networks and his background will facilitate multiple options for school and career, while his parents' financial stability will provide a safety net on his journey. In contrast, LeBron's path will be rocky. He will have to make the best of a less rich network with the hope of surpassing the achievements of his parents in income, job stability, and occupational prestige. Unfortunately, his family's lack of diverse and engageable connections, as well as financial stability, will likely not serve as a full catalyst to achieving the highest possibilities.

In the context of Rolling Acres, LeBron's lack of a safety net increases the odds that a misstep will land him in special education or get him suspended from school; later he may end up at a lower-prestige college or in the military. These were all common realities for black students in Rolling Acres schools. These outcomes may be less negative than the consequences of missteps that black males in inner-city areas face, such as dropping out of school, incarceration, and street violence, but it is important to recall that black families in Rolling Acres often cited moving to Rolling Acres as their method for avoiding common pitfalls and creating greater opportunity for their children. In attempting to move to opportunity, they were able to avoid one common set of destinies, but encountered another set of hazards along the way. Even in their ideal location, stewarding a black child toward safety and maximum opportunity remained a challenging task for black families.

FOUR

Making Your Public School Private

> "You wouldn't believe if I told you. You haven't seen
> anything! It was even worse at my old school. The
> problem is that they [affluent white parents] treat it
> like their private school."
>
> —PRINCIPAL BELL, BLACK FEMALE,
> CHERRY ELEMENTARY SCHOOL

The statement above by Principal Bell reflects one of her frustrations with being the principal of a diverse school with demanding parents. In particular, Principal Bell consistently dealt with a core group of affluent white parents who demanded educational customization for their children (classroom placement, priority in extracurricular opportunities, and others) and threatened to leave if their requests were not fulfilled; and she was among the district staff who feared these affluent families' exit. These demanding parents' engagement not only affected their children's lives but also influenced the chances that other families would want to customize their children's education.

In education research, parental engagement is often viewed as desirable and is associated with positive school experiences and schooling outcomes.[1] However, parental engagement is multidimensional, and beyond the positive image that is promoted there are negative dimensions as well, which affect the access of all families to a high-quality education. As the principal of Cherry Elementary, Ms. Bell understood this and recognized the advantages of parental engagement, but found that some types of parental engagement made the educational terrain between white and black and between rich and poor even more uneven. Understanding how individual and group parental engagement contributed to tense relationships between home and school and between families is key for understanding why Rolling Acres schools remain together but unequal.

In this chapter, I argue that the current literature on parental engagement has under-theorized the role of race by overemphasizing social class, and that current models lack sufficient consideration of the interfamilial influences of parental engagement—particularly concerted cultivation. I propose a model that captures interfamilial dynamics and reveals how home-school interactions change over time. The interactions between home and school dynamically shape the racialized roles of consumer and beneficiary. These roles help explain the grossly different experiences black and white families across social classes have in public schools.

I begin the chapter with a general discussion of parental engagement and the limits of models that emphasize social class. I follow by introducing a relational model of parental engagement that captures the role of race and intergroup relations and introduces the roles of consumer and beneficiary parents. To illustrate these processes, first I provide a case comparison of two black mothers from River Elementary and their different experiences with school volunteering. Second, I present a case study of parental organizing at Cherry Elementary that demonstrates how social networks can leverage information to the advantage of some families and constrain the educational opportunities of others. In both cases the role of race shapes differences in educational opportunity, even in well-resourced spaces. These examples aid in the elucidation of the power and latent effects of heightened and unequal parental engagement.

PARENTAL ENGAGEMENT

"Their parents just don't care." This statement is commonly touted as a reason for disparities in parental engagement between black and white as well as rich and poor. Parental engagement is often regarded as the educational Holy Grail—much desired but seldom acquired. The belief that engaged parents can help salve educational woes is, in part, supported by research findings that parental involvement and participation are associated with positive educational outcomes (e.g., test scores, fewer absences).[2] However, not all forms of parental engagement have equal significance, and not all forms are equally accessible.[3]

The social science literature distinguishes between the forms of parental engagement. A standard division is between parental involvement, which occurs predominantly outside the classroom or school, and parental participation, which occurs predominantly within the classroom or school.[4] The examples and models I present here encompass both participation and involvement in order to demonstrate that parental engagement is not always finite or neat; rather it reflects a complex relationship between home and school in which family background, school culture, and educational demands intersect and create divergent educational experiences.

Lareau and Weininger support a model of parental engagement that illustrates how differences in family background shape different cultural capital endowments, which moderate home-school connections. They argue that "students and parents enter the educational system with dispositional skills and knowledge that differentially facilitate or impede their ability to conform to institutionalized expectations."[5] Lareau first explicated this model in *Home Advantage* and further clarifies this approach in *Unequal Childhoods*.[6] She argues that middle-class families using concerted cultivation are well received and have favorable relations with schools, while working-class families that use natural growth have more antagonistic relationships with institutions. Figure 2 illustrates Lareau's model.

Lareau's model is parsimonious, but it notably underestimates the importance of race in home-school connections. Lareau and her colleagues do not ignore the role of race, but they are dismissive of it. In their study of parental social networks and school relations they argued that social class drove the relationship, with race holding little sway.[7] In *Unequal Childhoods* Lareau argued, "While race did have situational consequences for some youths, the power of social class was striking for all."[8] Across studies she argues that race is relevant only at the individual level, such as when an individual complained of discrimination or prejudice. This view is dangerously unsystematic because it ignores the pervasive influence of race on black and white lives and the relations between groups. As a result, when individuals must negotiate racial hazards, the causes of such hazards are seen to be (un)identifiable malevolent individuals, not groups or institutions. The failure to see the role of race in relations between white and black families is an important theoretical oversight and leads to empirical misspecifications of how parental engagement operates. The relationally

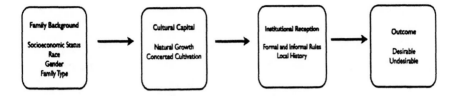

Figure 2. Annette Lareau's Model of Parental Engagement.
This diagram is a simplification of Lareau's model and cannot include
every possible factor that could occupy each box; thus it is a parsimonious
representation, not an exhaustive one. In addition, I chose to list some
categories that Lareau and her collaborators have consistently identified as
meaningful in the connections between home and school/formal institutions.

based analysis of race-related issues that I subscribe to would discuss the
relevance of race, not just to black families but also to white families, as
they operate in the same spaces and attempt similar tasks, like educational
customization.[9]

Last, the structure of Lareau's data across the aforementioned studies
precludes a more relational analysis of the roles of class and race. In *Home
Advantage*, few black families are represented, while in *Unequal Childhoods*
the middle-class black families sent their children to private schools, and
often not the same schools that white middle-class students attended. As a
result, suggestions about class primacy are warped because there are not sufficient black middle-class and white middle-class cases in the same spaces to
observe intergroup dynamics.[10] The data I collected in Rolling Acres allow
for a more relational consideration of parental engagement, which takes into
account race and class dynamics both individually and between groups.

A RELATIONAL MODEL OF
PARENTAL ENGAGEMENT

To fully understand parental engagement one must look carefully at relationships as they are affected by family background, cultural capital, institutional
reception, and desired outcomes, as well as the relationships between groups.
The process is not unidirectional (as it is often portrayed), with family background characteristics leading to stocks of cultural capital, which align with
institutional rules and result in a desirable outcome. Instead, I argue such a

simplistic model under considers the dynamics that exist between home and school and between different families in the same setting.

Schools are complex organizations with unique cultures that help shape and structure parental engagement. It is not enough to have a parent who is interested in being engaged; schools and their staff shape and broker what is appropriate or desirable parental engagement. This process invokes a structured protocol but is also discretionary because local schools and staff determine what is acceptable engagement, which of the desired outcomes are feasible, and which parents are desirable participants. School staff and the rules they set play an active role in determining which parents are engaged and what they receive from their engagement.

For example, formal rules can include school-wide policies such as how to request a teacher or classroom-level policies such as when baked goods can be brought to school. At the school level, formal rules are created by building administrators or dictated by the central administration. At the classroom level, teachers create policies and tasks that are administered by room parents—parents who volunteer to organize classroom matters. In Cherry and River Elementary Schools where I conducted observations, these formal rules were conveyed at the beginning of the year during school orientation, in PTA meetings, or in classroom newsletters. Once the rules distributed, it was assumed that all families understood them.

Informal rules of engagement were very important for home-school relations. For example, in each classroom I observed, particular days were available for parents to visit, and there were preferred forms of parental involvement; in addition, teachers determined when they were available for conversations with parents. I define many of these rules as informal because they were not written down or always shared; instead teachers would make the rules in an ad hoc fashion as the year progressed. Parents learned about them from the classroom teacher or from other engaged parents. In RAPS classrooms, both formal and informal rules for participation were rigid despite the fact that schools used many volunteers.

Many parents learned about a school's practices and opportunities via networks of parents. I found three types of networks at play: formal, semi-formal, and informal. Formal networks developed through organizations like the PTA or through "room parents." Room parents were groups of volunteer parents who coordinated volunteer opportunities, maintained phone trees, and served as brokers for the classroom teacher. For example, room parents would broker relationships with parents in their children's classrooms by distributing information about upcoming school events and volunteer opportunities. Semi-formal parent networks that began in organizations often extended beyond their original purpose; semi-formal networks made parents aware of extracurricular experiences and bridged geographic divisions through emails to parents about upcoming volunteer opportunities. For example, baseball team parents might use team activities to create bonds and share information with other baseball parents. Informal social networks tended to be organized around clusters of friends or other affinity groups, such as racially similar parents who discover common cultural interests or political leanings. They use these more organic networks to share information about negotiating academic hurdles and increasing educational customization.

Parental networks were not the only way that families acquired information about school-related information. A large amount of information about school-related activities was sent to students' homes by mail or with students in their backpacks. Mr. Marks, a white teacher at River Elementary, explained his perception of home-school correspondence, "There's a huge, huge, huge public relations marketing attempt. There isn't a kid . . . I mean a kid's got to be completely out of it not to be aware that [extracurricular activities are] available to him." In the view of Mr. Marks and other teachers I observed, the school provided sufficient information to families, and the responsibility of dealing with this information lay in the home. While Rolling Acres was consistent in its transmission of formal information, the reception of this information varied among families.

The Rolling Acres school district, like many other well-resourced school districts, features abundant extracurricular opportunities for students, including science clubs, scouting activities, and sports sponsored by the local city government. The communication of information to families is key to ensuring that all families have equal access to resources. These opportunities were expressed almost exclusively in written form (e.g., letters home, backpack mail, email). Among the parents in my sample, parental levels of education varied greatly between students in the same classrooms.[11] The majority of low-income families in my sample were single-income and single-headed; most parents had completed high school or some college. Middle- and upper-income families almost always had two incomes or a single large income and at least one college graduate.

Differences between families in education and family structure deeply affected how they used their time. Lower-income families had less time to read, process, and respond to materials sent home. This is not to suggest that the occupations of middle- and upper-income families were not time-demanding. Quite to the contrary, middle-income and affluent families' lives were very busy and heavily scheduled; however, these families relied on multiple social supports that gave them "more time" to engage their children and their activities. This time was made available by paying for costly childcare, having one parent stay at home, or hiring housekeepers to do basic household chores. All of these social supports cost money. Middle-class and affluent families used their economic capital to purchase time, which allowed them to juggle work, social, and familial obligations as well as process the large amount of information that came home about school and school-related matters.

On a typical day, children were sent home with homework assignments, homework logs, and numerous program announcements; this did not include information sent by regular mail and email. The different ways parents engaged with these school announcements became clear to me when I found that low-income families were not responding to mailed requests to participate in my research project. When I introduced myself to Mr. Clarke, an African-American grandfather of fourth-grader Vince, I asked him if he had received my letters. He replied offhandedly, "It's probably in a stack of bills." In contrast, middle-income parents that did not respond to mailings would often tell me they had seen and read the letter but had not gotten around to responding to me yet.

These small differences in availability of time, paired with educational attainment differences, led to widely divergent understandings of and engagement with local offerings. The administration of formal information, almost exclusively in written form, sorted families into and out of opportunities. It is important to note that there are other types of communication between families and the schools, such as parent-teacher conferences, but even the announcement of such events was conveyed almost exclusively via home mailings and backpack mail.

Information is a crucial resource that can be a gateway to other education-related opportunities. The structure of networks and the information that was transmitted to families allowed them to gain access to official school-related events as well as to information that was not official but was meaningful. During my time in the field I found that semi-formal and informal networks were very influential on the ability of parents to engage schools and achieve desirable ends.

EDUCATIONAL CUSTOMIZATION

A common goal of parents who engage schools is educational customization: the tailoring of their child's education to match their own ambitions and values. Nearly all parents are interested in their children getting a quality education, but not all parents are able to influence their children's educational pathway. While educational customization may appear to be an individual or family-level endeavor, in the aggregate the choices made by individual parents have collateral effects on other families in the same school. Sometimes the collateral consequences of customization result from casual oversight; at other times they are the result of families hoarding resources and opportunities. Pinpointing the difference between the two can be difficult. Nonetheless, analyzing the ways that educational customization attempts by families in Rolling Acres served to stratify educational resources between races and classes helps reveal the subtle sites of inequality production and reproduction.

Often parents engage with the school in order to monitor a child's academic progress and maintain a supple relationship with the school; they can also use their presence in and familiarity with the school as a basis for leveraging more educational resources for their children. In many districts this would look like parental lobbying for Advanced Placement or accelerated classes, but Rolling Acres Public Schools at the elementary level did not place students on different tracks.[12] Still, parents routinely lobbied to get their children access to the "best" teachers' classrooms and worked to curry favor with school staff in order to receive information about out-of-school opportunities.

This *desire* to increase the chances of their child's success cut across social class and race. However, I found that parents' *ability* to customize their children's education was influenced by class, but more importantly, circumscribed by race. As eager parents attempted to engage with schools to customize their children's education, their reception by school staff ultimately ushered parents into the role of consumer or beneficiary.

SHAPING BENEFICIARY
AND CONSUMER ROLES

Across racial and class categories I observed a healthy desire among parents to customize the educational opportunities of their children, but their
desires were met with institutional cultures and structures that guided parents into specific roles. Lareau argued that these differences were attributable to parental dispositions and child-rearing strategies that were social
class–based; I found, however, that these roles were race-based and were
more influential than parental disposition on educational customization.
Via observations and interview accounts, I found that parents, over time,
changed their strategies of engagement with schools based on their success
or failure.

It was common for white parents to assume the role of consumer. Consumer parents viewed schools as a customizable resource, and they fash-
ioned schools to fit their children's educational and social developmental
needs. The beneficiary role was more common among black parents in
Rolling Acres Public Schools. Parents in the role of beneficiary viewed
schools as a resource that had children's best social and educational development in mind and did little to customize their children's education. Beneficiary parents often followed the school's programming and suggestions
with the hope of ensuring that their children received a "good education."

Consumer and beneficiary roles resulted from interactions over time
between families and school staff and institutional norms. Parents may
have started out with similar ideas about the desirability of customizing
their children's educational trajectories, but their successes and failures
along the way signaled to them whether actually they had that ability. In
their repeated interactions with the schools, they learned which role they
were expected to occupy and maintained that role in their everyday negotiations with school staff and other families.

The home-school relationship develops and shifts through a recursive process. It is not a simple unidirectional or static relationship. It is iterative and
cumulative. As families engage and re-engage schools and their employees,
they are endowed with greater or less confidence in their ability to customize
their child's education. In the following pages I present a case study of two
African-American parents to illustrate how they were both ushered into beneficiary roles, despite their different class positions and orientations.

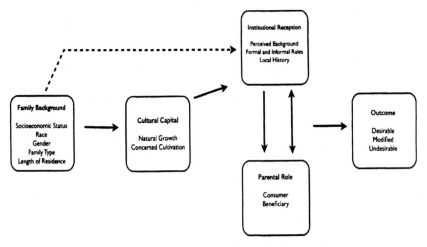

Figure 3. The Dynamic Nature of Home-School Relationships

PARENTAL ENGAGEMENT AMONG POOR AND MIDDLE-CLASS BLACK FAMILIES

Schools and their staffs are important brokers of parental engagement, particularly parental participation. Outwardly, schools and their staff say they desire high levels of engagement and participation from all parents; in my observations, however, I found that school staff worked diligently to decide how parents got involved and which parents were engaged. In this section I examine the ways staff treated two black mothers, one middle class and one poor. To capture the intersection of race and class issues, I rely in particular on Bourdieu's notion of habitus to make sense of their differing levels of success at engaging school staff.[13] Habitus is rooted in social class, and thus I differentiate their experiences by class, but these parents' ability to operate with authority at work and at school was circumscribed by race when they interacted with school staff and other parents. Race and class worked together to curtail parental engagement and educational customization opportunities for black families in the local public schools.

I first met Ms. Martin at River Elementary's open house. As I floated about the school, I stopped outside Mr. Marks's fourth-grade classroom to find him standing with his back to his classroom door, arms crossed, and repeating, "I will not discuss this with you now. We can set up a time to talk." After Mr. Marks repeated this several times, Ms. Martin left his doorway, visibly discouraged. I trailed her down the hallway, introduced myself, and told her I was doing a research project on River Elementary. She interrupted me to say, "You don't want to talk to me; I don't have good relationships around here." I reassured her that I was interested in all families' experiences, whether good or bad.

By the time I met Ms. Martin in the hallway I had known Mr. Marks for weeks, and he had advised me that there were several families he thought would be interesting for me to interview and observe; the Martin family was not on his recommended list. After my initial conversation with Ms. Martin, I returned to Mr. Marks's classroom to ask about her and the potential of including her in my study. He shuffled through the papers on this desk, did not raise his head, and informed me, "You can speak to her if you want." His non-ringing endorsement became more understandable over the course of the school year, when I came to learn that Mr. Marks and Mr. Tyler, the school principal, identified Ms. Martin as a "problem parent."

Problem parent was not a term that school staff used, but it was a category that described parents whose engagement was thought to directly conflict with institutional rules and norms. Their presence and advocacy were often eschewed or discouraged. The feeling of disdain that Mr. Marks and school staff felt for Ms. Martin was mutual. Ms. Martin felt that the school staff did not respect her as a parent and attempted to block her participation, which frustrated her. Over the course of four months, I watched her change from a concerned parent who actively attempted engagement to a parent who felt defeated by her blocked efforts and resigned to accepting whatever opportunities to engage that were offered.

Mr. Marks's disinterest in Ms. Martin contrasted sharply with his view of Ms. Towles, another African-American mother in his classroom. During the same open house at River Elementary where I happened upon Ms. Martin, Mr. Marks insisted I meet Ms. Towles. He repeated throughout the evening, with excitement, "You have to meet Ms. Towles, she's African-American and a lawyer!" A few hours into the evening Mr. Marks saw Ms. Towles's son Jeffrey, called him over eagerly, and requested that he bring his mother to meet me. Ms. Towles politely accepted my introduction, said we would talk later, and returned to her role as a parent volunteer at the open house. Throughout my time in the field, unlike Ms. Martin, Ms. Towles was a very engaged parent, but her engagement was rife with race-related hurdles at her son's school, which she negotiated successfully, in part because of her habitus.

Ms. Martin and Ms. Towles shared some characteristics but were also different in several ways. Both were single mothers. Both had limited contact with male caregivers for their children. Both were active in their children's education and desired to be more engaged. Importantly, their pedigrees differed. Ms. Martin was a fast-food worker and had completed high school. Ms. Towles was a practicing attorney and had multiple graduate degrees. These differences shaped their practices and the reception they received from River Elementary School staff like Mr. Marks and Principal Tyler and other families, and subsequently affected what they were able to achieve.

The confrontation between Ms. Martin and Mr. Marks that I observed at the open house was based on an incident earlier in the day. Ms. Martin had sent cupcakes to school with her daughter Raven to celebrate another student's birthday. While in many spaces this act of kindness would be considered normal and appreciated, at River Elementary and in Mr. Marks's classroom, following protocol was critical. In Mr. Marks's classroom all baked goods were arranged through room parents and were only to be distributed at specific times during the day. By sending the cupcakes with Raven, Ms. Martin had not followed protocol.

When I asked Mr. Marks in an interview why he thought Ms. Martin was so upset on that evening, he confessed that during the day he had chastised Raven for bringing in the baked goods and reprimanded her by saying, "Your mother knows better!" Raven, a quiet and sensitive girl, was hurt by the reprimand and public rebuke of her mother's efforts and related the day's events when she arrived home. Ms. Martin was angered and felt Raven had been mistreated because she was one of few black children in the classroom. Ms. Martin felt that Marks did not just correct the error but sought to embarrass her daughter. On the evening of the open house where I met Ms. Martin, I had observed her attempt to speak with Mr. Marks about the incident, which he refused to do by demanding that she make a separate appointment. This was not Ms. Martin's first run-in with issues at River Elementary, and the legacy of this incident and her past weighed heavily on her ability to effectively engage school staff and influence Raven's school experiences.

There are many forms of parental participation, but the type that was most desirable were teacher-sanctioned volunteer opportunities coordinated by room parents. When I spoke with Mr. Marks's room parents, two white stay-at-home mothers, they informed me that his classroom had high rates of parental participation. The room parents used an email list to relay information to parents and coordinate visits to the classroom. The school did not produce the list; instead it was created at the year's first open house, where attendees provided their email addresses. This contact list served as the master list for engaging parents in school functions and related opportunities. When I queried the room parents about its comprehensiveness, they informed me that most families were listed, but when I saw a copy of the list I noted that Ms. Martin and several other black families, with the notable exception of the Towleses, were not listed. When I mentioned this to one room parent, she replied that she would rectify the issue.

The missing contact information for Ms. Martin and the other black families may have simply been an artifact of their lack of attendance at the first open house, but it had consequences for their children's participation. The nearly exclusive reliance on written communication to convey information further posed a burden for low-income families, who may have had less access to email and other technology-dependent channels. The ability to participate in school events and school-related activities was moderated by the availability of information as well as the reception of school staff and other families. These subtle and cumulative differences in how information was transmitted and to whom partially explains why Ms. Towles was more visibly present than Ms. Martin as a parent volunteer throughout the school year.

The previous interactions that Ms. Martin had with Mr. Marks did not lessen her desire to participate in her daughter's class activities. Toward the end of the academic year, Ms. Martin indicated to Mr. Marks that she wanted to chaperone a field trip that the class was taking to the state capital. Mr. Marks informed her that the room parents had already lined up chaperones, but informed her that she could attend if she drove herself across the state to the capital and back. While driving was not impossible, it placed a differential burden on Ms. Martin who, at the time, still was not working and had a barely functioning car. Although Marks never directly said he did not want her to attend, in an informal conversation he told me, "I wouldn't mind [if she didn't come]."

This circumstance demonstrates how the formal and informal rules of his classroom were used to create differential expectations, as well as differential access to participation. When the field trip to the capital occurred, Ms. Martin met the students at the school, drove to the capital by herself, went on the walking tour with the students, ate lunch with them, and then drove back to Rolling Acres in her car with her daughter Raven as her passenger. When I asked Ms. Martin about the field trip in a follow-up interview, in a deadpan fashion, she replied, "It was all right." In her voice I detected no bitterness; instead I heard resolution that she had done what was necessary to participate, though she was aware that barriers to her participation had been erected. In the course of negotiating her issues with Mr. Marks and being denied the opportunity to chaperone, she never found River Elementary to be a welcoming place for herself or her daughter, but she remained.

Ms. Martin's relationship with Mr. Marks was not the only tense one she had at River Elementary. Although Mr. Marks did not know specific details, he told me that in Raven's third-grade year Ms. Martin had been banned from the school. When I questioned Ms. Martin about the ban, she said it was untrue, but told me that her previous interactions with the school's building staff had been strained. In Raven's third-grade year she had found herself dissatisfied with the educational opportunities and experiences available to Raven, and she went to the school to advocate in her daughter's behalf. Ms. Martin felt that school staff "brushed off" her complaints, so she then took her complaints to the RAPS district office. She used this strategy because she felt the district's administrative staff listened to her complaints, unlike the River Elementary building staff. Once her grievances were aired to the district central office, she said they pressured the school principal to respond to her issues. However, this approach was not sustainable because the district staff did not allow Ms. Martin to call them repeatedly, and after approximately three incidents encouraged her to deal directly with the school and its staff. The River Elementary staff was upset by her choice to complain to the district, and as a result she gained a reputation as a "problem parent." In the end, Ms. Martin was saddled with a school staff that resented her style of engagement and advocacy.

The barriers faced by Ms. Martin were not identical to those faced by other black parents, but were rooted in similar issues of institutional reception. When I asked Ms. Towles about her experience helping with a science fair at River Elementary she told me:

I was chairing the science fair and we . . . I was the only black on the committee. We had been meeting all along. The night we were setting up,
this lady [who] was on the PTA comes into the room and Mr. Tyler [the
school principal] was there, and Mr. Tyler pissed me off too. She walked
in and she says, "well you can't do this like this," and she started rear-
ranging everything we had worked to put together. And Mr. Tyler just
like . . . rather than saying, you know, "well, Sheila, these people are on
the committee. Ms. Towles is chairing [the evening's program], [the committee has] already talked about it, this is what they . . . I don't think you
should be in here doing this." He's like, "oh yeah, you are right. Let's move
this and move these tables around" and I was furious. I just walked out of
the room 'cause I thought I was going to kill him . . . Maybe I am a little
sensitive, but I thought it was, "Oh she's black, she doesn't know what she
is doing" kind of thing. You know because, other black women and I have
talked about this. They will tell you to chair but then they want to micro-
manage you and tell you how to do it. So yeah, I have experienced that
subtle racism, which is why I think a lot of black parents don't get involved
because they don't like that micro-managing. Tell me to chair something,
leave me alone, and let me do it.

Ms. Towles and other black parents were cautious about attributing what
they perceived as mistreatment to race. Sadly, they seldom found alternative explanations for why their efforts at the school were rebuffed or modified; they were aware that suggesting racial bias was viewed as "playing the
race card." As I discuss in chapter 5, in Rolling Acres race was invoked at
celebratory times but was taboo in conversations about discrimination and
intergroup power dynamics. As a result, race was an albatross that shaped
realities but was rarely fully engaged.

Ms. Towles endured the consistent racial microaggressions—the everyday small-scale experiences of discrimination related to race—yet continued
to participate in activities at River Elementary. Her education and occupation likely affected her ability to negotiate such forms of subtle racism.
As a public defender, Ms. Towles encountered disagreement, bureaucracy,
and compromise on a daily basis. In this way, her occupation fortified her
for dealing with these types of interactions. Though these circumstances
were not ideal and served to frustrate and challenge her efforts at her son's
school, her accumulated habits and skills allowed her to endure and maintain a relationship with the school.

Unlike Ms. Towles, Ms. Martin did not negotiate complex bureaucra-
cies or carefully broker arrangements at work. Her relationship with the

managers at her job had proved challenging. When I first met Ms. Martin she was serving out a suspension from her fast-food job because of two confrontations with her bosses. In the first incident she was told she could not read the Bible on her break. Ms. Martin recounted that the restaurant manager told her, "This is not the place to read this."[14] Martin responded, "[If you read this] you wouldn't have so much pity and so much evil and weakness in your life. Read Psalms and they should tell you, read the book of Romans, read the book of Joshua and you would really understand, you wouldn't have to feel the way you feel." Her manager did not appreciate these suggestions. And that was not the only run-in Martin had with her supervisors. She informed me that she observed a pattern of mistreatment of black drive-thru customers. When she spoke with her shift supervisor, another African-American, she felt her concerns about racial mistreatment were dismissed. Frustrated but not deterred, she repeatedly mentioned the differences in treatment but felt nothing was done to correct the perceived discrimination. Her outspokenness about religion and her sounding the alarm against racial discrimination led to her suspension and to tense relationships with her supervisors.

For a low-income wage worker, being suspended from one's job would be worthy of concern, but Ms. Martin seemed unfazed. She gladly accepted the suspension because she saw value in the messages she was communicating to her superiors. From her perspective, it was crucial that her managers know that her religious faith mattered and would not be shuttered. She also felt that black customers at her restaurant received less favorable treatment than whites and that the matter should be officially redressed. Although Ms. Martin believed her complaints were justified, her way of engaging people with power was contentious and of limited benefit to herself and Raven. The pattern of direct confrontation that Ms. Martin exhibited at work and at school created tense relationships and rarely resulted in desirable outcomes. The tension between her and Mr. Marks continued to build over the year, eventually ending her classroom participation and curtailing her broader engagement.

The cases of Ms. Towles and Ms. Martin display the different experiences of two parents who were dedicated to their children's education and wanted to engage with the school. They were received differently by the school staff and this led to disparate outcomes. Both mothers attributed their treatment to their race, but their responses to the discrimination they perceived were different. These experiences suggest that race mattered for both parents, but the depth of this racial effect was mediated by their habitus.

Ms. Towles's ability to both endure maltreatment and repeatedly negotiate this treatment is likely linked to her class status and her occupation as a lawyer. Although she felt she was treated differently from her white counterparts, she did have a presence at the school, which was useful in dealing with her son's educational needs. Ms. Martin, in contrast, behaved in ways at school that mirrored her behavior at work; importantly, in both locations her desires were at best rebuffed and at worst punished. Ms. Martin had a strong desire to foster and guide Raven's intellectual and social development, but her history of uncomfortable interactions at the school left her treatment to the school staff's discretion and prevented her from being an engaged advocate in guiding her daughter's path.

Both Ms. Martin and Ms. Towles had limited influence within River Elementary School, despite their desire for greater engagement. Their problems ranged from small matters like the cupcake incident to larger issues such as wanting their input to be as valued as those of their white counterparts. These experiences accumulated over time and influenced their approach to engagement and their subsequent attempts at educational customization.

For black parents of all social classes in Rolling Acres Public Schools, attempts to influence their children's educational experience was rife with challenges. Parents often interpreted their struggles as race-related, and being middle class only partially attenuated their experiences.

TEACHER SELECTION AND COMMUNITY-SCHOOL CONNECTIONS

The location that black families occupied in RAPS was further affected by the relationship between black and white families and competition. In this section I present a case from Cherry Elementary School about parental organizing and interracial competition for the resources of quality teachers.

Rolling Acres schools in the primary grades did not offer gifted or accelerated courses or programs. As a result, parents who wanted to customize their children's education often lobbied to get their child into a preferred teacher's class. The school maintained no official measures of teacher quality such as value-added scores; parents used informal networks to communicate with one another about the qualities of the most desirable and undesirable teachers. At an individual level of analysis, parental advocacy for desired teachers can be thought of as opportunistic foresight, but at the relational level this lobbying was a mechanism for triaging educational resources along racial and social class lines.

Teacher selection was a popular practice among parents but not among building staff. Each school building was responsible for determining its own protocol around teacher selection. In both of the schools I observed, principals did not prefer the process of teacher selection, but they still had to struggle to manage the individual and collective efforts of parents to do so. During the spring of each academic year, Cherry Elementary sent mailings to students' families announcing that decisions about the coming school year's classroom placement were being made. Principal Bell, the principal at Cherry, gave parents two weeks to return the parent input form to address the needs of their child in the classroom. The forms asked parents to identify students that their child worked well with, students that their child did not work well with, and special needs. Parents were not required to complete the form, and one sentence in the letter sent home read, "The same careful consideration in placement will be given to your child(ren) even if you choose not to return this form." The bottom of the sheet read, "Please do not request a specific teacher." The official letter to parents said that classroom assignments would be mailed five days before the start of the school year.

After the request forms were received, Principal Bell conferred with teachers and assigned students to different classrooms based on characteristics such as student performance, demographics, and special concerns.[15] Principal Bell retained ultimate oversight of the classroom rosters. When I asked her about the process of classroom placement and the short response time she explained, "I send a letter home. I don't want to make a big fuss, because I don't want everyone coming in here." Principal Bell viewed the letter as a reasonable way to minimize parental influence in the process of classroom assignment, but the short letter, outlined rules, and short turnaround time deterred only some parents. Despite these adjustments and the strategy, Principal Bell informed me that at her school a higher percentage of affluent white parents than other parents returned the classroom placement forms. She said that fast-responding affluent white families often ignored the stated rules and expressed a preference for specific teachers for their children. They then subsequently "checked in" with school staff and stopped by her office to advocate for their child's placement with a particular teacher. When I queried her about the unequal level of participation between black and white as well as upper-class and poor families, she told me, "I tried to get parents from the Mulberry Houses [the local low-income housing development], but they just didn't participate."[16]

During my time in the field there was a consistent narrative among black and white administrators and teachers that low-income families, who were predominantly black, did not participate in school matters, despite outreach. While I did observe notable differences in attendance at school-wide events, I did not find consistent evidence that school staff were actively pursuing, igniting, or rekindling relationships between poorer communities and the school. Instead, accumulated experiences as well as tales of disconnection discouraged continued pursuit of low-income and racial-minority families by school staff.

I experienced the tensions between Mulberry Houses and Cherry Elementary first hand as I attempted to recruit families into my study. I mailed additional introductory letters to families in the Mulberry Houses inviting them to an information session at the Houses' community center. Principal Bell agreed to attend the information session to visibly show her support for the research project. I arrived at the Mulberry Houses' community center approximately twenty minutes before the scheduled presentation. As I stood on the center's porch waiting for the complex's maintenance personnel to open the door, I saw a number of children playing in the parking lot, which was lined with townhouses with their doors propped open. I bided my time looking around the apartment complex, nearly all of which was visible from my perch. The houses were not like the fabled high-rise urban housing projects; instead they were low-rise gray townhouses. Had I not known they were subsidized housing, I likely would have as assumed them to be deteriorating apartments whose brightest moments were at least a ten years in the past. Surveying the complex kept me occupied, but my excitement about the information session soon turned to worry when neither maintenance personnel nor parents had turned up five minutes before the scheduled start time. As I stood, a 30-something African-American woman greeted me and asked, "What are you waiting for?" I informed her that I was doing an information session and asked if she had come over to join. She told me, "No, my kids aren't that old. I was just wondering why you were standing there." Her comment reminded me that I did not fit into the small community where faces were familiar, and my standing alone outside for twenty-five minutes likely seemed odd. She politely left me to wait on the porch by myself.

At 6:40, ten minutes after the session was scheduled to begin, a black Acura sports utility vehicle sped into the parking lot. The car parked next to the entrance and Principal Bell exited from the driver's side. I greeted her, and she asked, "Why are you outside?" I told her that no one had come to open the community center. She asked, "Well, have any parents showed up?" Sheepishly I replied, "Nope, just us." She blurted, "Typical. See, this always happens." She scanned the parking lot and then explained to me in a pleading tone that she had another obligation to attend. Her tone left me little choice; I obliged her request to leave and told her I would see her the next day at Cherry Elementary. She swept back into her car and sped out of the complex. I waited on the porch for another fifteen minutes and eventually left before any parents or maintenance staff arrived. I felt dejected but was not deterred.

Principal Bell's frustration with the non-attendance of parents was palpable. In her years as principal she had accepted that the strained relationship between the Mulberry Houses and Cherry Elementary was intractable. Though she was an African-American, her racial identity did not ensure a closer connection to the African-American families from the housing complex who attended her school. When I asked her if she thought her role as a black administrator was beneficial she responded, "Somewhat. I think some parents see me and feel more comfortable, but that doesn't mean anyone gets special treatment." Principal Bell's leadership could be a strong symbol to black parents that their presence was valued by RAPS, but it was not one that she relied on to connect to black families. Also, as a black administrator at a predominantly white school and with a predominantly white staff, her comment about special treatment reflects her reluctance to offer special patronage to black families. Principal Bell was not anti-black, but her position restricted her ability to advocate for black families.[17]

The black population at Cherry was heavily skewed toward the lower end of the economic distribution, despite being located in a well-resourced section of the city. When I asked Principal Bell to talk about the black middle-class families that attended Cherry Elementary, she interrupted my question to offer a list of six of seven family names and then began to slow with the naming. Her response was telling; she had interrupted my question and interpreted it as a request for a census of the black middle class who were enrolled. Even though she had been eager to respond, her census was quickly exhausted. Although there were middle-class black families in the school's neighborhood, many opted to send their children to non-public schools (a topic I take up in chapter 7).

At Cherry Elementary, families from the Mulberry Houses appeared detached from the school and detached from other families, particularly white and middle-class families. This detachment from the school was not replicated in social relations among families within the Mulberry Houses. Ms. Coleman, a resident of the Mulberry Houses and parent of Summer, explained her relationship with other Mulberry parents: "It's always known, if you go up there [Cherry], you can check on mine, and if I go up there I can check on yours [kids]. We sit and discuss the teachers and little issues that we might have. But that's the extent. I'm concerned with mine, I love them all, but mine is my concern." Ms. Coleman had not lived in the Mulberry Houses for many years, but felt that there were unspoken shared agreements about communal childcare and a web of social support. This type of communal caregiving suggests that families were not only familiar with each other in passing but had meaningful relationships that allowed for mutual benefit, even if an individual family or person was unable to monitor their child's well-being at school. In our interview, Ms. Coleman told me that parents utilized informal networks for childcare in the Mulberry Houses and that families got to know each other because children often played in the complex's driveways and common areas and visited each other's houses.

The relationship between Mulberry families and other families was important because school related information often traveled through semiformal and informal networks. When I asked Ms. Coleman about her relationship to the school and other parents, she responded:

> The teachers seem open and loving, but I can't say that about all the parents. Not all of them are friendly, they're not rude, but they have their cliques, I noticed there. I've gone to the picnics all the years and never end up talking to anybody unless I dragged [another Mulberry resident's] mom. They're there, they volunteer, I appreciate all their help, but they're

not the friendliest people in the world. You know you gotta go out of your way, you have to go "Hey Ms. So and So." Otherwise they sit right next to you and [do] not say a word.

The distant feeling that Ms. Coleman got from other parents in the school was not unusual. Ms. Towles said something similar about the affluent white families at River Elementary: black parents who were engaged seldom felt fully incorporated or welcomed by white families, who were the most regular participants. Ms. Coleman suggests that "the cliques" they formed were exclusive and that it was not a malicious rebuffing of her presence, but still she was not part of their networks.

In interviews, parents said that parental networks were largely homogeneous, both racially and economically, and I noted the same thing in my observations. Thus the flow of information and support was also stratified by race and class. Parents organized and lobbied in ways that highlight how race- and class-stratified parental networks blocked access to equal educational opportunities.

AVOIDING MS. BAKER

During the winter of the school year at Cherry, conversations about Ms. Baker, a fifth-grade teacher, began to brew. Ms. Baker arrived at Cherry Elementary in the academic year that I began my observations and had a commanding presence in the school: she was an African-American woman in her early thirties and nearly six feet tall. She sported a short cropped haircut, and every day that I saw her she was dressed professionally in a skirt and turtleneck. As I conducted interviews with parents at Cherry Elementary, I first heard of "problems" with Ms. Baker and was alerted that a number of parents were concerned that she might be their children's potential fifth-grade teacher.

Although it was Ms. Baker's first year at Cherry, she was not new to the district; she had worked at several schools in her previous three years of employment there. To some parents her short tenure at each school signaled a problem and raised a red flag. Many concerned parents raised the issue of her reported absences from school and from her teaching responsibilities. Aly Stone, a white parent at Cherry Elementary and a substitute teacher in the Rolling Acres district, described Baker's past performance as a reason for concern:

The first thing that I learned was it's her third building in three years and I'd been to her other two buildings. I know that in her last building she would go out for lunch and not come back and leave her kids unattended. It's not like she told anybody, it's not like she told anyone "I'm not feeling well" and it's not like she went out and called a sub. She'd just leave and not come back. How can a teacher do that? How can the district allow her to be in charge of kids? I guess that didn't really happen this year . . .

Ms. Stone's information about Ms. Baker's classroom absences was based on reports she had received from other teachers at Ms. Baker's former schools. As a substitute teacher, Ms. Stone held both insider and outsider roles in the school. Early in our interview she acknowledged that her dual role created some tension and suggested that as an employee of the district she was not free to divulge her insider knowledge to other parents in the school. Despite this, later in the interview she said that she had shared "some information" with other parents at Cherry Elementary who were concerned about Ms. Baker's being their child's fifth-grade teacher. Ms. Stone was able to stoke concern about absences, although she acknowledged that the issue had not yet come up at Cherry Elementary.

Several parents repeated the rumors of Ms. Baker's past absences to me, and a few even said that she had been chronically absent in the present academic year. Perceptions of Ms. Baker's actions seemed to be more important to parents than verifying the validity of the claims against her. In an informal interview with Principal Bell I inquired about Ms. Baker's absences during the year; Principal Bell said there had been no unexcused absences and that concerns and rumors from former buildings had followed Ms. Baker to Cherry Elementary.

The "evidence" surrounding Ms. Baker's poor performance could at best be classified as second-hand conjecture, but it was used to coalesce concern. Mr. Sommers, another Cherry parent, commented, "There is this huge groundswell of dissatisfaction and lack of support for this individual [Ms. Baker]. It seems like with this many people they [parents] just can't be out to get somebody."

The "groundswell of dissatisfaction" with Ms. Baker was a product of two phenomena: second-hand information and fear. The parents that I spoke with at Cherry wanted to ensure that their children had access to a high-quality education, and they believed having Ms. Baker as their child's teacher would compromise this. As more parents became concerned about Ms. Baker, they used informal and semiformal networks to move from individual grievances to a collective response. The collective response to concern about Ms. Baker was not shared by all parents; I believe the disparity in concern was based on lack of information, rather than lack of desire. I explore the role of networks in organizing against Ms. Baker and discuss their consequences below.

PETITIONING TO AVOID MS. BAKER

Concerns about Ms. Baker quickly moved from individual consumer families to organized groups of parents. The collective response was spearheaded by parents in the wealthy Beaver subdivision. The Beaver subdivision, which was constructed in the 1990s, is situated less than a mile from Cherry Elementary. It is composed of single-family houses, and its residents are largely white, but there are also a number of Asian and Asian-American families. Much like the geography of the Mulberry Houses, the geography of the Beaver subdivision created an opportunity for the formation of parental networks based on weak ties.

While the Mulberry Houses relied on fictive kin for social support and problem solving, in the Beaver subdivision relations were amicable but appeared much less collectively oriented around tasks like childcare and home-school connections. Instead, families regarded their own children as their private concern, rather than expecting any communal responsibility for their rearing and care. This is not to suggest that mutual aid was not an important feature of Beaver, but it was more discrete in nature, such as the shuttling of children and their friends between extracurricular activities and home. Weekly communication between parents, particularly mothers, within the subdivision was common, and this community served as an important source of information about school and extracurricular activities. Each parent I interviewed in the subdivision said there were families that they were close to, and there was a sense of general camaraderie among the households.

Through weak social ties, discussion of Ms. Baker's alleged transgressions traveled and ultimately coalesced into an actionable concern.[18] Parental disquiet was formalized by the creation of a petition that was circulated among Cherry Elementary parents. The petition featured two demands: (1) the investigation of Ms. Baker and (2) assurance that the children of the parents who signed the petition would not be assigned to Ms. Baker's classroom, regardless of the results of the investigation. This petition signaled a move from individual to collective concern and reflected how a private grievance could become a public concern and then be formally pursued. The signees were self-interested, of course, but they were also able to find common ground for advocacy. The dual approach allowed signees to advocate for an investigation that could benefit all families at Cherry, and at the same time demand that their children receive special treatment.

In the minds of concerned Cherry parents, the assignment of their child to Ms. Baker's class would be unconscionable. When I asked Ms. Stone the hypothetical question, "What if your son were placed in Ms. Baker's class?" she offered a nearly knee-jerk response, "I'll pull him [out of school]." This was a common response among parents who had signed the petition or were concerned about Ms. Baker. I would then follow up and ask, "Where would you send your child to school?" Some parents said private school, other said a charter school, and some even said they would move to another district to avoid Ms. Baker's classroom!

The threat of exit is a common response to perceived failure of a system to respond to constituents' needs. In the book *Exit, Voice, and Loyalty*, Albert O. Hirschman outlines the ways that people respond to organizational decline.[19] Individuals or groups may choose to exit by moving themselves and their resources, or they may speak up to voice their concern about the current operations. While the exit option is not new to education, in smaller school systems like RAPS it is still very consequential. Choosing to leave Cherry Elementary would have had significant race and class implications for classrooms and for the school as a whole. At Cherry, affluent parents wielded the exit option throughout the process of developing and enacting a voice option (the petition). Parental pressures at the school level and the district level, as I discussed in chapter 2, were influential forces on educational opportunity. At the building level, principals at both Cherry and River Elementary Schools said they felt pressure to satisfy affluent white parents who consistently threatened exit.

Principal Tyler told me that the threat of exit was constant and was sometimes framed as a request for special patronage. He said, "I've told you before that I've had [Caucasian] parents come through the door and say, you know, 'I could have my child go to any school but I want them to go here.'" While not saying directly that they would leave the school, the implicit message was that they had options and RAPS was only one of many. Although both Cherry and River were public schools, white families held disproportionate sway. To the school staff, the economic, social, cultural, and human capital influences of white middle-class and affluent families' contributed importantly to the Parent-Teacher Association, the volunteer labor force, the donation of resources (e.g., guest lectures, classroom materials, treats), and test score dividends, to name a few. Principal Bell shared Principal Tyler's experience and added the suggestion there was pressure from the school district to retain the most affluent families within RAPS, which pressured building staff to keep them satisfied. As a result, principals were constantly doing a delicate dance of listening, response, and selective action.

At the close of the school year, three parents representing the petitioners met with Principal Bell to discuss their concerns about Ms. Baker. Principal Bell told me, "They were not interested in talking to Ms. Baker, and they weren't interested in hearing that Ms. Baker was a good teacher. They weren't here for that." Principal Bell described the meeting as one that was fueled by rumors and involved a number of incidents from Ms. Baker's previous schools, not her performance at Cherry. When I asked Principal Bell if tussles with families were common, she responded, "You wouldn't believe if I told you. You haven't seen anything! It was even worse at my old school. The problem is that *they* treat it like their private school." Principal Bell stressed "they" to emphasize that she was talking about a cadre of affluent white families that were organized and agitated consistently. While not all affluent families were directly involved in agitations, the agitators gained legitimacy by having others sign on to petitions and back their concerns.

Importantly, the threat of exit, which motivated a great deal of school response, was not available to all families. Black middle-class families told of making requests and demands that were seldom granted. In fact, some families that exited Rolling Acres Public Schools indicated that their exit threats were met with little resistance, which subsequently led to some families' leaving local public schools. Enrolling in private schools allowed them to take on a consumer role where their presence was considered valuable. I take this up further in chapter 7. Diligent advocacy by families has to be aligned with capital endowments that schools and their staffs view as viable and valuable if educational customization is to occur.

Although the subdivision was the nucleus of activism, all of the families who lived there did not know about the petition against Ms. Baker.

As efforts to address the allegations against her increased, conspicuously absent from the signers of the petition were non-affluent and non-white parents. In my interviews with residents of the Mulberry Houses and other African-American families at Cherry Elementary, none of them revealed any knowledge of the situation with Ms. Baker or the petition. The flow of information between parents of different races and class backgrounds, despite engagement with the school, appeared never to have reached parents outside of the wealthy white Beaver subdivision and select families attached to the geography-based social network.[20]

Full information about the efforts to avoid and investigate Ms. Baker did not reach families like the Rosenbergs—a multiracial Ecuadorian and Jewish household—who lived in the Beaver subdivision. Their son, Tim, was enrolled in a number of different sports with other families from Beaver, but the organizing efforts had not reached them. When I asked Ms. Rosenberg about Ms. Baker and the petition, she said, "I never heard about any of that [the petition, the organizing, the meeting with the principal]. I heard a parent mention something at a baseball game, but nothing like that. " As we talked, I asked Ms. Rosenberg what she thought other parents at Cherry considered her son to be ethnically and racially. She responded, "Well, they think of my son as white, but they don't know what I am. I've heard them whisper and wonder." She believed her ethnic identity (Ecuadorian) as well as her husband's (Jewish) made them outsiders to white families at Cherry.

Economically and educationally, the Rosenbergs were on par with and surpassed many of the affluent white families in the Beaver subdivision, but they were not fully integrated socially, despite the fact that their son played in the same bands, attended the same camps, and played on the same sports teams as the children of white Beaver residents. When asked about this exclusion and her son she responded, "I think it's the parents. They're racist. The kids, they don't care, they learn it from their parents." Ms. Rosenberg saw her family's unique ethnic identity as a marker at Cherry Elementary and in Rolling Acres as a whole. While her family had achieved economic and professional success, she and her family were not often read as white; she was Ecuadorian-American and her husband was Jewish. Their ethnic and racial uniqueness placed them in a precarious location in a predominantly white school. The experiences of Ms. Coleman (Mulberry Houses) and Ms. Rosenberg (Beaver subdivision) reflect how social networks functioned to prevent information from reaching poor families and families of color, despite their close proximity and concern for their children's education.

The accusations against Ms. Baker were never substantiated, but the agitating parents and the co-signers successfully avoided having their children placed in her classroom. Ms. Baker did not return to Cherry the following year, possibly owing to the scrutiny that she was under. Most important, Principal Bell also gave in to the petitioners' pressure to not assign their children to Ms. Baker's classroom. This small acquiescence would have been significant if Ms. Baker had returned; since minority families were not equally tied in to the Beaver social networks, they would most likely have been assigned to the classrooms least desired by others.

The case of Ms. Baker demonstrates that parents within Rolling Acres were actively engaged in attempts to customize their children's education. At some times this advocacy was collective, but not necessarily inclusive. Parents used networks in their daily lives to communicate about school, sports, and neighborhood events, but not all families were given equal access. The concerted efforts of the Beaver subdivision's parents could be read as an exemplary use of social capital, but if not viewed relationally the dynamics of opportunity hoarding and exclusion would be overlooked. The intersection of parental engagement with its collateral consequences for the stratification of education-related resources is essential to understanding how some families acquire greater resources and how other families may be left unaware that they have not received them.

CONCLUSION

The data and analysis presented in this chapter make it clear that parental engagement is not equally accessible to all families. Previous research has demonstrated the importance of parental engagement, but much of the literature has overlooked the ways that race and class, combined, affect family engagement. Research by Annette Lareau and others has identified class as the central factor in determining parental engagement with schools; but I found that connections between homes and schools were equally if not more greatly shaped by race. Looking at parental engagement over time, rather than cross-sectionally, illuminates the ways that cumulative experience shaped perceptions of families and their ability to customize their children's educational experiences. These perceptions helped assign parents to the roles of consumer and beneficiary that resulted in grossly different educational experiences for black and white families in Rolling Acres Public Schools.

Social networks were key for parental engagement and advocacy, but the composition of those networks and the strategies they used had collateral influence on other families. In contrast to previous research on social networks suggesting that the black middle class and white middle class possess similarly rich networks, I found that white middle-class and affluent residents were able to utilize class and race-exclusive networks to leverage their influence on local schools. Although families of color, across class, were connected to social networks, their connections did not allow for a similar level of information or advocacy. As a result, economic and racial minorities did not have the same information, they could not advocate as freely, and their needs were not as dynamically responded to as those of white families across class statuses.

In Rolling Acres, educational resources (such as information about teacher transgressions and special sessions with administrators) were treated as a zero-sum game. Affluent white families worked diligently to hoard those resources for their children and limit resource access to racial and economic minority families. Because information, teachers, choice, and volunteering opportunities mattered for customizing education, the competition for them was subtle yet significant. Given that the family circumstances of black and white families are unequal, additional stratification of educational resources could serve to deeper embed inequality. While some parents were empowered, the most vulnerable families, the black and the poor, were disempowered.

Black families and white families, despite living in the same city, did not have similar home-school relations. All families began the process with the goal of increasing opportunities for their children, but the roles they filled and the experiences they had were separate and unequal. This outcome is not inevitable; schools and their staffs could change their institutional cultures to improve the relationships between home and school. "A good education" was the outcome that nearly all families desired for their children, but the cultures of the schools in Rolling Acres made this accessible only to a select segment of the population.

FIVE

A Few Bad Apples Are Racist

On a warm May afternoon, Summer and Monique sat in the classroom at Cherry Elementary after the other students had filed out for lunch and recess. This was not an odd occurrence, since students often had additional work, asked to stay in, or wanted to have a one-on-one conversation with the teacher, Ms. Jackson. Today, however, Summer and Monique sat sullenly as they awaited a reprimand from their teacher. Normally chatty, today Summer and Monique sat in silence. They were the only two African-American girls in Ms. Jackson's classroom, and they tended to spend great amounts of time together inside and outside of school. As I prepared to go outside to observe recess, I watched Jamila, a petite biracial (black and white) girl from the neighboring fourth-grade classroom, slip into the room. She sat down with a look of disgust on her face. As she took her seat, Ms. Jackson began to speak in an even yet demanding tone. Earlier in the day, Summer, Jamila, and Monique had been involved in an incident during which they called another student "white trash." Ms. Jackson, an African-American woman, asked all the girls to imagine, "What would I do if someone called me a name similar to that?" She then instructed the girls to "Write about how racism is connected to the name you called that young lady!"

The three girls sat at their desks poised to write, but none began moving her pen. As they sat, Ms. Jackson busied herself tidying up the room; she then continued, "You know, when I was little we were the first black family in town. They tried to keep us out. The kids did name-calling too. You can be racist! When you call them 'white trash' it opens the playing field." The girls sat with their pens resting on their papers, positioned to write, but their hands were not moving. With their blank faces they looked like sailors on deck waiting for a storm to blow over their weather-battered ship. Then one of the girls broke the silence. Jamila retorted, "They can call me names because I know I'm not [those names]." She continued, "I'm half white anyway!" Ms. Jackson stopped mid-pace, spun around, and said, "But your parents didn't raise you to have a trashy mouth." Pleased with having gotten "a rise" out of Ms. Jackson, Jamila's mouth crocked into a smirk and she began giggling. Ms. Jackson, likely realizing her monologue had not moved Jamila or the other girls, decided to shift her approach.

"Think about that little girl and if she goes home and tells her parents. They'll be mad and at your doorstep later." Jamila quickly spurted out, "But she started it." Ms. Jackson barked back, "Doesn't matter who started it!" As Monique and Summer sat silently watching Ms. Jackson and Jamila joust, Ms. Jackson realized that she was losing this battle with a 10-year-old on racial ethics. "'Why It's Bad to Call People Names,' write that down as the title," Ms. Jackson commanded. As the girls wrote their titles, Ms. Jackson walked over to her desk to retrieve some papers. When she returned to the girls, who were now grudgingly writing, she stopped by Monique's desk, looked at her paper, and said, "Good start!"

Ms. Jackson asked Jamila, "Did someone touch you?" Jamila responded, "No." Ms. Jackson then commented, "I'll fight for you . . . if you did nothing wrong." Jamila diverted her eyes from Ms. Jackson's and slowly scribbled on her paper. The girls continued to write slowly in silence with little discussion until Jamila's homeroom teacher, Ms. Marsh, entered the room. Ms. Marsh was a white woman in her mid-fifties and a teaching veteran. She began to chat quietly with Ms. Jackson and raised her voice to comment audibly, "They should write about how they would feel." Ms. Marsh pulled up a chair next to Jamila. Ms. Jackson then dismissed Summer and Monique to get lunch from the cafeteria. They jumped from their seats and bolted out of the room. Ms. Marsh asked Jamila, "Do you go to church?" Jamila nodded in response. "Are they all black people?" She shook her head no. "Do they teach you that [name-calling]?" Jamila sat in silence, letting the question go unanswered. "Do you usually talk like that? I want you to think about why you said it, because you don't usually do that. Do you usually talk like that?" Each successive question and comment pierced the hard exterior that Jamila had portrayed to Ms. Jackson. Ms. Marsh continued, "Was it because you were with Summer? Monique?" As she questioned Jamila, tears began to stream down her face. "It's so unlike my Jamila. You're a kind and sweet girl. You know I care, right?" As Jamila dried her eyes and sniffled, Summer and Monique returned to the room with lunches. As the lunches arrived, Ms. Marsh backed away from questioning Jamila, and the girls sat at their desks and ate their meals. Ms. Marsh and Ms. Jackson then went together into the hallway.

As I sat in the room with the three girls, they began to talk among themselves. The somber mood moments earlier, which resulted in Jamila's crying, quickly disappeared. Monique leaned back to talk to me as she ate, then Jamila and Summer turned to me. I asked them, "What happened?" None of them offered a response. Then Monique explained they had "an issue" on the playground with some white fifth-grade girls. She recounted that Summer was the first to call the unnamed fifth-grade girl "white trash," and then Jamila and Monique echoed her epithet. As they told the story, none of the girls appeared remorseful; instead, their tone conveyed vindication. After they finished describing the incident, the teachers returned, the girls finished their lunch, and they wrote until the recess period ended, without any more talking.

Not long after the incident, I had the opportunity to interview Summer and Monique about issues of race in their school. Both said at first that race was not an issue, but later revealed that race did matter at their school. Ms. Jackson and Ms. Marsh highlighted Summer and Monique's roles in hurling a racial slur and demanded they write an essay on why racial slurs hurt, but their response and the assignment treat this incident as if it were an isolated, if not anomalous, occurrence. These type of approaches do little to address the ongoing issues of race that permeate the educational environment.

When incidents like this playground issue arose, adults tended to focus on the children identified as the racial transgressors. They often suggested that there were a few "bad apples" or that a child had had "a bad day" but were reluctant to identify race as an issue with children. When Ms. Marsh asked Jamila if she had learned to say "white trash" in her church congregation, she was hinting that her church was monoracial and could have been a source of racial bigotry. Despite Jamila's denial that her congregation was monoracial, Ms. Marsh and Ms. Jackson continued to focus their attention only on the black girls in the incident. By not concentrating on both sets of participants in the conflict, there was little chance the teachers would learn what had caused the issues between the black and white girls or that they could do any deeper work on addressing racial issues. In their focus only on those perceived to be the racial transgressors and not on the dynamics of relationships, teachers and parents brought their own sets of racial beliefs and assumptions, which influenced how they framed and understood youth's racial perspectives and tensions.

As I discussed in chapter 2, the race-blind policies of the district and the colorblind ideology of its adults shaped the official policies that were put in place at the district level, but at the school level teachers, school staff, and other adults were responsible for how race was lived and engaged in classrooms and at home. This chapter explores how the asymmetries in race socialization (at home), as well as treatment (in school) along racial lines in classrooms, shaped the experiences of youth. Teachers and other staff considered racial issues to be "normal" and "occasional" and consequently stressed that there was not a "race problem" at their schools or in their classrooms.

Rolling Acres does have a race problem. However, the problem is not the presence of episodic racial antagonisms as teachers and white adults would suggest; rather, Rolling Acres' race problem lies in the asymmetries in racial understandings and the resulting terrain on which schools and everyday lives operate. Several scholars have begun to explore the role of racial meaning and race talk in youth development and schooling.[1] However, these studies draw from analyses of middle school and high school students who have more developmentally advanced ideas about race and have been socialized toward adult notions of racial meaning; or these studies emphasize the role of institutional influence on racial meaning but do not fully incorporate youth voices. To better understand the everyday meanings of race we must examine how youth and adults leverage racial meaning in the post–Civil Rights moment.

In previous chapters I have discussed how racial ideology affects policy and how racial beliefs operate as background factors; in this chapter I foreground racial thinking, race talk, and racial response at the group and school levels. I explore contemporary race socialization among black, white, and multiracial families. I look at how youth make sense of racial messages from adults and explore the racial worlds they create and negotiate. I conclude the chapter with a discussion of the racial worlds that emerge at the intersection of adult and child worlds and how race talk becomes a meaningfully commodified resource.

RACE SOCIALIZATION BY BLACK PARENTS: THE ODDS ARE AGAINST YOU

The Cultural Ecological Model (CEM) pioneered by Signithia Fordham and John Ogbu suggests that the messages black parents pass on to their children influence how they see the world and how they engage in or disengage from formal schooling.[2] Fordham and Ogbu argue that both active messages (those directly told to youth) and passive messages (those observed by youth) inform youth that racial barriers are pervasive. According to the CEM, black youth observe the struggle and limited life opportunities of their parents and other black adults and decide that formal paths, such as education, are not tenable for blacks in America. As a result, even among the black middle class, knowledge of race-related barriers, among other factors, drives academic disengagement and results in underperformance among black youth. The CEM view of racial socialization suggests that race-conscious socialization negatively affects worldview and mobility.

However, not all social scientists share such a fatalistic view of black parents' race socialization. Diane Hughes and colleagues, in their extensive meta-analysis of ethnic socialization, found that messages about racial barriers were popular, but messages about racial pride were among the most common race socialization messages for black families.[3] They argue that socialization messages can serve to buffer biases as well as instill a greater individual and group identity.

In Rolling Acres, I found that black families stressed racial barriers more often than they sent their children messages of racial pride, though both were present. The observed emphasis on the presence of racial barriers may be tied to the amount of interracial contact that black youth in Rolling Acres had. The expansion of the black middle class and greater access to historically white suburban areas forced black middle-class adults to develop strategies to negotiate racial and class hazards.[4] As a result, messages may have morphed to emphasize the negotiation of race-related barriers with the hope of making black youth more mobile, not less.

Although there is a popular emphasis in society and the media on the declining significance of race, and the election of Barack Obama to the presidency was considered by some to signal the dawn of a "post-racial" United States, this type of racial reasoning was not common among black parents in Rolling Acres.[5] There, all the parents of black children acknowledged that race still had importance in shaping their lives. Most agreed it would continue to influence their children's lives, despite their desire for it not to do so. The duality of this belief—the inevitability of race factoring in and the hope that it would not matter—still led these parents to socialize their children to the harms of racism that they might encounter.

Ms. Downing explained to me the messages she passed to her son LeBron regarding the social order of the United States:

> I tell him [LeBron] that every day. First of all, [he has] so many strikes against him. He's black. He is a black man and he is living in a world of white rules, 'cause every rule, every law comes from a white person and they ain't come from black people and white people setting down the laws and stuff together. Like I told him, this world is made . . . it's a cruel world out here you know, and this world is made for white people's opinion only. What they say is right or what is right is not right.

Ms. Downing held a structural view of race that stressed the disparate power of whites to influence blacks' navigation of the social world. She taught her son that white people used their power to define "right" and "wrong" in American culture, but their definitions did not necessarily map on to the moral categories of "right" and "wrong" in which she believed. She was not hesitant to share with her son that the rules and scales were tipped in favor of whites. Ms. Downing and others talked about racial inequality in terms that were not common to the everyday experiences of youth—for example, her reference to "laws." Although her son and other children are aware of the law, the critical race perspective that Ms. Downing employed is beyond the everyday reality of the average 10-year-old. While Ms. Downing's frequent reiteration of the imbalance in law and social order does represent a more extreme position, her message was echoed by many black parents.

When I asked black parents about the sharing of their individual experiences with discrimination and oppression, most informed me they did not talk about specific details with their children because it would not be developmentally appropriate. Black parents' willingness to discuss structural inequalities without a "personal face" may have been a double-edged sword. On one front, it heightened their children's awareness of racial hazards and unsettled racial naiveté. On another front, non-personal narratives reduced the chances that their children would learn specific strategies for negotiating racial issues.

When parents did attempt to have conversations with their children about the role of race, they said that their children often rebuffed them. Ms. Towles talked about an ongoing conversation she had with her son about growing older and race's relevance:

> I have tried to relay to him the importance of knowing his background, the importance of him understanding who he is and where he comes from and what it is to be a grown black man in society, and it's really strange because he doesn't feel like that is a problem. He doesn't feel it is [an] issue, and again I think that is from being in Rolling Acres Schools. But you know when I say to him, "well Jeffrey you know when you are six feet tall and a lot heavier, people will view you different and they will react to you different." [Impersonating Jeffrey's voice] "Oh I don't have any problems." Everybody thinks that. Yeah, because you are 9 and cute and you are cuddly. But when you grow it isn't going to be the same. In his mind he doesn't get it; he doesn't see that.

Jeffrey was not alone in his suggestion that race did not matter in his life and that his parents' perspective was outdated. Ms. Towles attributed this difference in orientation between black adults and their children to the environment of Rolling Acres schools, where discussion of race rarely touched on the role of power or social stigmas that faced black students. Black families dealt with two types of truncated racial conversations: those that revealed their own failures as a way of conveying the need for the negotiation of barriers; and those related to school, where conversations about race and power were eschewed in favor of conversations about ethnic differences. These *truncated race discussions* were not exclusive to black families; they also occurred in white families, albeit in a different way, which I discuss next.

RACE SOCIALIZATION BY WHITE PARENTS:
HOPING FOR COLORBLIND CHILDREN

In stark contrast to black parents, who wanted their children to be socialized to racial hazards, most white parents told me of their desire for their
children be colorblind and not see the race of other students. Ms. Stone, the
white mother of Rick, beamed with pride as she said, "He [Rick] doesn't
classify his classmates based on their ethnicity or anything." To Ms. Stone,
her son's ability to not notice the ethnicity (or race) of his classmates was
progressive. Ms. Stone was raised in a racially segregated (predominantly
white) school and neighborhood. She thought her son's colorblind approach
to social relations was desirable, but this was not to suggest that differences
at school went unnoticed.

Many white families boasted about International Night. International
Night was a celebration of students from different countries at their schools
as an example of Rolling Acres' vibrant racial and ethnic diversity. Families from more than forty heritages brought dishes to the event, but many
of these dishes reflected the white families' different national and ethnic
backgrounds. Their highlighting of the ethnic identities conformed neatly
to Mary Waters's notion of "optional ethnicities."[6] Ethnic background was
meaningful at celebratory cultural events, but it was rarely a topic of conversation at other times.

When I asked white parents, "Have you tried to teach your child about
his or her racial or ethnic identity?" with few exceptions, white parents
greeted my question with hesitation and then questioned me.[7] They asked,
"Do you mean that he's Irish [or another ethnic group]?" "What do you
mean by that?" And "Well I haven't really thought about that, let me think."
In post-interview discussions, both white men and women explained that
they were "caught off guard" by the questions on race socialization. Their
initial hesitation and later reflections demonstrate the pervasive nature of
whiteness, which allows white Americans to seldom think about their own
racial and ethnic identities.

After their initial hesitations they answered my question, and their
responses fell into three categories. The first category included responses
that concentrated on ethnic identity (e.g., being Polish, Jewish, or Dutch).
One such response came from Ms. Courtlandt, who described the conversations she had with her daughter Lisa and how they came about:

COURTLANDT: A little bit. Her dad is one hundred percent Dutch, and she has asked questions about what background is she and we have talked a little bit. I am more Irish and Norwegian background. So we kind of told her you are half Dutch, you are a quarter [Norwegian] and a quarter Irish. So we have had conversations about it but I don't know if it is something that she . . . I think she has asked about it but whether she is really aware of it I can't say.

INTERVIEWER: And how did the conversations about her ethnicity emerge? Was it a conscious decision?

COURTLANDT: I think she asked about it. But it wasn't like something that we sat down, had books out, it just came up and we told her and then off she was. So whether it really stuck, I don't know.

The Courtlandts, like other white families, were willing to discuss their ethnic identity around holidays, as part of scheduled cultural events, or when directly queried. These conversations about ethnic identity were largely limited to descriptions of the regions from which families came, foods made and eaten, and customs that were practiced. This type of cultural frame conveyed pride, but did not acknowledge that ethnic background is linked to differences in race relations, treatment, and privileges.

A second category of responses came from parents who said they did not teach their children about their ethnic and racial backgrounds:

INTERVIEWER: Have you tried to teach Danny about his racial or ethnic background?

MR. MORRIS: Teach him about being white?

INTERVIEWER: If that is his racial background.

MR. MORRIS: Teach him, I guess in . . . I want to say no. I mean, I guess you teach by actions, he's just a person with white skin. I don't tell him there's a certain way you act because you're white or nothing like that. I don't know how to answer that.

For Mr. Morris, racial identity was not a topic he actively thought of as a necessity for his son's development. The blind eye that Mr. Morris turned to race is likely linked to his own perception of whiteness and his lack of awareness of its role in his own life. Race scholars have argued that whites' ability to be "de-raced" has allowed them to maintain power by not acknowledging the privileges that they enjoy as a function of their skin color and not acknowledging the consequences that others suffer on account of their gains.[8] The invisibility of whiteness, in part, is what endows it with its social power. When Mr. Morris does talk about race with his son, the conversation is truncated. The discussion among whites did not explore how being white mattered. Instead it highlighted that being white, or any other race, should *not* matter. The concentration on the ideal by Mr. Morris and other parents socialized children away from noticing the current power of race and did not equip them for the realities of negotiating racial tension.

As I discussed earlier, most white parents did not believe that their children were ignorant of race despite the use of the label "colorblind." Instead they desired that their children not think of race as consequential in their social interactions. Descriptions of active colorblind socialization constituted the third category of responses. Below is an excerpt from an interview I conducted with Mr. Neilsen, Laura's father:

INTERVIEWER: Have you tried to teach Laura about her racial or ethnic background?

MR. NEILSEN: No. We just try to teach her that, you know, when anything has come up that it's, you know, there's no issue, you know. There is no issue! So . . . I don't know if that answers that directly, but we've certainly tried to support the fact that there are . . . there's no color at school.

Mr. Neilsen desired that Laura see all children as equal and that race have no significance in her life. While this is a noble goal, it was likely unattainable. Laura's mother, Ms. Neilsen, told me earlier that in second grade an African-American classmate had bullied her daughter. The Neilsens did not mention any possible racial component of the bullying; instead they ignored race and stressed that race did not matter. After our discussion of the incident, Ms. Neilsen began to question out loud if their choice to actively socialize her daughter away from race being meaningful was the "correct" decision. She worried that the altercation had affected Laura's view of African-Americans given her limited exposure to them, but since she and Laura had had no explicit conversations about race Laura had no basis on which to combat potentially negative thoughts about African-Americans. While the Neilsens had fears about these passive messages about race, these fears were not significant enough to motivate in-depth conversations about race with their daughter.

The halcyon characterization of race that white parents provided their children did not necessarily coincide with their personal beliefs about race. White fathers, in particular, believed that race mattered and would affect their children's ability to get ahead in the United States. White fathers were more likely than white mothers to think their race mattered in their jobs and would affect their children's chances in education and occupation. One white father explained that race had no importance and that everyone was equal, but at the close of our interview lamented that race mattered too much in how promotions were given at his job as an engineer for an automotive company. He told me, "the problem is minorities, well . . . unqualified minorities, you know what I'm talking about, like not you, but unqualified minorities get promoted quicker."[9] While white adults claimed that race did not matter to them, when probed, they admitted that race was meaningful, particularly when they were "overlooked" or experienced "reverse discrimination."

Within a number of white fathers' assessments of their sons' mobility was an implicit belief in their own children's ability and the lesser ability of minorities. Public conversations about the achievement gap reified beliefs that whites excelled while blacks lagged behind. The gap was invoked by parents who spoke of "disruptive students," as well as "students who slowed down the class," who were presumed to be black (recall Ms. Tolliver's discussion of the achievement gap in chapter 2). These quiet background assumptions animated parents' desires for their sons to get ahead. They feared that their white sons would face barriers to promotion like those they themselves perceived in the workplace. These fathers and mothers were less concerned about race being a barrier for their daughters because they believed girls would benefit from gender-considerate Affirmative Action. This did not stop fathers from highlighting race as a negative factor within Affirmative Action for their sons. Parents, particularly fathers, were willing to share these perspectives with me over time in interviews, but they consistently told me that they did not share their views with their children. Even if parents acknowledged that they did not pass these messages explicitly to youth, it is not hard to imagine that they convey these sentiments in other ways, such as in conversations overheard by their children at home.

MULTIRACIAL SOCIALIZATION

The expanding multiracial population is fertile ground for rethinking racial group membership, socialization, and the meaning of race. According to the 2010 census, 2.9 percent of Americans identified themselves as belonging to more than one race. Black-white families were the most common type of multiracial family in my study. Most often, mothers were white and fathers were black. Given the expanding conversation on the complexities of multiracial identity, what parents tell their children about the meaning, value, and costs of race is essential to understanding the racial landscape of Rolling Acres.[10] A great deal of the race socialization among multiracial families came from mothers and began while children were young. Among black-white biracial families, I found a tenor that was different from that in white households and near to, but not identical to, that in black households.

White mothers stressed the importance of their children knowing that race did matter. Most white mothers also expressed a desire for their children's skin color to not matter, but they tempered this message by saying that race-related hurdles were "real." This view was present even among mothers who were reluctant to say that their children were "of color." These mothers did not want their children to face racial hurdles, and they believed that teaching their children about the social meaning of race was important for navigating the social world. They seldom actively endorsed the "one drop rule"—one drop of black blood makes a person black—but they passively accepted the rule by socializing their children in ways that were more closely aligned with black families' practices than with those of white families.

The messages they conveyed expressed a desire for children to understand that race could hinder them, as well as their personal desire that race would not matter. It is important to note that the majority of white mothers with biracial sons stressed that they were treated as "black boys" in school and throughout Rolling Acres.[11] Ms. Conley, mother to David, a biracial boy, when asked how she talked to her son about race said, "I don't know, we been having—he's always been aware of his situation [being biracial]. And I teach him about struggles that black people went through, and I think he's still kind of young though to really grasp it." Ms. Conley informed me that these conversations came up when they watched television or listened to the news. Unlike black parents, biracial parents often voiced the opinion that Rolling Acres was an ideal place to raise children. For example, Ms. Conley said:

> I like the diversity in Rolling Acres and like my kids being biracial. I don't want them in a real rich or real white type area. I wanted somewhere where they can really see different things going on. Different cultures, community displays and things like that. I think Rolling Acres is really perfect for that.

For multiracial families, Rolling Acres was a city where multiraciality was not uncommon, which they viewed as desirable, but they were aware that race-related barriers still existed. For white mothers and fathers of biracial children, socializing their children who are often read as black will likely hold challenges as their children experience racial realities that their parents did not experience growing up white. Multiracial families' approach to socialization lay strategically between that of black families and white families. They conveyed an interest in non-racialized experiences while simultaneously cautioning their children that race could matter.

BLACK YOUTH: BAD APPLES AND BAD MOMENTS

The messages that adults passed to youth are only part of the calculus of racial meaning within Rolling Acres and its schools. Children also used information from other settings—school, their social networks, and popular media—to make sense of race in their lives. Black children, who were socialized by their parents to see race as a hazard, had to deal with a competing public script that race should not matter. Following the Civil Rights Movement, there was a strong emphasis on reducing overt racist attitudes, and in the 1990s multiculturalism highlighted the value of ethnic diversity by stressing the celebration of different cultures. As a result, having an ethnic identity was popular, but the bridging of racial divides seldom occurred. Children in Rolling Acres were aware that racist attitudes were not desirable, so their discussions of race often de-emphasized race as meaningful. When they did concede that race mattered, they tended to discuss racial conflicts. Among white youth, silence allowed racial issues to be ignored yet simultaneously fester beneath the surface. Among black youth, silence allowed racial issues to be viewed as important in special cases, such as when a individual in their classroom exhibited a racist attitude, but race was not central to their everyday lives. Below is an excerpt from an interview with Jeffrey, an African-American male at River Elementary.

INTERVIEWER: At your school do you think it is important what race you are?

JEFFREY: No. Not at all.

INTERVIEWER: Okay. Do other students at your school think what race you are is important?

JEFFREY: Yes. Remember the kid [one of his African-American classmates] that I said that would call me little white boy? He thinks that blacks are tougher than whites and Hispanics are weaker than whites. And he thinks that different races are stronger than other races and other races can earn more money. He thinks that white people can earn a million dollars in four weeks, then come Hispanics, then African-American[s].

INTERVIEWER: And how did you learn this? From things he said? Have you gone to school with him for a while?

JEFFREY: Last year he was in my school and we rode the same bus and he sat in the same seat as me. Three people to a seat and [in] ours we had two people to a seat, him and me. And he would talk about that sort of stuff and say stuff about our bus driver and she was white. . . .

Jeffrey told a narrative about another African-American boy in his grade who saw race as important. Jeffrey refused to identify the boy even when I probed for more details. Through conversation and prolonged interaction with the other student, Jeffrey believed that the other boy was negatively fixated on race. Jeffrey's first profession that race did not matter was his own belief, not his classmates'. This belief operated alongside his being called "little white boy," an explicitly racial label.[12] Among the black students in my sample, Jeffrey advanced the most colorblind narrative about the significance of race in school and as a factor that influenced getting ahead in America.

At home, Jeffrey's mother, Ms. Towles, stressed that race mattered, but Jeffrey responded to his mother's contention by retorting, "Things are different now, Ma!" His mother acknowledged that times have changed regarding race, but she had concerns that he would not understand that race was not just a problem "inside black people's heads." She attempted to allay her concerns by stressing that later in life Jeffrey would "get it." She and other black parents worried that teaching youth in Rolling Acres that race was not an issue would later be consequential. Their concern was not unfounded, given that teachers and other school officials often quelled race talk, rather than explore its contours. When race was discussed it was framed in ethnicity-centered ways, which aligned well with the messages that white families passed to their children, but not with those of black families. If it was not framed in ethnicity-centered ways, race was only presented as meaningful when an individual treated another badly, which individualized racism.

At the beginning of the chapter I introduced Summer, an African-American girl who had been involved in a racial incident on the playground. When we sat down for an interview, I asked her if she thought race mattered at her school:

SUMMER: No, but sometimes . . . no.

INTERVIEWER: Okay, 'no, but sometimes . . .' tell me what you mean by that.

SUMMER: Because once, it, it was in, um, the third. Yeah, it was in the third grade when my friend Alexandra, like I had Chinese friends, I had five friends until stuff happened. I had Lisa, Agnes, this Chinese girl Christine, and Ami. One day, I wanted to play with them and then they was like, "My mom said not to play with you cause you are, like, she said 'we're not allowed to play with people like you.'" Then I was like, "Why not?" and then . . . I think they made it up and then they got in really big trouble cause it was racist cause they was like, "My mom told me not to play with black Barbie dolls or nothing like that." Then they got in really big trouble. So the principal called home and all this stuff.

Summer's account of the experience she had playing with a racially mixed group of girls stands in contrast to her initial answer of "no, but sometimes . . . no." Her reservation about saying that race mattered was a common one and came from the desire to disavow race's influence, but it was tempered by the reality that she had in fact experienced racism's bite. Considering race meaningful and acknowledging that racism is persistent are often regarded as taboo. For children like Summer, discussing race as meaningful would betray her stated belief that "everyone is the same." Later in the interview, Summer explained that the two girls who made the comments to her, Lisa and Agnes, were both white. Summer, Lisa, and Agnes had been in the same classroom for several years, so she felt their rejection of her based on her skin tone was peculiar. She regarded them as friends but acknowledged they did not spend time together outside of school. Among youth, even when school-based interracial friendships were identified, interracial friendships did not mean they spent time at each other's houses. Friendships tended to be divided along race and class lines.

Summer did not think that the two girls had actually been told not to play with her but could not pinpoint where the girls would have gotten that idea or why they would mention it. Summer explained that she did not come to regard Lisa and Agnes as racist or assign their sentiments to other white students. Instead, Summer stressed that their opinions were simply misguided and that they were still nice girls. Despite maintaining that they were nice girls, she broke ties with them shortly after the incident.

When I asked Summer how it made her feel, she said, "Pretty bad, like, 'Dang, I don't have no more friends now.' So then, that was when me and Monique [a black classmate] had met." Summer's recounting of her shift in friendship networks did not ring of bitterness; instead it conveyed disappointment. In Monique she found a playmate who lived in her apartment complex, shared her race, and did not exclude her because of her skin color. During my time in Rolling Acres, Summer and Monique had a close friendship, and their mothers also began to develop a friendship. The relationship between Monique and Summer can be characterized as homophily—the idea people who are alike seek out one another—in a cross-sectional survey. But from Summer's account we learn that her failed attempts at brokering sustained interracial friendships led her to choose an African-African as a close friend.

Both Jeffrey and Summer initially attempted to suggest that race did not matter to them. Only after probing did they identify schoolmates who thought race was important; and both worked hard not to characterize their schoolmates' transgressions as representative of all their classmates. Instead, they dealt with racial antagonisms as contained altercations, which were due to "bad apples" or good girls having a "bad moment."

WHITE YOUTH: OTHER PEOPLE'S PROBLEM

Race's role was equally downplayed by white youth, but beneath their moderate attitude lay a different logic about racial responsibility. Black youth tended to view racial incidents as individual issues, whereas white youth worked diligently to not be seen as racist. When white students did commit racial transgressions, they disassociated themselves from the offenders and were reluctant to identify the perpetrators:

> INTERVIEWER: And do you think there are students at your school who think what race you are is important?
>
> ROBERT: I know there's one.
>
> INTERVIEWER: OK. And um, how do you know that there's one?
>
> ROBERT: Because he announced it to everybody.
>
> INTERVIEWER: OK, describe how you announce . . .
>
> ROBERT: He! He did! During recess. He told everyone to come around him so he could announce that he didn't like black people.

Robert was careful to make it clear that he was not the child who had said that race mattered. His interjection demonstrates that even by the fourth grade there was a public stigma associated with those who attached significance to race. For children, race mattering became nearly synonymous with racial antagonisms. Repeatedly they said that race mattered but should not, and that children who saw race were negative and different from other students. I believe this view was informed by adult notions of race, which prioritized acute incidents rather than everyday subtle differences in "doing race."

White youth, like black youth, initially suggested that race did not matter in their everyday lives. However, after probing, they said that race did matter to some of their peers, often their black classmates. While black students tended to shy away from attaching behaviors to racial groups, white students were more willing to make group-related statements about race. Below I quote from the interview with Lisa, a white student from an affluent family.

> INTERVIEWER: Do you think what race you are is important at your school?
>
> LISA: No, it's just how the inside is.
>
> INTERVIEWER: OK.
>
> LISA: Like if you're nice or mean and . . . people will want to be your friends or people won't want to be your friend so . . .

> INTERVIEWER: Do you think other students at your school feel the same
> way or something different than you?
> LISA: Some people think that maybe if . . . some people think
> if you're like African-American, then you're usually like a
> little meaner and a little tougher.

Lisa reluctantly acknowledged that "some people" thought that black youth were meaner and tougher. I asked Lisa for the names of people who shared this belief, but she declined to reveal them. By declining, she shielded the perpetrators from any potential retribution. White children were often more hesitant than black children to discuss racial antagonisms in detail or to identify individual actors. When they were willing to share, they kept stories anonymous or only referred to groups in general. A number of white students indicated that when race did matter it was because of black students' behaviors, and that if other whites said that race mattered, it was because of blacks' perceived behavior.

In an interview with Matthew, a white male from an affluent family, he told me the following:

> INTERVIEWER: In your school, do you think what race you are is important?
> MATTHEW: Um, no.
> INTERVIEWER: Do you think other students at your school think the same
> way?
> MATTHEW: No.
> INTERVIEWER: You think they think differently?
> MATTHEW: Yeah.
> INTERVIEWER: OK, tell me why you think so.
> MATTHEW: Well, um, sometimes uh, they'll . . . they won't let other
> kids play basketball . . . and that's the reason why.
> INTERVIEWER: And when you say they. . . which kids are you talking
> about?
> MATTHEW: Um, a lot of the black kids who play basketball.
> INTERVIEWER: Won't let the [interrupts] . . .
> MATTHEW: Mostly. Most of the time they'll let us [white boys] play, but
> maybe they'll do it once or twice, won't let some kids play.

Matthew's discussion of the basketball court as an exclusionary space was repeated in my interviews with white male students and parents. During recess, boys and girls were allowed free play, and boys tended to flock to the basketball court. The children, with light supervision, played pick-up basketball games of five-on-five or simply shot around. While observing at schools, I did not observe the explicit exclusion of whites from basketball games. In fact, on most days, I observed that there were more white students than black students on the court at any given time. Nonetheless, Matthew expressed concern that exclusion from basketball signaled that his racial background was important and was used against him in determining his opportunities for equal playing time.

Sporting options for boys at recess typically included basketball, football, and playground games. Among these choices, basketball was a top pick for many of the African-American boys. The saturation of images of African-American basketball superstars via television and the funneling of African-American males toward basketball as a career option likely led children to reify the ideas that basketball was a natural space for black youth.[13] Thus it is likely that black boys were also perceived to have greater ability and were granted greater leverage in deciding who was "picked" to play. These youth-centered spaces are arguably the most fertile for understanding youths' racial worlds, since they do not suffer from high levels of adult intervention.

In the case of basketball and Matthew, he felt he was excluded because he was white. Matthew then told me he had filed a formal complaint about his exclusion with his teacher. In Matthew's classroom, formal complaints were handled in classroom meetings. Using a system known as "I-messages" students would place their comments about problems in a box. For example, Matthew might have placed a message in that box that said, "I felt left out on the basketball court today when [student's name] wouldn't allow me to play because I was white." A clear consequence of the "I-message" system was that Matthew would be placing himself at the center of an accusation with a racial tone. When I asked what had happened with the "I-message" he put in the box, he said he withdrew the complaint before the teacher could discuss it with the class. I inquired about how the situation was handled after that, and he said that it had been resolved but did not want to talk about how. Matthew's mother, Kerry, told me that Matthew was disturbed by the exclusion but did not wish to create a stir about it. Matthew had said that his exclusion was resolved, but his mother suggested otherwise. His mother's belief that the issue bothered him may signal that instead of dealing with the exclusion, Matthew quietly accepted it.

The accumulation of quiet dissatisfaction with exclusion at the hands of African-American classmates could lead white students to an ideological position that African-Americans are more invested in the perpetuation of racial inequality. This is a position that has been advanced in popular dialogue and exhibited by white adults.[14] While the empirical costs of such a phenomenon, if it is true, are difficult to measure, it is important to understand because it contributes to asymmetrical racial understanding between whites and blacks. These asymmetries in racial understanding form the fabric of Rolling Acres' racial world.

CONCLUSION

To understand race in Rolling Acres, and in most spaces, one must suspend belief that there is one racial reality. In this chapter I have analyzed racial attitudes using race- and age-based groups. The interactions between these groups created a quilt of racial worlds in Rolling Acres. The community's group-based identities endowed their racial worlds with meaning, and the clashes and coalescences between them matter in the racial discourse, which lays the foundations for claims of racial relevance and everyday practices and policies around race. The racial narratives that exist in Rolling Acres jibe nicely with post–Civil Rights era rhetoric and frames.[15] Yet these frames are not the limits; they provide the ground on which ideas about race's meaning and value are contested and eventually monopolized. Both white and black residents engage race daily, but fears that their group will be taken advantage of in the contemporary post–Civil Rights moment cloud their ability to discuss what it means to "do race" and its collective consequences. John Jackson would label such a phenomenon racial paranoia.[16] He describes racial paranoia as the collective outgrowth of the suppression of outward racist and racialist attitudes and the emergence of political correctness.

All of the families in Rolling Acres had to respond to the racial paranoia of the contemporary period, but white frames provided the foundation for the everyday lived experience of race. By this I mean that the frames of white adults carried the most social weight and thus shaped the dialogue and policy responses within schools. Both white parents and teachers erred on the side of claiming that race was not an issue, save in exceptional cases.

This persistent disavowal of race's relevance allowed their own race-related benefits to be ignored. Also, white adults' endorsement of colorblind frames socialized children, both black and white, to see the mention of race as taboo.[17]

As a dominant socializing space, schools taught youth what race should mean, when race was relevant, and who was responsible for using race improperly. Ms. Jackson, an African-American teacher, and Ms. Marsh, a white teacher, used the occasion of a racial incident on the playground to suggest that racism was accessible to all students, including black students. This runs contrary to significant sociological research arguing that racism, in the contemporary moment, is much less an individual attribution of prejudice or bias and more a feature of a social system of stratification welded together by powerful institutions and select individuals.[18] The teachers' emphasis on individual acts of prejudice and discrimination as the litmus test for racism allows power inequalities to be washed from the discussion. Instead, racism becomes the domain of any one individual who opts to discuss race or contends that race matters. This is particularly meaningful for the racial worlds of youth who dealt with race daily, but worked diligently to disavow its significance.

In contrast to previous generations of black youth, the black youth in twenty-first-century Rolling Acres were less likely to endorse their parents' claims that race mattered in everyday life; instead they subscribed to the idea that race should not matter, and if it did matter it did so only to those who were "bad apples." While black parents often believed that their children would eventually recognize the truth of the parents' claims about race's role, it is equally possible that these youth will come of age viewing their parents' navigation of racial discrimination and messages of racial pride as a product of their parents' attachment to race, rather than as a feature of being black in America.

The white youth in Rolling Acres were equally primed to take advantage of colorblind ideologies through their endorsement of racism as episodic. If they were to engage in conversations about race, they likely would invoke the optional ethnicities and narratives of diversity that they heard from their parents. For them, consideration of race and racism could become synonymous, which would further silence dialogue. In these ways racial understanding and talk were truncated and monopolized by white-endorsed ideas of racial paranoia. The collective truncation of race talk and asymmetrical racial understanding meant that families in Rolling Acres often talked and walked around race, but seldom dealt with it in ways that could lead to systematic and individual interventions. The ways that race was discussed and not discussed created homes and schools where race was rendered invisible, yet nonetheless consequential in the everyday lives of white and black.

SIX

Culture as a Hidden Classroom Resource

Mr. Marks, a white teacher, sat at the front of the classroom with a reading group composed of three students: Jimmy, Becky, and Jeffrey. They were the top three readers in a class of twenty-two. They sat ready to pounce in response to the question Mr. Marks was formulating. Moments earlier they all read ferociously in their seats and now waited to demonstrate their intellect. Finally, Mr. Marks broke the silence and asked, "So what connections did you see?" He turned to Becky, a blond white student, and she quickly responded, "In the story they mentioned mums, and my mom has talked about mums before." Mr. Marks chimed back, "Yes, as a child I remember we had mums growing near our house." He then nodded to Jimmy, a white student, to solicit a connection. Jimmy thought for a moment and offered, "The main character in the story plays with family members, and I play with family members." Mr. Marks contemplated and then nodded in agreement. Next up was Jeffrey. Jeffrey, an African-American student, who brightly replied, "Yes! They talked about neon lights. And there are neon lights on the bottom of cars." Mr. Marks froze, hummed as he thought through Jeffrey's answer, and replied, "No, that's not right." Jeffrey rebutted, "The lights on cars that are on the ground." Mr. Marks responded,

"No Jeffrey, sorry that's not right." Marks quickly rejected Jeffrey's answer and asked another student in the group for another reading connection. Jeffrey squirmed in his chair in frustration but offered no second retort; instead he remained silent for the remainder of the reading lesson.

That scene could represent an ideal learning environment, given that it has a committed teacher, a small group of students, and a lesson that encourages making real-life connections to reading materials. However, it actually provides a glimpse into the way bias remains present in contemporary classrooms. In this case, Jeffrey, the only African-American boy in the highest reading group for his class, offered a connection from the reading to his life that was correct but was not understood by his teacher. Jeffrey was referring to "ground effects," which are neon lights that hang from the undercarriage of cars and illuminate the pavement beneath. Unfortunately, Mr. Marks did not recognize this reference and therefore rejected Jeffrey's suggestion. Mr. Marks found Jeffrey's answer incorrect, and rather than ask Jeffrey to think of a different connection or to further explain what he meant, he shuttered their exchange.

In this instance, Jeffrey's cultural cache was squelched by Mr. Marks's own limited cultural vocabulary; and this is part of a larger issue—culture as an educational resource. While no teacher can always be culturally competent, an emphasis on making real-life connections raises both prospects and hazards for learning because it makes culture explicit, and in this case, a metric for student assessment. These types of interactions are increasingly common in classrooms, as students make connections between texts and their social environments and prior knowledge. Although these strategic connections represent advances in pedagogy, they cannot offset bias in teachers' cultural toolkits.

As suburban public schools become more diverse, it is critical to understand what happens in classrooms. Education policy and discourse have focused more and more on resource provision and test scores, and less and less on how classrooms, schools, and micro-level interactions matter for school equity. In this chapter, I explore what inequality looks like in day-to-day experiences by documenting and interrogating the role of culture as a resource. My goal is twofold: (1) to recenter the importance of the classroom in discourses of resources and academic experience, and (2) to explicate some of the multiple ways that culture shapes schooling in diverse settings.

CULTURE AS RESOURCE

Inside classrooms, culture operates as a resource between teachers and students. Teachers, both intentionally and unintentionally, draw from their cultural toolkits to develop strategies of interaction, which include giving feedback, responding to student behavior, and relating in other fast-paced ways. Following the work of Ann Swidler, I argue that culture does not determine the actions of teachers;[1] rather, culture provides a toolkit for teachers to draw from, which helps structure their strategies of action. Put another way, teachers draw from what they know, or believe themselves to know, to influence how they interact with different students and their families.

The racial and economic diversity of Rolling Acres makes the need for a flexible cultural toolkit very important. The class and race positions of teachers influence how they view students and families. This is significant because, in moments of conflict or disagreement, a teacher's reading of an individual family can result in a student receiving the "benefit of the doubt" and educational opportunities, or it can produce the opposite outcome. While teachers may not actively think of themselves as controlling educational resources, their day-to-day classroom activities affect students' opportunities to learn.

Self-fulfilling-prophecy research has argued that teachers' expectations could influence the treatment of students and subsequently affect their performance. Although there have been mixed results in empirical investigations of "Pygmalion effects," it is still important to examine how the dynamics between teachers and students can shape educational experiences. The teachers I observed were painfully aware of issues of racial and class inequality and stressed that they wanted to make sure those issues did not create problems in their classroom. Each drew from his or her own cultural toolkit to determine paths of action in the classroom, but because those toolkits were not always appropriate, the teachers' actions often disempowered racial and economic minority students.[2] Although I would not classify any of the teachers in Rolling Acres as knowingly prejudiced, their own cultural toolkits coupled with their assumptions and anecdotal observations of others created an environment ripe for the promulgation of bias and unequal treatment.

BIAS

The terms prejudice, discrimination, and bias all have a long lineage in social science literature. Twenty-first-century legal and policy discussions have centered on more structural accounts of disproportionality in school discipline, special educational classifications, and school segregation. Though worthwhile, these measures of disparity are often used as evidence of contemporary discrimination despite questionable signs of prejudice; these quantifications of disparities capture but one type of difference observed in schools.[3] Here I am interested in the micro-level differences that can occur without prejudice or animus but are often rooted in bias.

I use "bias" because it can occur at both the individual and the structural level and because it does not require cognitive animus. Miles Hewstone and colleagues argue, "Intergroup bias refers generally to the systematic tendency to evaluat[e] one's own membership group (the in-group) or its members more favorably than a non-membership group (the out-group) or its members."[4] Bias, as an analytic term, is grounded in intergroup and intragroup relationships, which can occur with or without intent. A careful ethnography such as Mary Jackman's *The Velvet Glove* has shown that animus or hostility need not be part of discrimination and that sentiments of fondness toward the oppressed are often part and parcel of contemporary social relations.[5] She argues, "The everyday practice of discrimination does not require feelings of hostility, and, indeed, it is not at all difficult to have fond regard for those whom we subordinate, especially when the subject of our domination accedes to the relationship compliantly."[6] The functionality of the relationship between the dominant and subordinate often operates at the micro level without consideration of emotional and structural dimensions. For this reason and others, I have little interest in trying to locate animus, which is often the litmus test of legal investigations of discrimination.[7] Instead, I am interested in how everyday discourse and actions between people draw from dominant social frameworks to justify, ignore, or make palatable biases and discrimination. In addition, my inquiry into bias does not assume that a singular social identity lies at the core. An intersectional approach that considers how race, class, and gender bias may influence treatment simultaneously or individually is necessary.[8]

Also, where one looks for bias shapes what is found. Maureen Hallinan wrote this about tensions in levels of analysis:

Tension between individualistic or microlevel perspective and a structural perspective continues to be played out in these debates. An individualistic perspective attributes blacks' underperformance primarily to individual, family, and cultural factors associated with the black race, while a structural perspective concentrates on the impact of social structure on the black experience.[9]

These tensions can be mitigated by analysis that looks at culture and structure as mutually informing and relational, rather than viewing them as opposing mechanisms or explanations of inequality. For this perspective, I draw from classroom observations to explore how individual actions relate to larger structural issues. The treatment students receive does not occur in a vacuum; at any given moment, teachers are weighing multiple factors in making decisions.

Each day teachers I observed began implementing their lesson plans, but these plans were frequently renegotiated in response to students' dispositions, students' comprehension, and administrative demands on scheduling (e.g., breaking for elective classes, fire drills, or impromptu conferences). As teachers negotiated these competing needs, how they spent their time and how they interacted with students shifted. Across the three classrooms I observed, the teachers acknowledged revising their plans daily to fit the needs of their students, and all mentioned times when behavioral issues caused them to discontinue lessons. The connections between teachers' assessment of students' behavior can easily color their perception of student engagement and evaluation. I found that teachers were both susceptible to and responsible for the maintenance of inequality in classrooms in ways that they did not notice. Many of these interactions were guided by ideas that operated beneath the level of consciousness, but were nonetheless structured to perpetuate inequality.

CULTURE, PRIVILEGE, AND PEDAGOGY

Ms. Reno, a white teacher at River Elementary, having returned from a family vacation over spring break, decided to use part of class time to present a slideshow of her trip. During the slideshow, she asked, "Boys and girls, what's that?" in reference to a statue by a body of water. One student responded with the correct answer and shared that his family had a summer home near the statue. The photos included pictures of Ms. Reno and her family, and occasionally she asked the students to make connections between the photos and readings the students had done during the year. She spoke casually about her husband, children, and various locales she had visited. She encouraged students to interject with stories about their own experiences on spring break.

Most of the communication between Ms. Reno and the students came from white students who relied on their families' spring break vacation experiences to answer her questions; few black students responded to her questions. When she turned to directly querying some black students about their spring break, she learned that their holidays fell into two categories: staying at home during the break or traveling by car to visit family. None of them said they had gone on a stand-alone spring break trip. Taking a family vacation during a weeklong break connotes a level of class privilege because the cost of travel is high and because only parents in high-prestige occupations likely have the flexibility to take time off from work. Pedagogically, making connections between lived experience and coursework is ideal, but when they are rooted in class privileges these connections can create unequal classroom experiences.

In a conversation I had with Ms. Reno about the slideshow, she never mentioned that the large majority of children who participated in the discussion were white. Her obliviousness to this fact represents the type of common cultural blind spot many teachers exhibited. Ms. Reno's goal was to expose students to new locations and experiences. This was a noble goal, but she likely missed her target demographic of poor and minority students, because they did not participate. Even with a conscious intent to treat students equally and engage them in making real-world connections, teachers facilitated the development of closer relationships with privileged students and families than with minority students and families in their classrooms.

Gloria Ladson-Billings has fervently made a case for culturally relevant pedagogy (CRP) as a necessary approach in education.[10] CRP calls for teachers to use students' environments and cultural experiences to build learning environments where academic success is normative. Although some regard this as "just good teaching," in fact, when looking at the teaching strategies of Mr. Marks and Ms. Reno we see that good intentions are not enough to produce good teaching. Rather than engage the culture of all students, they drew nearly exclusively from their own perspectives and experiences to craft exercises and determine a student's competencies. The race and class privileges of these teachers remained hidden unless one looked carefully at real-time interactions. Neither considered him- or herself prejudiced, and their philosophies of teaching indicated that they wanted to make sure all students had an equal chance to learn; but their practices produced something different. Mr. Marks and Ms. Reno developed stronger connections with their economically and racially privileged students. Whether through references to mums or vacation locations, bonds between teachers and students were iterative and endowed with meaning over time.

Given past research, it is a fair assumption that, owing to the greater degree of connection between teachers and privileged students, minority students would be called on less frequently and receive more negative feedback (e.g., "no," "that's not right," shaking of the head) than their majority counterparts. However my systematic observations demonstrated that the opposite was true (see Appendix A). Students from minority backgrounds received less negative feedback than those from non-minority backgrounds, but at the same time rarely got pushed to correct their answers. When black or poor students did not answer correctly, Mr. Marks and Ms. Reno often did not tell them their answers were wrong; but neither did they guide students toward the correct answer. Instead, they offered very neutral commentary such as "hmmmm" or nonverbal cues that communicated the answer did not fully respond to the question. White and affluent students were told vocally they were incorrect and then were given feedback that led them through the process of finding the correct answer. This counterintuitive finding was contextualized by Mr. Marks when we discussed his relationship to black families. During his interview, Mr. Marks said:

> There was a time when I would correct kids' black vernacular and say, "That's not standard middle English, and to make it in this world you've got to speak and write standard middle English. When you go to the neighborhood you can say anything you want. When you go into the work world you know you have got to conform to this standard of communication. If you don't, it will put you at a disadvantage." I have kind of pulled back on that a little bit. All I do is do my best to move kids along in reading, teach them how to write.

He continued,

> But I never correct [black] kids. When they say, there goes the doorstop. You know, "Where is it going?" I don't do that anymore because I don't want to offend anybody. I don't want the kids to think, well this guy

doesn't respect the way I talk. Who knows? I have some pretty percep-
tive kids. They might think if he doesn't respect the way I talk he doesn't
respect the way my family talks because that is the way my family talks.
I mean where do the kids learn it? You know they learn it in their homes
and neighborhoods primarily. So I'm real careful not to say anything to
my students of color that would hurt their feelings or make them feel
inadequate because of things that are part of the way they are.

There are a number of complex things occurring in Mr. Marks's commentary on not correcting African-American students' speech. In his own
estimation, he is balancing culture, academics, and developmental issues.
While he recognizes the necessity for students to speak what he calls "standard middle English," he suppresses his inclination to correct students
under the guise of cultural sensitivity.

On multiple occasions I observed well-intentioned teachers shift their
standard praxis for the perceived benefit of their minority students. In
this case, Mr. Marks wanted to assure black students that he did respect
the homes they came from, but worried about their future opportunities
based on their use of language. In response, he opted to virtually eliminate
negative feedback and process correction for language use when dealing
with African-American students. Mr. Marks applied what I call a *sliding
standard*—a standard that is relaxed as part of a rationalization—to his
black students. Mr. Marks was concerned about being labeled "prejudiced"
or offending blacks, so he disengaged from correcting them, one of his
primary functions as a teacher. This change could occur for a moment,
or in his case became part of his regular pedagogical practice. While Mr.
Marks sees culture as centrally important, applying a sliding standard can
be considered unequal treatment and potentially allow differences in language skills to build. This balancing of culture and academics among the
teachers I studied was often posed as a trade-off between pedagogy and
cultural sensitivity. The district itself had conducted cultural sensitivity
training, but the everyday machinations of culture and pedagogy were very
complicated.

Mr. Marks's fear of offending African-Americans was likely not unique
to him and arguably could be found among many teachers in the work-
force. Mr. Marks viewed himself as fair and considered his response to
be culturally sensitive, but he never mentioned making an effort to discuss such changes in practice with other teachers or supervisors. As white

teachers in diverse classrooms, Mr. Marks and Ms. Reno made their own decisions about how to incorporate students from diverse backgrounds; in some cases their practices may have provided a disservice rather than a service.

On another occasion, Mr. Marks asked Jeffrey, who was African-American, to select the story that they would read next in their reading group from a short list of African-American folktales. After Mr. Marks's request, Jeffrey appeared mildly confused, but selected a story. Mr. Marks proudly informed me that the menu of African-American stories was intended to take account of Jeffrey's background, despite the fact that Jeffrey had no familiarity with any of the stories. This type of "singling out" occurs when students of color are small in number and teachers believe that encouraging their participation, via this practice, is being culturally sensitive.

In Rolling Acres and in the United States at large, conversations around culture and race were often cut short or silenced for fear of causing offense or guilt.[11] Fear of causing offense or being accused of student maltreatment was at the core of many troubled relationships in River Elementary and Cherry Elementary. Although these teachers' jobs would not necessarily be in jeopardy for maltreatment, their social reputations could come under fire if they were perceived to treat students differently because of their race.

Shelby Steele argues that, in the post–Civil Rights era, the rules around social relations, not simply racial relations, are regulated by fear of being labeled a perpetuator of inequality.[12] He says that this culture of fear and guilt has limited the ways we talk about and respond to inequality and stigmatizes whites who fear being accused of racial discrimination. Steele's argument poses a challenging consideration: in the context of education, can one expect white teachers to negotiate race-related cultural issues with success, or are the stakes so high that avoiding reprimand supplants the work of creating culturally respectful classrooms? There is no easy answer to such a question, but further understanding of how white teachers make sense of race and how they make decisions can be useful to offsetting the imbalance.

In the classrooms that I observed, teachers seldom successfully juggled both race-related cultural sensitivity and consistent high academic standards, although other studies have found that this is possible. Numerous scholars have argued for the importance of culturally relevant approaches to education *and* the maintenance of academic standards.[13] However, the teachers in my study tacitly viewed cultural sensitivity and standards as oppositional. Their inability to maintain both creates a lose-lose situation for their students, who receive neither culturally grounded and affirming teaching styles nor consistent quality instruction.

DISCIPLINE AND DESERVING FAMILIES

The sensitivity that teachers employed in calling on students was conspicuously absent in their disciplinary practices. Mr. Marks and Ms. Reno were quick to discipline black students for their social behavior. This was surprising considering the large literature on differences in punishment between minority and non-minority students and the district's historical documentation of differences in discipline rates between African-Americans and whites.[14]

None of the teachers in my sample suggested that punishment of students was unequal or that the process of student punishments in their schools was racialized. However, my in-class observations revealed that students from racial and economic minority backgrounds did receive differential treatment when issues of behavior arose. These differences were closely tied to the family background of the students. All three teachers in my sample drew from their partial knowledge of the students' family backgrounds to interpret their home lives and allowed these perceptions to heavily influence the manner in which they interacted with and reacted to students in their classrooms. These perceptions of family background, particularly whether families were "engaged" or "disengaged," were powerful and consistent throughout my months of observation in classrooms.

Family background is thought to shape schooling in many ways; in particular, home life is believed to shape academic performance.[15] I also found that teachers used their perceptions of their students' home lives to dictate certain in-school treatments. These perceptions thus intervened between the family's actual home life and student achievement.

Across the three classrooms I observed, teachers used assumptions about their students' family backgrounds to rationalize differences in behavior and academic performance. While the Pygmalion effects research suggested that priming of academic evidence produced a "self-fulfilling prophecy," I found that teachers did not need experimental priming to shape their interactions with students. They relied on their own beliefs to shape the classroom.

Mr. Marks often hosted a lunchtime "study period," which was a time for students to get special assistance with their schoolwork, but most of those who attended were students who had not finished their homework and were mandated to stay. This type of arrangement was common at Cherry and River Elementary Schools. During the morning, Mr. Marks would request that students turn in their homework or walk around and ask each student if her or she had completed the work. If a student responded positively, he would continue on to the next student. When a student answered in the negative, he would stop and have a small conference with the student.

Though I was not able to overhear every conversation, I noticed that the tenor of conversations varied. I first noticed this difference when one morning, Megan, who was white, did not have her reading log. The weekly log required parents or guardians to certify that their child had read independently outside of school. He allowed her to go out for recess instead of mandating that she stay in to do her reading, as he had done earlier the same day with Byron, who was African-American. Byron consistently did not have his reading log signed, and he would tell Mr. Marks that his guardian had forgotten to sign it. Despite Byron's request to go outside, Mr. Marks mandated that he remain inside for the lunch study period. Later, Mr. Marks told me that Byron routinely did not have his reading log signed and that he was unsure if he was reading at home, though he was a "strong reader."

Later that same week, I watched Mr. Marks question Jeffrey, another African-American boy, about his unsigned reading log. Instead of quickly bypassing Jeffrey as he had done earlier with Megan, or mandating his attendance at study time as he had with Byron, he reprimanded Jeffrey, saying, "Jeffrey, you and your mother know this has to be signed! Make sure you bring it in tomorrow." Initially I was puzzled by Mr. Marks's different treatment of the three students. Later Mr. Marks clarified his strategy for dealing with homework, telling me, "Jeffrey's mother is a lawyer and is usually busy." Marks said he "knew" Megan's family and that she was likely reading; he did not "know" Byron's family but he knew "he had issues at home," so he questioned if Byron was reading. In Mr. Marks's estimation, he judged the "legitimacy" of excuses on the basis of his past experiences with the students' families and his perception of the strain present in the students' homes. Ms. Reno and Ms. Jackson also employed this strategy in the classroom.

Mr. Marks attempted to maintain a fair classroom and emphasized following the rules to students and parents while using considerable discretion in day-to-day matters (recall the cupcake incident recounted in chapter 4). Over the course of the year, teachers had multiple opportunities to acquire information about the students' families. Having more knowledge about a family arguably should lead to better relationships between home and school, but these stockpiles of information can cut in both directions. For Byron, his actual ability as a reader was not used as an indicator of the likelihood that he was reading at home. Mr. Marks's perception of his mother's inconsistent review of the reading log ensured that Byron would spend his recess reading rather than playing outside with his classmates. In contrast, both Jeffery and Megan enjoyed their recess times with little issue, largely by virtue of their perceived home environments.

Small differences in treatment like these can lead to the accumulation of benefits for students from families that were perceived to have "legitimately busy" schedules. Students from backgrounds that teachers perceived to be "illegitimately busy" had their parents classified as neglectful and thus rarely received the benefit of the doubt. Although teachers may not have actively thought about this distinction between legitimately and illegitimately busy families, these two types mapped closely onto occupational prestige and perceived socioeconomic status. I heard teachers mention parents' white-collar occupations as a legitimate cause of students' incomplete assignments, but rarely did I hear teachers suggest that students' being in a home where multiple children were present or where guardians held multiple jobs were acceptable reasons for not completing their homework. Mr. Marks relied on social class to determine his actions, though he would also on occasion use race as part of his decision-making. The dynamic manner in which race and social class affected the classroom suggests that teachers were responsive actors, but not necessarily sensitive to how their treatment advantaged some and disadvantaged others.

Ms. Reno also utilized background information to rationalize differences in student behavior. The largest student behavior issues were in her classroom. When I asked her about changes in student behavior during the course of the year, she was eager to tell me about Adam, a white student. Throughout the year, Adam struggled with his interactions with other students and often was contentious with Ms. Reno. She explained that in a meeting early in the school year with Adam and his father, the father said, "Adam, we're not in Russia anymore, you don't have to fight for bread." She said that over the course of the year Adam's outbursts and aggressiveness began to decline; she attributed Adam's shifts in behavior to his becoming comfortable with the classroom environment and the cultural adjustment from Russia. However, when I discussed Adam's life with his father, he informed me that Adam had *never* lived outside of the United States. Adam's father was raised in Eastern Europe but moved to the United States for graduate school, years before Adam was born. Ms. Reno misidentified Adam's background and thus applied a lenient approach to his behavioral issues. This misidentification gave Adam greater behavioral leeway, which he frequently pushed to and beyond it limits. Other students, particularly black male students, often found themselves with less disciplinary leeway.

Ms. Reno attributed Adam's behavior to his cultural background (via his family's nationality) and was lenient, but considered the behavior of Scott, an African-American, to be unacceptable. She routinely attributed Scott's behavior to an unstable home life with statements like, "He's got a lot going on at home." Scott was Ms. Reno's second largest behavioral challenge behind Adam. Ms. Reno said that Scott began the year acting very studious and respectful, but that his behavior spiraled downward over the second half of the school year. Ms. Reno suggested that Scott's parents' strained relationship negatively affected his behavior and led to inconsistent messages about school behavior from his parents. When issues of discipline arose, Ms. Reno was quick to refer the problems to Mr. Tyler, the school principal. Nearly daily students milled around the classroom, talked to other students, and did not respond to her cries of, "Boys and Girls! Quiet!" She struggled with classroom management, and on a number of occasions her classroom felt as if it were on the edge of chaos.

To deal with these issues, she used a classroom behavior incentive system involving colored cards. Students with a green card had full privileges (e.g., they could get drinks of water from the hall, go the classroom closet, etc.); students with a yellow card received limited privileges (e.g., they were allowed to move around the room to others' desks or go to the bathroom); students with a red card had no privileges (e.g., they had to stay in their seats and could not leave room). Each morning all students started with green cards, and throughout the day when indiscretions occurred she would tell the offending student to "move your card." By moving their own cards, students remained aware of their behavioral standing; still, many disputed Ms. Reno's disciplinary decisions, but were rarely successful in convincing Ms. Reno that their cards should not be moved. At the end of the day, three boys, two black and one white, regularly reached red card status.[16]

Ms. Reno's attempts to manage her classroom were marginally successful because they allowed classroom sessions to continue, but students who lost privileges seldom changed their behavior to comply with her rules. In addition, although the system was designed to be equitable, the students who regularly misbehaved (and who commonly reached yellow or red status) tended to be disciplined more quickly than students who typically had few behavioral issues (who commonly retained their green cards and occasionally were demoted to yellow).

Scott consistently closed the day with red card status. On several occasions, I witnessed Scott behave identically to other students, but he received more severe discipline. For example, on a spring afternoon, Scott got in trouble and was sent into the hallway. On his way, he shoved an empty chair that skipped about two feet ahead of him. Ms. Reno shrieked, "Scott! Go to the principal!" She then commented to me that she was appalled by his behavior and that it was endangering other children. Later that day I witnessed Adam "drop kick" a chair about three feet. Ms. Reno had little reaction except to say, "Adam, what are you doing?" Adam returned to his seat and continued the lesson, while Scott sat in the principal's office.

I did not discuss the difference in treatment with Ms. Reno, but it became clear that she often reprimanded Scott more severely than she did other students. One possible explanation is that Ms. Reno's relationship with Adam's parents was solid, and his parents had flexible cultural capital at the school. Adam was new to the school the year that I observed. Upon entry, his parents had lobbied the school to provide Adam with classroom assistants—paraprofessionals whose job was to work with the classroom teacher and Adam to keep him on task. When I asked the principal and teacher about how Adam had received assistants, they informed me his parents had been persistent. Often in RAPS, persistence, by the right families, was rewarded with having demands met.

Ms. Reno did not have a good relationship with Scott's family. Near the mid-year mark, Ms. Reno had a contentious interaction with Scott's mother and then decided she would contact her only sparingly to deal with

Scott's behavior issues. Instead, she would only contact his father when issues arose. When discussing the disciplinary plan that both of Scott's parents and Ms. Reno had developed for Scott, Ms. Reno commented that the agreed upon plan did not have support from his home, so she hesitated to call his parents. Since she had a tense relationship with his family, she often sent Scott to Principal Tyler's office to "cool down" or for him to be picked up. The perceived severity of Scott's actions was only exacerbated by calls from the principal and Ms. Reno's lack of desire to interact with Scott's family.

Ms. Reno used her perception of Scott's and Adam's home lives to structure how she interacted with them. In the case of Adam, her perception led to greater leniency. In the case of Scott, it resulted in more visits to the principal's office, but few calls home from the classroom teacher. To casual observers, the limited relationship between Ms. Reno and Scott's family would suggest that Scott's family was uninvolved. In fact, Ms. Reno's inability to manage this particular relationship, not parental negligence, led to reduced contact between them.

Interpersonal conflicts between teachers and families were serious factors in understanding who participated in RAPS. Across all three classrooms, teachers told me that low-income and black parents were inaccessible and uninvolved. However, I was able to contact, speak with, and interview many of these "difficult" parents. Teachers commonly referred to their students' families as "involved" or "uninvolved." These categories remained largely mutually exclusive and durable, with the "uninvolved" being herded into the beneficiary role where they held limited power to intervene.

Ms. Jackson, an African-American teacher, was not an exception to this pattern of using family background to inform and sometimes to justify differential treatment. I originally selected three classrooms, two with white teachers and one with a black teacher, so that I could observe whether there were differences in thinking, teaching, and treatment of black students due to the teachers' race matching. Though research evidence on "race-matching teachers" and academic achievement is mixed,[17] I hypothesized that a black teacher would likely be more sensitive to the needs of or issues among the black student population. In analyzing my observational notes and interview data, I found very few occasions when Ms. Jackson used her racial identity to forge additional bonds with black students or families in her classroom. This is not to suggest that Ms. Jackson's race did not sometimes aid in facilitating connections with black families. But these connections were usually the result of parents' perception that she was more approachable, not the result of her extending herself to them. Of the black families in the classroom that mentioned feeling a strong tie to Ms. Jackson, none of them offered evidence she was more approachable than teachers in the past. Instead, these parents perceived a tie to Ms. Jackson that was related to what she represented racially.

Ms. Jackson expressed a clear desire in interviews to work in a school that served African-American students, but her behavior toward black students and the ways she used family background to inform her interactions was consistent with that of the white teachers in my sample. In large part, I attribute this similarity in use of family background to Ms. Jackson's social class. As a middle-class black woman with a young child, she spent limited time outside of the school day engaging in school-related matters; instead she opted to be with her family. Also, she did not live close to the school, and at the close of the day she left the building shortly after the students were dismissed.

The majority of the black students in Ms. Jackson's class lived in the Mulberry Houses, as did the majority of black students who attended Cherry Elementary. In contrast, most whites in the school lived in middle-class and affluent subdivisions and neighborhoods. In an attempt to deal with this racial and economic segregation among the school population, Ms. Bell, the principal of Cherry Elementary, hosted multiple school-related events at the Mulberry Houses, though they were sparsely attended. Principal Bell stressed the need to connect Mulberry parents to the school, but Ms. Jackson did not mirror this commitment in her actions. When I interviewed Ms. Jackson in the latter part of the academic year, I asked if she had visited the Mulberry Houses. She said she had intended to, but had not yet done so. When we discussed differences in student performance, she identified the students from Mulberry as her low performers.

Ms. Jackson's perspective on the underperformance of black students in her classroom relied on a family-based cultural rationale. She attributed black student underperformance to a lack of motivation among the students, as well as their parents. While she identified the lack of motivation as geographically concentrated—she said that students from Mulberry were the worst performers—she did not take the initiative to visit the housing facility. Her lack of relationships to her students outside of school was consistent with her espoused approach to families, which she developed in her past experiences as a teacher.

> INTERVIEWER: Are there some students and families that you interact with more than others? And if so how did that relationship come about?
>
> JACKSON: Nope. I leave here, I interact with my family. I didn't want to get too . . . I almost did that at my last school, but it would have been a mistake I think. A student was like real sweet, my pet, and her parents, her mom was really nice. She would come in to pick her student up and we almost developed a friendship there, but it was too hard then after school in the summer to continue that. I don't want any kids to feel like, "oh no, she is not calling me anymore" so I just go home. Leave the kids alone.
>
> INTERVIEWER: Have you found that some families are more willing to contact you than others?
>
> JACKSON: Not necessarily. There are just some that aren't as involved with their kids' education, so they won't contact me. I have one student in particular, my learning disabled student, and she. . . . Her mom has the blinders on. She doesn't want to hear anything bad about her child, [that she] can't learn like the others, and so she really doesn't want to come up here.

Ms. Jackson, like the other teachers in my sample, tended to view parents and families in a binary fashion: involved or uninvolved, helpful or harmful, aware or blind, caring or not caring. These binaries were consistent across my observations throughout the year, even when evidence was provided that those perceptions were wrong.

These categorizations of families were rigid and often impervious to actual changes in engagement or disengagement during the year. Even when conflicting or new evidence surfaced, teachers seldom allowed it to affect their characterizations of or actions toward students. It is reasonable to assume that a teacher's knowledge of families can positively affect students' behavior and performance, but with limited and/or inaccurate information this knowledge can be detrimental to developing relationships or developing effective responses to families' needs and circumstances.

ACHIEVEMENT GAPS

"Achievement gap" was a term that commonly appeared in local papers, was uttered at school board meetings, and haunted Rolling Acres residents' consciousness. Most teachers were keenly aware of the achievement gap, and I wondered how this affected their work inside the classroom. When I asked Mr. Marks what he thought caused the achievement gap, he responded, "I have been teaching a long time and it's a very complex problem. I think the problems of American society in general are, by and large, connected to the problems we have with kids in school." He continued: "They need a whole family unit. It is not just [white] American kids, but in my experience there have been a much greater percentage of African-American kids who come from single-parent families than my Caucasian families. But I am not going to lay the whole thing on the family problems. That's certainly a part of it." In his general comments during our interviews, Mr. Marks discussed family background, differential early childhood preparation, and test bias in standardized measures as causes of the gap. His explanation could have been torn from the pages of a research report on the gap with one key omission: the role of school processes in perpetuating the gap.

Publicly, teachers were said to be a source of bias, potential culprits, or allies in reducing the achievement gap. Mr. Marks recalled an article in the *Rolling Acres Courier* in which one of his former African-American students, a middle-class youth, was quoted. Mr. Marks had been nervous that his former student would implicate him as a cause of the achievement gap and was relieved to find out that the student had not mentioned him. He proudly touted this example as verification that he played no role in the issue. In general discussions of the gap, classroom teachers described wider structural issues with the social world (e.g., economic inequality, family structure, test bias). However, when I asked Mr. Marks about the gap within his classroom, he (and other teachers) quickly suggested that cultural differences in motivation and family values were at the core of inequalities.

Ms. Jackson thought that culture and effort were at the core of the achievement gap problem. She drew from her own life to explain this. Ms. Jackson's family had moved to a suburb from a city while she was in second grade. She had two older brothers who were enrolled in the local suburban public schools ahead of her. Ms. Jackson said that her academic

performance was on par with that of her white peers, but that her brothers'
performance lagged far behind. At first, I thought Ms. Jackson was going
to suggest that her brothers' early education in the city had underprepared
them for a more rigorous suburban curriculum. Instead she said that their
underperformance was due to a lack of motivation from her parents.

> My brothers, they started fourth and fifth grade in that district, they
> always had a[n] [achievement] gap. I think cause they are very capable and
> I think the pressure didn't come from home as much. The pressure from
> home from my parents was behavior. "I don't want to hear the teachers
> complaining about your behavior." I mean they weren't pushed to exceed,
> you know, their performance or improve their grades. So I think it was a
> lack of motivation from the parents in seeing their children succeed in my
> family.

Ms. Jackson felt that her parents' concentration on the boys' behavioral
issues subtracted from their academic performance. Despite her parents'
focus on discipline, Ms. Jackson said that her brothers routinely misbehaved, were unmotivated, and did not do well in school. Black boys are
routinely disciplined more often and in more punitive ways that white boys
and black girls.[18] Ms. Jackson could have looked to disciplinary disparities
or differences in school quality as partially explanatory when it came to
personal explanations of gaps; instead she eschewed these structural explanations in favor of more individual cultural deficiencies. She believed that if
her brothers had been more motivated and her parents had pushed harder,
they would have succeeded. This explanation was mirrored in her discussion of black students and families in her classroom.

When I asked her if there was an achievement gap in her classroom, at
the mid-year mark, she was unsure. After walking to her desk and retriev-
ing the most recent state standardized test scores, she informed me that
some of her lowest achievers were indeed African-American. As an explanation for their performance, she then proceeded to list all the low performers and provide an individual narrative about each of her black students.
These narratives identified behavioral or motivational issues as the root of
their low performance. In identifying the educational inequalities within
her own classroom she used an individual lens and did not mention larger
structural issues like class, race, and gender.

Teachers' explanation of disparities in achievement rarely relied on the
cumulative advantages that the white and affluent accrued or the structural

disadvantages that black families inherited. Rather, they hinged on the individual failings of black students' backgrounds. By individualizing issues of student achievement, teachers arguably could identify individual levers for change. However, armed with semi-accurate information about students' backgrounds, teachers' individual-based interventions were unlikely to be successful. By categorizing underperformance as individual, lacking accurate information about families, and subtly valuing cultural similarity, teachers reified group-based differences in treatment between black and white and between poor and non-poor students.

THEORIZING DIFFERENCES

This chapter has demonstrated that racial and economic minorities in RAPS experienced school differently. The different assessments and treatment of academic performance (teacher feedback), behavior (student discipline), and culture (perceived family background) cumulatively contributed to the marginalization of the minority students. Although teachers understood the overarching structural issues that led to embedded inequalities, they failed to bring this larger understanding into their characterization and treatment of students. I observed similar patterns of difference in treatment across all three classrooms. Mr. Marks, Ms. Reno, and Ms. Jackson thought of themselves as culturally sensitive teachers who created diverse classrooms for quality education. In fact, their classrooms created unequal experiences for black and white students.

These differences in treatment, particularly race-based differences, need not be rooted in explicit racial animus or intentional mistreatment. Implicit stereotypes and bias may be at play in leading to differential treatment.[19] I agree with Lincoln Quillian, who writes, "evidence suggests that for behaviors where conscious regulation is difficult, such as body language or decisions made under time pressure, implicit biases are likely to influence behavior even among subjects with neutral or positive explicit attitudes toward the target."[20] For this reason, the classroom is an important environment in which to observe implicit bias, given the fast-paced nature of much of the interaction. Teachers often respond in ways they are not cognitively aware of when disciplining or giving student feedback. To a degree, their actions provide an unmediated view of how bias operates when it is not checked by social conventions. Harvard University's Project Implicit on implicit bias finds that, across racial groups, there is substantial pro-white and anti-black bias among adults and children across races.[21] Their findings demonstrate the pervasive nature of the system of racism, which privileges being white as the highest ranking in the social hierarchy and the most socially desirable. Being implicitly biased does not mean that people are unable to change, but it does suggest that these implicit attitudes are difficult to shift.

The relationships with families and treatment of students that teachers maintained were complicated. All of the teachers in my sample cared about the children's well-being in their classroom, but their actions in some ways betrayed their intent. A teacher's implicit association of group membership with desirable academic or behavioral performance perpetuated the lauding of some students and the chastisement of others. This is not to suggest that these implicit biased associations are immutable or absolutely consistent across classrooms or individuals. I believe that the backgrounds of each of the teachers I observed influenced their relationships and behaviors toward students and families, and each one had his or her own cultural toolkit for managing classrooms and relationships.

The explicit prejudices of yesteryear's classrooms were not present, but the RAPS classrooms still favored the white and affluent. Whereas earlier research captured malicious treatment of youth by hate-filled teachers, in today's classrooms one is more likely to observe inequality in a subtler form. RAPS teachers and school staff were attuned to issues of social inequality, but they seldom incorporated their social scientific knowledge when discussing their own classrooms. Instead teachers saw educational inequality in their classrooms as a function of individual student issues or family issues. The differences between what they believed about the gap abstractly and how they understood it in the classrooms concretely may be a key source of divergence and critical to figuring out how teachers could be influential in reducing the gap.

CONCLUSIONS

Classrooms remain an important stage for inequality. From in-school suspension to academic standards, many everyday decisions affect students' performance, behavior, and experiences. Teacher bias is not a new concern, but questions about its prevalence have fallen away from mainstream dialogue about educational inequality. In many ways, this shift from concentrating on the role of in-school treatment has led to a refinement of the research on external factors that affect educational inequality. But this has come at a cost; without looking carefully at student experiences in schools, we will have an inadequate understanding of the multiple spaces of inequality and the intersecting layers.

There is a complex tangle of inequality at play in the relationships inside classrooms that is linked to both structure and culture, micro and macro. There is a hazard in zeroing in on one while excluding the other. The classroom is a terrain where biases hold immediate sway and lead to accumulated consequences. There are no easy solutions to such complex educational dilemmas, but they must be tackled because many students and teachers are forced to grapple with them daily in diverse settings.

SEVEN

Black Exodus

> In reality, black folks have no sort of social power in
> this town. There's not a positive symbolic status of
> black folks here. There's not a way for mobilization
> around issues. I think there's strong class divides, but
> I think the black middle class in this town are highly
> against being associated with black poor people. So all
> that means that when it comes to school settings or
> issues of full rights, people kind of withdraw to their
> respective corners . . .
>
> —MR. ORANGE, *AFRICAN-AMERICAN*
> *FATHER, PRIVATE SCHOOL PARENT*

Mr. Orange was a professor at a local university and raised two sons in
Rolling Acres with his wife. Having arrived in Rolling Acres as an adult,
he was surprised to find that black social influence in areas ranging from
schools to municipal services was very limited. Mr. Orange voiced concerned over the class-based fault lines that divided the black community,
which he believed undermined the collective social capital of black families
in Rolling Acres.

When I began my study of Rolling Acres, I expected to find more black
middle-class families with students in the local public schools. I soon found
that the black middle-class students that attended RAPS were part of the
black middle-class core: largely from working-class backgrounds and in
non-white-collar jobs. I soon learned that many black middle-class families that were "blue-chip"—earning upwards of $50,000 individually, often
college educated, and in white-collar professions—opted out of public
schooling.[1] This chapter explores the educational experiences of these black
middle-class families who opted out of Rolling Acres Public Schools and

the influence of their non-presence in the public schools on the educational prospects for all black students.

Class divisions among the black community had an acute influence on educational inequality in Rolling Acres. First, differences in social and economic resources allowed many middle-class and affluent black parents to opt for schools of choice (private, religious, and charter schools). Second, the exodus of black families with high amounts of social, economic, and cultural capital served to concentrate less well-resourced families in Rolling Acres Public Schools. As a result, the social capital that a unified black community would have to offer was absent in Rolling Acres. To develop this argument, I begin with a discussion of perceptions of the RAPS school system, followed by an examination of the factors that influenced black families to leave RAPS and enroll in schools of choice. Last, I discuss the collateral consequences of black upper middle-class exodus from public schools on the educational possibilities for blacks in Rolling Acres.

APARTHEID EDUCATION

> "You see we've had many white people ask us [why do you
> send your children to private schools], especially people
> like from Rolling Acres and not from Rolling Acres,
> "Rolling Acres has fabulous schools!" And we just flat-out
> tell them, "There's two systems. It's an apartheid system."
> —MS. TURNER, *AFRICAN-AMERICAN MOTHER,*
> *PRIVATE SCHOOL PARENT*

Ms. Turner, though a bit hyperbolic in her characterization of the local racial climate, was not the only black parent to stress that educational opportunities in Rolling Acres were heavily stratified. As an affluent black parent, she and her husband became accustomed to their white city mates inquiring about their insistence on sending their children to private schools. The reputation of Rolling Acres Public Schools among white families was stellar, yet among black families, particularly the black middle class, RAPS was viewed as hazardous for educating black children. Many of the black families I spoke with shared the sentiments of families like the Turners, who found Rolling Acres idyllic for its social affluence, but dangerous for its subtle yet insidious race issues.

Exploring their rationale for opting out of public schools and opting for schools of choice is a complicated undertaking. Their rationales were diverse, but there were some consistent themes: the private schools offered educational customization, a more welcoming institutional reception, specialized curriculums, and fewer race-related issues such as the achievement gap. The families who were involved in the public school exodus were aware of the potential toll that their exit could have on others in RAPS, but typically said that their children's individual needs outweighed their commitment to engaging with the education issues of the wider black community. The social worlds of black families who sent their children to schools of choice and those who sent their children to RAPS rarely overlapped. The exception appeared to be when the few black upper-middle-class families from RAPS mingled with black upper-middle-class families who sent their children to schools of choice in locations such as church and fraternal organizations.

TWO PHONE CALLS AWAY

> The system [RAPS] was not the best around race issues. I just heard, you know, a ton of reports, again, from people who warned us saying that being in a small city you can talk with people, you can get information on a lot of stuff pretty quickly here. And a lot of that I feel like, dealing with the black community, everybody's two phone calls away, removed from everybody else. So you find out stuff, and just over the years, that the public school system was not the easiest place in the world for a black kid, in many ways, detrimental.
> — MR. ORANGE

Among the black middle class in Rolling Acres, there were very few degrees of separation. Social life revolved around a few central social institutions—the church, the neighborhood, and a few elite extracurricular activities like Jack and Jill.[2] While many point to the success of the black middle class as an example of achieving the American Dream, black families in Rolling Acres consistently told me that achieving middle-class status did not mean an end to race-related barriers. Black middle-class and affluent families were particularly attuned to the hazards of educating black children in a predominantly non-black space.

In my conversation with Mr. Orange, I asked him about his decision to send his son to a private school in Rolling Acres. He said, "I think in a general sense, but in regard to Rolling Acres Public Schools, [the schools are] not comfortable environments for black kids." In Mr. Orange's perspective, successfully ushering a black child through school, whether it was an urban or suburban public school, was a harrowing task. Black families, from lower to upper incomes, were cognizant of race-related issues, but the families with higher socioeconomic status had greater resources (both economic and cultural) for managing these issues. A great deal of research suggests that socioeconomic status matters for school performance, and an increasing body of work highlights the importance of wealth on educational outcomes.[3]

In Rolling Acres, financial resources gave families the option to choose among local public, religious, charter, and private schools. Mr. Orange and Ms. Orange held stable employment as professors and earned enough to pay for private school for their sons, and they were pleased with their eldest son's school. However, even with choice and financial resources, they still faced hurdles in private school.

Because Rolling Acres was not a bustling metropolis, the Oranges and many other families found limited educational options, and these few options featured a different set of hazards for their children. In larger cities and urban centers like Chicago or Detroit, Mr. Orange's concerns would have been animated by class-related fears of violence, crumbling school infrastructure, and potentially out-of-date pedagogical materials; in Rolling Acres, the Oranges' fears were more race-based. Within Rolling Acres, tales of black students being treated differently by teachers because of their race, social conflicts between students around racial/ethnic tension, and reports of public school officials ignoring the concerns of black parents abounded, and they informed the choices that black families with greater amounts of capital (economic, social, and cultural) made. A tight-knit community facilitated the flow of information that parents used to inform their school choices, sometimes without consideration of its larger implications for community-wide black education-related social capital.

SCHOOL KNOWLEDGE

As discussed in chapter 2, race-related issues in education were often made widely known by local media such as newspapers and websites. These public conversations about educational disparity led to what I call "public knowledge." Public knowledge includes general communications about educational inequalities that were accessible to all or most, such as newspaper articles and news stories, but were not based on personal experiences.[4] In contrast, "local knowledge" refers to information about educational inequality discerned from first-hand experiences or from experiences of close relations. I distinguish between public knowledge and local knowledge because most families in Rolling Acres, black and white, tended to refer to "things I heard" or "something I read" as the rationale for their school choices, rather than to personal experiences. The city's media often discussed educational inequality in sensational ways, which suggested that the achievement gap was anomalous. Using both public and local knowledge, many black middle-class families deduced that local public schools were not an ideal setting for their children.

The Turner family drew from both public and local knowledge to make decisions about their three children's schooling. Over the course of their residency in Rolling Acres they sent their children to both public and private schools. When I asked Ms. Turner how her family decided where to enroll their children and with whom they discussed education, she told me, "I was lucky because the church I go to, there's a lot of educators in there. There's a lot of people that talk and are giving helpful suggestions and so on and so forth, so other parents have told me, you need to pay attention to this, you need to watch out for this, you need to do this."

Within Rolling Acres, there were two black churches that were central to social life. The churches' denominations were different, but they shared similar congregational demographics. The majority of each congregation was composed of middle class blacks. On any given Sunday, the church parking lots were filled with cars featuring license plate holders that named historically black colleges and universities, sororities, and fraternities. Many of the middle-class and affluent black families that I interviewed for this study attended one of these two churches. The African-American church, arguably, is the most influential social institution in black life.[5] Rolling Acres churches were not simply religious centers; they served as locations for social organizing and also provided outreach services. Although the congregations were composed primarily of middle-income blacks, the churches' social programs, including tutoring, youth field trips, food drives, and local cultural tours, were targeted at low-income and working-class families.

One example of a church-related offering was a tutoring program headed by an affluent African-American woman, Ms. Taylor. Ms. Taylor no longer had school-age children but had sent two children through the RAPS system. The tutoring program was co-sponsored by a local civil rights group and had been in existence for a number of years when I began observing. She routinely gathered African-American college students to tutor children and arranged transportation for the students to the program on Saturdays. She co-coordinated the program with her husband, who was retired. The program ran on a meager budget, was volunteer-based, and was a true labor of love. When I asked why she chose to keep the program going even after her children were grown, she responded that there was a need in the community and she was there to fill it.

Ms. Taylor was a community figure in her own right. As a former educator, she saw firsthand how black children were seldom given an equal chance for success in the local public schools. As a longtime resident of Rolling Acres, she believed that RAPS could be negotiated successfully with vigilance. She and her husband had stewarded a son and a daughter through local public schools, into prestigious colleges, and into high-prestige careers. Ms. Taylor's stories about school negotiations, based on her experience as a parent and as an educator, were a source of information for younger black middle-class families. She was not the only black community elder who shared stories of navigating racial pitfalls; such narratives were common among black parents who negotiated RAPS both successfully and unsuccessfully. Ironically, her stories may have influenced a number of families' decisions to opt *out* of RAPS rather than attend. While she and her husband made the decision to send their children through RAPS, this decision appeared less common among young upper-middle-class black families.

Late in my fieldwork, I spoke with Ms. Taylor about my research and mentioned that her name had come up in several conversations. She was intrigued and asked in what context she was mentioned. I told her, "Just conversations about negotiating RAPS, that kind of thing. People said you were very helpful for advice on the schools here, though some mentioned that what you told them helped them decide not to send their kids there." Her look turned from excited intrigue to concern as she scrunched her forehead. She said, "L'Heureux, that's not why I tell people about these schools, so they can send their kids to private schools. You have to stay and fight." She was a firm advocate of public education and was concerned that black children's plight would only get worse if black families with economic resources opted out of public schooling and left poor and working-class blacks in RAPS. The city's present black middle class admired the careful choice she had made to send her children to RAPS nearly fifteen years prior to my study, but they were not inclined to emulate it. Informational, economic, and social capital set many black middle-class families on a road to school choice.

All families viewed education as important, but middle-class families had the luxury of considering private or religious schools. Rolling Acres was predominantly white and affluent, and its schools were nationally recognized. For white middle-class parents, it was an easy choice to send their children to the public schools; however, black middle-class families often felt obliged to choose non-RAPS educational options. Mr. Turner explained his frustration with the racially segmented schooling opportunities of Rolling Acres by discussing a conversation that he had with a white co-worker:

> [It's] irritating that I'm black and you're white. Why can you send your kids to this [public] school for free and we spend $16,000 a year at someplace like the Wimberley School? And you get just as good of an education as my kid for free. And you know, I don't think I have that same option because my kids are black; I really don't. Because I think that my kids would be looked upon a little bit differently than your kid . . . And I think that the expectations would be different.

Mr. Turner was not alone in his frustrated assessment of Rolling Acres Public Schools as biased against black children. While he and other parents knew that educational opportunity abounded, they also knew that black children did not have equal access to opportunities within their city. The decision to send children to schools of choice was hard, but it was one that many of the best resourced black families in Rolling Acres made.

SCHOOL CHOICE

Increasingly, school choice has been at the center of national attention, particularly for poor families and families of color.[6] Often the school choice debate is framed around failing public schools and the need for greater options for poor families. However, in Rolling Acres, public schools were succeeding, yet black families often felt compelled to consider school choice. Whether families were sending their children to public schools or schools of choice, the goal was to ensure access to high-quality education.

Many low-income and working-class black families listed better educational opportunities as a rationale for moving to the district. However, after a short time in the district's schools, they too came to see, first hand, the concerns that other longer-standing black residents of Rolling Acres had. Their initial aspirations for a high-performing school district that provided the best education for their children was soon met with the realities of segregation, opportunity hoarding, and colorblind rhetoric. These issues surfaced for all families, but a limited number of black families had the resources to exit public school.

Rolling Acres is a small city, and although the educational options were not abundant, there were several school types from which to choose. One of the most prestigious and costly choices was a private or independent school. Private schools included longstanding preparatory schools that catered to the city's elite and newer small independent schools, which featured specialized learning environments and approaches to teaching. Private schools had the most selective admission criteria among the school types. Applicants were often required to take an entrance exam that featured some form of intelligence test; and often both the students and the parents were interviewed to ensure that the family would be a "good fit" for the school's learning environment. A number of private schools charged annual tuition of between $12,000 and $15,000 in the early elementary grades. Tuition was higher for children in the higher grades. Thus, though private schools were desirable, access to them was severely limited by economic and social capital.

A more accessible, yet still selective, schooling option for black families was a religious school. Families that opted for religious schools tended to stress the schools' culture of strict rules, moral and ethical guidance, and more reasonable costs. Religious schools typically topped out at $3,500 annually, roughly a quarter of the cost of local private schools. If families met the requisite criteria, particularly the ability to pay tuition, their children could be admitted to local religious schools.[7] However, if students had academic or behavioral issues, religious schools had the right to deny admission.

Last, charter schooling was an emerging option in Rolling Acres. Charter schools were not restricted to the curriculums of RAPS. Each one had an individual mission statement and enjoyed some freedom to create unique educational environments. The most visible differences between the local public schools and charter schools were place-based learning opportunities, school philosophies, and class size. With only a few charter schools available, admission to these schools was competitive. Because they were technically under the control of the state's Department of Education, they could not restrict admission. Instead, they used a lottery-based system of admission, which was designed to randomize attendance.[8] Once admitted, parents and students had to maintain good standing by following agreed upon family guidelines. There was no charge to attend a charter school, but fundraising was essential to keep the programming going, so parents often contributed both their time and their money.

A major dividing line between the three types of schools of choice was the financial cost. Families with the greatest financial and social resources tended to send their children to private schools; families with lesser means opted for religious and charter schools. There were, of course, exceptions to this pattern, but wealth stratification among schools of choice was still observable. Parents in schools of choice suggested that, by attending these schools, their children would continue the tradition of educational success and financial stability that they had achieved. In this way, schools of choice were a primary location where the fragile black middle class could maintain status, whereas public schools were viewed as zones of hazard where parents' past gains might be squandered.

"COOL" CONCERNS

The hazards of raising black boys loomed large in families' minds. Both fathers and mothers stressed repeatedly that raising boys was different from raising girls. When queried on the distinction between raising boys and girls, parents and guardians told me that boys required greater supervision than girls, for both cultural and structural reasons. Parents perceived that black boys were treated differently by school staff, and they also worried that black boys' peer networks would suppress their academic potential and influence their social behaviors. In many ways, parents feared that a culture of "cool" would ensnare their black boys.

Richard Majors and Janet Billson argued that black males developed a "cool pose" as a coping mechanism for dealing with exclusion from opportunity in larger American society. They explained, "Cool pose is a ritualized form of masculinity that entails behaviors, scripts, physical posturing, impression management, and carefully crafted performances that deliver a single, critical message: pride, strength, and control."[9] Cool pose dispositions serve to bolster black males' opinions of themselves, but this self-affirming disposition may not be valued in wider society. For example, the choice to wear baggy clothes, create hip-hop music, and express oneself artistically may be read in predominantly white spaces, like Rolling Acres, as emulating the "gangsta" lifestyle.[10] From a social psychological standpoint, Majors and Billson looked at the cool pose as both helpful and harmful; however, the black parents of Rolling Acres homed in on the negative aspects of cool pose, which for them was exemplified by hip-hop culture.

Mr. James, the black father of a son and daughter, Justin and Angela, expressed his concerns about sending Justin to local public schools. He said:

> I am at war with "cool." The reason why is because I went to Rolling Acres Public Schools and I understand what "cool" is. So the definition of "cool" is you sit down in your chair, kind of slumping, right now you have pants that are off your tail. And you're not smart and you don't go to school. And so, I don't want my kid to go through that, and he hasn't. And that's one of the reasons we made the decision to take him out of that environment [public schools]. At this age right now [age 10] is when they start the process, you know the little kids at church that are his age now, they have their hats kind of in back, and they're "cool." And they talk a totally different language now. Last year, it used to be regular. Now they're "cool." That's my struggle! And my struggle when I was in school was to kind of remain part of that world as well as be plugged in to my world, which is going to school and doing well in class. But most of the people did not know, most of the people from the "cool" world, did not know that that was what I was doing.

Mr. James, and other black parents, felt that black boys were sucked into a cultural vortex that valued the aesthetic of cool over school achievement. Although this view is reductionist, it was a dominant frame used by well-to-do black residents of Rolling Acres who spoke of the cultural dilemmas of black boys. Styles of dress were often used as a marker that connoted how serious a young male was about his academic career and his future. Sagging pants and hats worn backwards signaled allegiance to a hip-hop version of cool that was assumed to be anti-intellectual.[11] In parents' interpretation, the notion of hip-hop cool was tied to the racial authenticity of boys, which suggested if a young black boy did not dress in a certain way, listen to particular music, and speak in certain forms they were not accepted among black cliques. Most of the critiques of black male modalities of cool came from parents and teachers, but youth rarely drew distinctions between children and their orientations toward school and mobility based on their dress. Through an adult lens, cool was sabotaging the future of black boys; for families with greater resources, one way of avoiding having a son struggle with cool was to enroll him in a school of choice.

During my observations, black and white males demonstrated culturally similar practices. For example, they often listened to hip-hop or pop music. However, black boys' wearing of certain styles was read differently by adults than when the same styles were worn by white boys in Rolling Acres. Black parents who sent their children to schools of choice routinely said that it was extremely difficult to be both cool and high-achieving in public school. However, they said that in schools of choice students were often bound by a culture of high achievement and a sense of cool that was not anti-intellectual. Although there is no way to determine whether their estimations were accurate, the accuracy of their claims is less important than their perceptions, because their perceptions drove them away from public schools.

Much of the repudiation of cool by black middle-class families may also be tied to intra-racial class divisions. Cultural attachments to cool have often been linked to poor and working-class modalities of cultural expression. In contrast, the black middle class have relied on the politics of respectability to identify "appropriate" cultural behaviors that they perceived would allow for the successful negotiation of racially unequal environments[12]—for example, the use of Standard English that does not rely on African-American Vernacular English (AAVE), clothing that is demure, and script-switching to fit a given setting.[13] For middle-class black adults, the preferred coping mechanism was to identify and enact appropriate cultural scripts. These scripts were meant to mitigate racial hazard in nonconfrontational ways, which stands in contrast to the adoption by youth and the poor of cool poses that were perceived as oppositional.[14]

Black families that opted out of RAPS worried that if they sent their children to RAPS they would be lumped in with the black poor and working class. If they were lumped together, these parents worried that their children would receive fewer opportunities than local white families across the class spectrum. Thus, middle-class black families were desperate to locate educational institutions that would give their children desirable individual attention, rather than treating them like a member of the lumpen minority. Fear of cultures of cool and the resulting treatment from school staff created an environment where parental hypervigilance was necessary, which troubled black RAPS exiters.

AVOIDING HYPERVIGILANCE

While it is common for families in high-performing school districts to imagine that local schools serve all of their children well, this is often not the case. Both black and white middle-class parents knew that educational benefits would not magically accrue to their children by virtue of attending a "good school." As a result, black families who wanted educational returns from the public schools participated in a process of "hypervigilance" to ensure that their children were treated fairly. I use the term hypervigilance because parents often expressed that having a black child in the RAPS system was, as one parent put it, "like having a part-time job," because of the daily racial micro-agressions that they and their children had to negotiate. An orientation towards hypervigilance was not the only necessity for ensuring quality schooling; as noted earlier, the social, economic, and cultural capital endowments of families mattered.

In Rolling Acres Public Schools, black parents contended with unwanted individualized attention in the form of special education classification. In one of the classrooms I observed, by fourth grade, 50 percent of students already had Individualized Education Plans (IEPs), which set them on a different educational trajectory than their mainstream classroom peers. Mr. Green, who was African-American, a college graduate, and a blue-collar worker, had moved to Rolling Acres near the time of our first interview; he explained the process he encountered in RAPS.

His daughter, Candy, was enrolled as a student in Mr. Marks's classroom. Mr. Green was called in for a parent-teacher conference by letter.

He and his wife arrived excited to learn about Candy's progress since her arrival at her new school. The progress report they got was dismal; they were told that Candy was several grade levels behind in reading and was in need of immediate assistance. When the Greens attempted to inquire about the next steps, Mr. Marks hurried them out and told them he had another appointment but they could email with him about next steps. They later told me that Mr. Marks was minimally helpful. They expected him to assist Candy in reaching grade level, but he instead encouraged them to enlist their daughter in pullout instruction for reading. Feeling as if they had few choices and little recourse, they acquiesced to his request, which resulted in Candy's IEP and separation from a number of her classmates, particularly white classmates.

Black youth who attended RAPS were rarely ushered up the educational hierarchy; instead they were routinely shuffled into special needs classes at disproportionate rates. Rolling Acres was no stranger to the overrepresentation of black children in special education, but this did not garner the same public outcry as the achievement gap. In part, this was likely because the black parents with the greatest resources to make noise in local media venues chose to wield their influence in non-public schools and customize their children's educational pathways there.

In order for the Green family to ensure that Candy received the proper educational attention, they would have to practice hypervigilance. Nationally, African-American students have been found to be over-referred to special education services, which sometimes occurs because schools fear being accused of "underreferral."[15] This double-edged sword meant that the Greens would have to be very aware of Candy's educational needs and options to aid her progress. In addition, intervening on her educational behalf would require some significant monetary expenditures. If the Greens wanted a second opinion, they would need to locate appropriate alternative testing facilities or a professional, which would be financially costly. As new residents, located in a largely working-class black neighborhood, the Greens did not have the deep social, cultural, and economic resources necessary for successful intervention. As a result, they were unable to challenge Candy's classification, and she was placed in special education programming while her parents were ushered into a beneficiary role.

Ms. Turner, an affluent black mother, argued that the families who could be hypervigilant and had the high stocks of capital necessary to successfully guide their children through RAPS and advocate for the best educational options tended to opt out of the system because the amount of effort necessary for achieving the best results was overwhelming. She commented, "It's kind of sad, because only the ones who really push for it [educational customization] are the ones that are very confident and very educated. The ones that aren't very confident and very educated, they listen to that bull [what school staff tell them about their children and denials of customization requests]." Educational customization was available to black families in public schools if they were able to put their social and cultural capital to work, if they practiced hypervigilance, and if they were received favorably by school staff. Unfortunately, this perfect storm of conditions was rare for the black families, particularly working-class and poor ones. Still, even having everything in their favor did not mean that the black middle-class families got what they wanted; it simply meant they were more equipped to battle the school system. These clashes over education customization could tire families over time. Black parents needed to be hypervigilant to avoid educational woes, but the vigilance required to avoid mistreatment did not necessarily mean children would receive a good education; it simply meant they avoided some hazards. Getting their children the attention that would put them on a path to optimal educational achievement was a linked but separate task.

DESIRED INDIVIDUAL ATTENTION — CONSUMERS

Parents' choice to not enroll their children in public school was not based only on the negative factors associated with public schools, but also on the advantages of schools of choice. In traditional public schools, staff often unconsciouslly yet consistently lumped all black children under the rubric of poor, but this was not necessarily the case in schools of choice. The single most consistent reason parents gave for enrolling their children in schools of choice, particularly private schools, was the individual attention that they received. Mr. Turner commented, "They push the kids, they push the kids individually. The class sizes are relatively small. There's time for one-on-one. And they have certain expectations for the kids. And the kids that are far behind those expectations, they try to get a plan to get those kids to that level."

Black middle-class parents questioned the low expectations that RAPS seemed to have for black students, and they perceived the average level of academic encouragement to be greater in schools of choice than in public schools. Not all schools of choice pushed black children to their intellectual limits; instead, parents often said they needed to "remind" staff to challenge their children to ensure their academic development.

Many of the parents that I interviewed in traditional public schools saw their role in education as supporters with limited capacity to advocate for their children; in contrast, parents in schools of choice said that advocacy was a primary responsibility. Ms. Brown, a black mother whose children were enrolled in private schools, described her role in her children's education. She explained her duties as, "Selecting what schools you want to go to. What classes you want to take. How they're going to prepare you for life. How do you manage the teachers? [What] complementary skills outside of school that you need to succeed in school, from academics to athletic to social? Be a coach slash mentor. But a consumer, I see myself as that. The teacher is not only there to serve my child, but to serve me."

The consumer role did not mean schools of choice were oases; black parents also had to practice a race-related vigilance around curriculum and course placement. Given that schools of choice were predominantly white, issues of race remained salient between students and staff and among students. However, in schools of choice, parents felt that their vigilance was meaningful because schools often responded to their concerns and demands without stigmatizing them. Not all of their requests were granted, but there was fuller engagement around issues of concern. When I asked Ms. Davis, the black mother of a biracial son, Kenneth, who attended a charter school, about her role in her son's education, she responded:

Well, he has a particular personality. He's a bit fidgety. He's got a lot of energy. He's outspoken. That's not a good combination for every setting. So I try to make sure that he gets put into settings that bring out his best form. I get the impression that people have ideas about the way my son should be treated, or the way my son should think about the world, and it's my job to make sure that they understand that if I'm paying for it, then he should be heard, and respected. So that's pretty much what I do, I stand around and make sure that they understand it, and we're gonna move along as happy campers at school.

Ms. Davis was a single black mother who held a PhD and worked at a local chemical lab. She opted to send her son to Acres Charter School, which was located on a campus that resembled a nature preserve. She felt her advocacy for her son paid off in the charter school world. Her first attempt at advocacy was getting him a space in Acres Charter School. Initially, Kenneth had not been offered a spot at the school. In the year she applied, because the number of applicants exceeded the number of slots available, the school used a lottery system to grant admission. Kenneth's name was not selected, and he was placed low on the waiting list. Ms. Davis was not willing to take the initial rejection as a final answer, and she called daily to speak with school administrators about getting him a spot. She told me that her advocacy ultimately led to Kenneth's admission, even though other students were ahead of him on the list. Ms. Davis worked around the rules at Acres Charter, much like affluent white parents worked around the rules in RAPS to get their preferred teachers. Her demands were not met with resistance; instead they were considered and often granted.

Once enrolled at Acres Charter, she felt that the staff provided a flexible curriculum and used a behavioral system that fit Kenneth's needs. Ms. Davis feared her son would have been pushed into a special education program for behavioral issues if he had attended a traditional public school, but in the charter school, the staff was able to deal with him differently. She stressed to the school that it needed to respond to her son's needs. She was an active advocate and routinely threatened exit in order to get the school to respond.

She recounted an incident when her son conflicted with a substitute teacher and she was called in to meet with the principal. While the meeting began as a progress report on her son's misbehavior with the substitute teacher, by the end of the meeting she was able to get the principal to concede that the substitute teacher was ill-equipped to deal with her son's educational needs, not that her son was misbehaving. Ultimately, this resulted in the principal agreeing to have Kenneth sit with him daily until the regular teacher returned from leave! While this is an extreme case, it demonstrates that as a parent she felt empowered and the school was responsive to her family's individual needs. In a traditional public school, Ms. Davis likely would have been considered a troublemaker and penalized for persistently challenging the school's informal and formal rules. At her son's small school, she received no such rebuke or reprimand.

Given the predominantly white environments of many schools of choice, one might expect race to be dangerous terrain. However, Mr. Orange offered a counterintuitive observation about school racial composition and discussions of race. In talking about his son's private school he said, "An advantage is that the white teachers in the school are not uptight about race. So even though racial issues arise, and they sometimes do wrong things, they're not defensive. That alone creates opportunities for the kind of education that I couldn't get elsewhere." At the Oranges' son's school, staff were aware that the school lacked diversity, and rather than opt for a colorblind approach, they acknowledged issues of race when they arose and worked to create greater space for race-related dialogues.

Ms. Orange related another story of racial inclusion. She told me about a storybook her son had created that featured a monkey as a central character. The storybook told the tale of a mischievous monkey and his travels. On the concluding page it read, "That monkey was me" and featured the head of her son on monkey's body. The storybook was drawn by all students in the classroom, but she and her husband found the association of her son and monkeys problematic. She was initially irate and concerned because of the long history of associating black people with monkeys and apes, so she went to school to discuss the matter with the teacher. In discussion, she found the staff very sensitive to her concerns and apologized for the incident. Not only did the staff express remorse for their oversight, but they also invited her and her husband in to share more about cultural diversity and race relations in classroom and in school-wide forums.

The response of the Oranges' school contrasted greatly with how teachers in RAPS likely would have dealt with a similar issue. As discussed in chapter 6, Mr. Marks, Ms. Reno, and Ms. Jackson seemed more concerned with avoiding racial missteps than dealing with the role of race in their classrooms. In chapters 2 and 5, I discussed how Rolling Acres public schools were often colorblind sites, which influenced black middle-class parents' perceptions of the prospects of equal education. These sets of public and local knowledge helped influence upper middle-class black families to not enroll their children in public schools and to subsequently concentrate on their children's individual education at the expense of a citywide effort to ensure black educational opportunity.

BLACK SOCIAL CAPITAL?

The local media and school board's attention to the black-white achievement gap often hid the significance of social class. Just as general differences in average social class between black and white influenced achievement, differences in wealth within the black community of Rolling Acres influenced networks and resources that black families held. Black middle-class and affluent families tended to maintain distinct social networks that were race- and class-exclusive. From schools to sports, the social capital that black families wielded in Rolling Acres was splintered along psychological and material lines.

The black affluent and middle-class parents who were able to send their children to schools of choice often utilized education as a source for maintaining social status and ties, and to create opportunities. In contrast, low-income and working-class black families whose children attended local schools saw them as pathways to mobility. This difference in views meant that black families in Rolling Acres saw schools differently; as a result, the basis for organizing and challenging the status quo was splintered. For the black middle class and affluent, because their economic gains and educational attainment had already been solidified they were most invested in maintaining and expanding those gains. In contrast, the black working class and poor were using schooling as a motor to propel their future mobility and were often battling to keep their children afloat in local schools. With public concern about black schooling centered on seemingly intransigent achievement and disciplinary gaps, black middle-class families tried to avoid these issues more than use their social capital to resolve them. Although black parents across class lines were concerned about their children's performance, this did not mean that their common concern produced a unified political agenda or coherent race-based social capital.

There were few spaces other than the city's schools where the black poor, working class, and middle class interacted. In the church sanctuary on Sundays one could find a variety of social classes, but interactions were still segmented along class lines. Black middle-class adults often headed the Rolling Acres School Board and local civil rights groups, but their ability to represent the interests of the black poor was limited. A few spokespeople for the black Rolling Acres community advocated from their organizational positions, but without school-aged children or children in the public schools, their advocacy inevitably appeared weak. Grassroots attempts to form black parent advocacy groups were undermined when the black poor and working class, who were the target, did not attend or take leadership roles.[16] There was a clear need to address black educational issues, but little ability to mobilize across class lines existed.

William Julius Wilson argued in *When Work Disappears* that, with the exodus of the black middle class from the inner city to more suburban areas, poorer black inner-city residents fell into more concentrated poverty, their social ties with more successful black families weakened, and many of their role models disappeared. In Rolling Acres, the distance between the black poor and the black middle class was physically much smaller than in Wilson's constellation. At the same time, the social distance between the black poor and working class and the black middle and affluent class was a sizable chasm. The issues faced in RAPS were often known and negotiated by individual members of the black affluent and middle class. They seemed not to desire to engage in hypervigilance for other black families' children to achieve what were potentially limited educational returns. Instead, they often opted for schools of choice to maximize opportunity for their own families. The more the black middle class concentrated on their individual children's schooling, the less likely black students in Rolling Acres could benefit from the collective social and cultural capital in the city.

The divisions between black public school attendees (mainly poor, working-class, and black middle-class core) and black school of choice attendees (mainly affluent and "blue-chip" blacks) served to further rupture any race-based social and cultural capital that the RAPS black families had. The black poor suffered most from this divide in losing powerful and experienced education advocates, as well as citizens who knew how to navigate day-to-day barriers in a predominantly white and affluent city. The black middle class, in turn, missed out on the benefits of collective political power because it was known that their advocacy was undermined by their lack of authentic connection to the black poor. In response, the city's political apparatus was able to look at them as representatives of minority or fringe groups with little collective bargaining power. While all black parents were concerned about race-related educational inequality, few were able to act on behalf of the collective good.

EIGHT

Hope in the Promised Land

I sat with Mr. Downing in his living room on a winter afternoon to discuss his son LeBron's future. He beamed with pride as he described his daughter's pending enrollment in community college, a first for his family. He was optimistic about LeBron's educational trajectory, despite his personal knowledge of the limits of Rolling Acres Public Schools. With a restrained assuredness, he told me that he had successfully ushered multiple children through schools in Rolling Acres.

Mr. Downing spoke with the confidence of poker player who had a royal flush stashed as others bet against his odds. His secret to success was a local high school for students with behavioral issues. With just over three hundred students and a long-standing relationship with its principal—a respected African-American male leader in the community—Mr. Downing thought this school would provide LeBron's best chance to attend college. He liked the small size of the school and told me when LeBron's older sister was a student there she had received positive individualized attention, a sought-after but seldom achieved experience for black families in the Promised Land of Rolling Acres. I asked if he thought LeBron should attend the school even though he had no known behavioral issues. He said with a laugh,

If you find success someplace, you use it until it is not there anymore. I know the principal is not going to live forever but, you know, hopefully [if he leaves] there will be somebody else in that system out there who is going to take the same path and attitude and get the same results. For almost 33 years he has been [that person] in the system.

Mr. Downing, like most black parents in Rolling Acres schools, spent a great deal of time learning how to work *around* the schools their children were assigned to rather than *with* the schools to set their children on a path to educational success. In contrast, white families were able to work with their local schools and were seldom rebuffed in the pursuit of educational access and success. While Mr. Downing desired to take advantage of all that Rolling Acres offered, like many others, he knew that simply sending a black child through RAPS without hypervigilance and lobbying was folly. His choices were informed by the blockages in the system that faced black families, both poor and middle class. He had witnessed them first as a student in Rolling Acres Public Schools, and later as a parent. The goal of breaking the cycle of receiving a second-class education in a first-class school system was a difficult one to achieve and often carried consequences even for successful strivers.

Mr. Downing's intention to send LeBron to a special needs high school to gain individualized attention may seem extreme; in reality, it was a rational response to the institutional reception, segmented social world, and resource hoarding his family contended with daily. Even if Mr. Downing has found a "secret formula" for his own family's success, his chosen path cannot be followed by all in the district and is hardly sustainable. To ensure wider-scale success more systematic reforms must take place. In this final chapter, I discuss paths forward toward more equitable schooling experiences in Rolling Acres by identifying levers for change that could move its citizens closer to equality-inducing practices and policies.

The portrait I have painted in this book of the educational and social landscape of Rolling Acres may appear bleak. From a seemingly intractable achievement gap to numerous failed attempts at desegregating schools, the problems of Rolling Acres are readily apparent. Despite these failings, there is a strong potential for reforms that could lead to greater equity in schools and the social world of black and white residents. This final chapter is as much about Rolling Acres as it is not. Every district, every school, and every family has idiosyncrasies that make the inequalities that are produced unique, but they also have common mechanisms that produce these inequalities.

MINDING THE GAP

Nationally and locally, a concentration on the achievement gap has robbed schools, their staff, and families of a chance to fully deal with issues of race and class in schooling. High-stakes testing—the use of standardized tests to make critical decisions about the fate of schools and/or students—have hastened the pace that schools work to create desirable results. One key issue is that results desired by higher levels of governance, like improving state standardized test scores mandate rapid change but do so without a full understanding of what caused the gaps. The fevered concentration of ratcheting up test scores can suppress the opportunity and responsibility of schools to explore how race is operating within *their* schools. This top-down presure (e.g., from the Board of Education) curtails the potential for bottom-up problem solving (from communities and classrooms).

At both Cherry and River Elementary Schools, racial tensions played out subtly yet significantly. Teachers and white parents often observed that race was not an issue of concern; and when it did arise it was a situational issue. In reality, the racial fault lines ran deep through the lives of youth and adults. Students were shuffled into different classrooms (via teacher sorting, special education classification, and other methods) in ways that created school-based racial segregation. This segregation within schools was one of many factors that led to students' different quality of interaction with teachers. Classrooms were not the only spaces where race mattered; race was present on the school playground, in extracurricular activities, and within neighborhoods. Black and white children lived under the constant influence of race, but there were little said about these racialized realities outside of discussions of the achievement gap. A concentration on the achievement gap may appear to address racial inequalities, but it does little to deal with the divergent worlds in which black and white families lived. Race was typically considered to be only a category of achievement disparity, not a lived reality that guided lives.

The racial landscape of Rolling Acres was virtually silent about and resistant to in-depth conversations about race. Most parents, children, and teachers regarded race as a taboo and thus allowed conspicuous acts of racial differentiation to affect the quality of in-school and out-of-school experiences with little response. Emphasizing the achievement gap allowed white adult citizens to feign concern, but it did little to resolve the failure of subgroups within the school system. Most parents that I interviewed and observed admitted to concern about educational quality overall, but they were fixated on their own children's performance.

Education remains a domain where self-interest often trumps communal concern. For this reason, "achievement-gap mania," as it has been called by Rick Hess, seldom produces action-worthy concern among families that perceive their children are not on the failing side of the gap.[1] In addition, the achievement gap's emphasis on outcomes is often cast as an individual failing or group failing, which allows families whose children are performing well to opt out of acknowledging their role in perpetuating inequality.

The single most significant gap in Rolling Acres was not the achievement gap; it was the gap between the citizens who acknowledged their role and responsibility in contributing to educational inequality and those who did not. True traction on inequality in suburban settings must build understanding about the relationships between groups and how bonds, or the lack thereof, between them serve to embed inequality. Within these bonds, the paths of resources can be understood and potentially altered to produce more equal schooling.

MAKING RESOURCES WORK FOR ALL

Resources matter. However, resources do not matter in a simplistic input and output fashion. While quantifying per pupil expenditures and number of faculty are important for understanding differences between schools and school systems, when we look beyond those differences we find that resources follow multiple pathways between home, school, and local communities. From this study of Rolling Acres, we can see that resources are shaped and leveraged based on the racial and class terrains that families inhabit. Resources were in ample supply, but people's access to them varies greatly. A relational resource perspective can help us understand when, how, and why resources affect the schooling experiences of students and adults.

Charles Tilly's model of opportunity hoarding is a useful heuristic for understanding how the resources of Rolling Acres were leveraged by whites and kept blacks from equal access to them. Tilly stated, "In opportunity hoarding, the clique excludes people on the opposite side of the boundary from use of the value-producing resource, captures the returns, and devotes some of the returns to reproducing the boundary."[2] Similarly, I found that white families, in both covert and overt fashions, guided the paths of not only their own children but also school staff and citywide efforts around education. Through this control of resources they were able to increase their children's educational opportunities and simultaneously, consciously or unconsciously, through hoarding steer black and poor families into less desirable educational situations.

In the previous chapters I described how many of the educational resources present in Rolling Acres were not as accessible to racial and economic minorities as they were to those who were affluent and/or white. There are methods for ensuring greater reach of resources that cost little but require additional effort on the part of schools and districts. Looking at these problems from a relational resource perspective can help locate blockages in the pipe that runs between resource provision and the taking up of resources.[3] Uncovering the junctures where resources become diverted can be critical to producing greater equality of opportunity and potentially greater equality of outcome.

Resource provision often occurs behind the scenes, with schools or districts identifying supplemental educational services such as tutoring, enrichment clubs, and off-campus resources. Typically, families that are closely connected to schools are perceived as involved and are notified first about these kinds of resources. Families without an equal connection to schools are left out of the loop about programming. As discussed in chapter 4, information is often only conveyed in one format and stratified along racial and economic lines. Lack of knowledge about available programming, particularly low- or no-cost programming, can marginalize low-income families from academic and social opportunities within a city.

At the school and district levels, a current and constantly updated list of school-related programming and resources should be made available to all families. This list should feature pertinent program information, including descriptions, faculty sponsors, deadlines, and requirements for participation. After the list is compiled, it should be distributed to families via multiple methods, ranging from backpack mail to robo-calling. Sharing these lists in multiple formats will provide the greatest access.

Resource value is critical to ensuring that all families are able to fully engage available educational supports. In many cases, when a resource is available its utility or value is not made readily apparent. Consistently, black and poor families in Rolling Acres made rational decisions about how they spent their time, where they sent their children, and how their choices influenced their children's life chances. However, because of the stratification of information, these parents sometimes lacked an in-depth understanding of the multiple contributions that extracurricular programming or other school-related activities could offer. Although I found no evidence that racial minority and economically disadvantaged families did not value education or extracurricular activities, I did find that they valued them in different ways than their affluent white counterparts. Their different value systems were not simply the result of background and orientation differences; rather often they were tied to the families being ushered into beneficiary and consumer roles.

In chapters 3 and 7, I discussed how schools and schooling were often viewed differently by families with a history of higher education attendance. These background differences will only grow if schools and programming do not explicate their value in ways that resonate with more relatively deprived residents. Rolling Acres residents were in the city by choice, and often voiced a strong desire for educational opportunity; but often they lacked equal opportunities or the resources to grasp onto it. Schools and other programs can expand their patronage and the breadth of benefits by making sure a that a resource's value is clearly and completely articulated to as many as possible.

Resource utilization is the final area that the resource engagement model takes into account. Once an opportunity has been made known to the public, its value articulated, and access made available to all, unevenness in who is able to take advantage of the resource is commonplace and often results in uneven engagement. Minority families routinely expressed concern about the gap between the existence of a resource and information about how to gain access to it.

In the field, I found that programs that had the most consistent participation from low-income families tended to provide things like transportation, meals, and even childcare for siblings of the children who would be in attendance. These items are not luxuries but the necessary organizational scaffolding that gives all a chance to participate. This scaffolding can be as basic as providing clear rules of participation in programs to providing bus passes to participants.

The examples above drew from supplemental out-of-school resources, but resource provision, resource value, and resource utilization are equally applicable to in-school resources. In chapter 6, I outlined the consequences of teachers using *sliding standards*. They did so under the guise of accommodating student differences, but a more academically effective response would have been to use one standard and share it with students and parents. Also, teachers could co-create learning goals and daily practices for students to do at home that would support their in-school work. Such strategies—to establish a common vocabulary, a common standard, and relational trust—have been shown to improve school culture, feelings of community, and overall student achievement.[4] These relationships of trust must be built, supported, and worked at iteratively.

Shifting how a school or a district approaches resources can serve to equalize opportunity and move many families from beneficiaries to consumers. The aforementioned suggestions are some of the easier and clearer paths that schools can take. Still, there are larger system-wide changes that must be addressed by residents, school staff, and district officials. I outline some of these challenges below.

AVOIDING POLICY CO-OPTATION

In Rolling Acres, as in many diverse areas, the belief that race should not matter governed not just how individuals and families interacted with each other but also how education policies were formed and transformed. While educational inequality was a common concern for black and white, rich and poor, agreement on how to redress these disparities was not shared. With increasing public concern about failing schools and student subgroups, districts like Rolling Acres were pressured to increase the performance of its minority students.

In understanding the district's recent history of policy interventions, public response to policy suggestions was key. In the 1980s, 1990s, and through the mid-2000s, Rolling Acres' proactive attempts to break patterns of school segregation and resource stratification were met with resistance. Across three decades, sets of affluent white residents practiced a version of concerted cultivation that allowed them to reroute the actions of the Rolling Acres School Board and local school officials away from desegregation and race-targeted interventions and were able to maintain segregation, thus hoarding opportunity. Throughout the 1980s, anti-redistricting advocates stressed that rerouting children into more racially balanced schools would disrupt the local ecology of Rolling Acres. In the 1990s a similar group of anti-change advocates argued that providing more access to supplemental educational resources to black children would disadvantage non-black children. Time after time, a vocal resistance to equity-targeted policies reshaped the district's efforts.

Resisting change is often easier than creating change. Both those who were active opponents of change and those who held little opinion about it were lumped together in discussions of equity policy changes. Affluent white change resistors did not have to appeal to racial unity like the White Citizens' Council in the Jim Crow South or anti-busing advocates in Boston in the 1970s; they simply had to invoke a narrative about the loss of community. Their invocation of destroyed communities quietly implied that the neighborhoods and schools that residents had come to know and love were ideal. The absence of explicit racial animus and their argument that change would disrupt "normalcy" made their narratives seductive and emboldened organizing against change. The appeal to maintaining community allowed real-life segregated neighborhoods and classrooms to be overlooked.

At nearly any level of analysis, be it citywide demographics, classrooms, or social networks, a clear portrait of separate social worlds was evident, yet many whites overlooked this. Their own backgrounds mattered for this because many grew up in middle-class and affluent predominantly white neighborhoods. As a result, when they looked at their children's communities and schools, the few families of color were hyper-visible and lent credence to their skewed perception of racial diversity in their children's schools. These parents used the presence of some diversity as a signal that equity had been achieved. The white residents' belief in achieved equality coupled with narratives of potential community destruction provided the perfect storm for the maintenance of de facto segregation.

Vocal dissenters framed attempts at desegregation as the meddling work of outsiders who did not fully understand Rolling Acres. Anti-redistricting advocates organized both formally and informally to block proposed changes. The spontaneously formed organizing and committees were never successful in completely eliminating attempts at redistricting; however, they were very successful at altering the proposed policies.

Anti-change advocates were able to have their voices heard and in one case were tasked with drawing up alternatives in an official capacity. Their transition from concerned citizens to active policy agents demonstrates the power that *select* residents were able to wield within Rolling Acres. Lobbying by a few parents who were very influential was enough to maintain stratified communities and schools. However, for others—particularly the black and the poor—these interventions by the influential buried any hope of repairing deep social and educational divides and arrested their mobility.

A common quandary in RAPS was how to frame equity policy in an attractive manner. Rolling Acres' representatives assumed that "equity," as a value, would be sufficient to garner support from its residents; this was very inaccurate. Rolling Acres Public Schools must not only think and work hard on designing strong policy; they must take an active role in framing and communicating their policy preferences to the city's residents. Admittedly, this may seem ambitious for a local school district, but research suggests that the only way to gain sufficient support for work on equity is to identify the common ground between residents.

In recent years, scholarship about advancing support for race-considerate policies has offered some useful insights. The Opportunity Agenda has suggested four communications strategies for improving discussion about black males.[5] I believe these same strategies are useful for thinking about equity policy in general in Rolling Acres. Opportunity Agenda's four strategies for expanding opportunity are: (1) lead with common values, (2) highlight community, (3) lift up systematic causes, (4) highlight clear solutions.

The values of "increasing opportunity" and "shared community" can be used in reframing for race-conscious policies. From the 1980s through the 2000s, RAPS was routinely seen as a school system that was disrupting community, rather than growing it. Pro-actively promulgating messages about how the community could benefit from equity policies would be a good start in avoiding this perception with future policies.

RAPS must also be aware that racial paranoia is pervasive and will influence residents to avoid or remove racialized language and to suggest "race is not a problem." RAPS must systematically document the disparities between groups and over-share these facts to the point of saturation. Providing consistent messages and saturating the public with knowledge about the gap will make it more difficult for colorblind narratives to dominate. This saturation must deconstruct the narrative that school inequality is the result of individual failures and point out that inequality is bigger than individuals. In the past, the district has done some of this, but its variety of messengers and incoherent messages were quickly co-opted by squeaky wheels. Missteps by advocates like the Achievement Gap Administrator, who framed equity policies as only beneficial for removing disruptive children, played into the frame of black residents as culturally different, and made culture rather than structural inequities the area of concern.

Finally, residents must feel they are part of a shared solution to a community issue. Policies must be clear and understandable to all. Squeaky wheels often gathered attention and used venues like local media to frame equity policies as "outsider meddling" and as non-beneficial to the majority of residents. RAPS must work to frame equity policy in terms of opportunity expansion and collective good, not collective costs. If done in a concerted and systematic way, this could influence the potential to organize and usher in meaningful policy change.

After re-messaging, coalition work must be reconceived. While well meaning, equity advocates, in the past, tended not to have strong ties to the black working class and poor in the city's schools. These marginalized communities were rarely given voice in newspaper articles or community forums, and they were seldom consulted about how to improve Rolling Acres schools in ways that would benefit them. Their silence allowed affluent whites who opposed drastic change to hoard local political power as they customized schools to favor the affluent and white. In many cities, not just Rolling Acres, the needs of the most vulnerable are often overlooked. Incorporating working-class and poor people into policy construction and leadership roles will increase numbers for advocacy and will make suburban poverty visible. These changes in messaging and coalition work could lead to the production of meaningful equity policies that reach their targets and improve schooling for all.

RACE AS A RESOURCE, NOT A TABOO

Rolling Acres has a race problem—actually multiple race problems. The school community's inability to discuss race and acknowledge both the individual and the structural roles of race keep it from engaging all residents head-on. The dialogue about race in the post–Civil Rights era is often truncated, and deeper conversations are essential.

In Rolling Acres, residents rarely discussed the everyday mechanisms that produced and reproduced inequality. Black residents talked about racial hazards and concerns with other black residents but did not have these same conversations with whites. Black adult residents attempted to instill their children with an understanding that their race would shape the friendships they had, the opportunities they encountered, and how they would be received by the world at large, just as it had shaped their parents' lives. To their chagrin, black youth rebuffed these messages in favor of the colorblind narrative that race *should* not matter and prematurely concluded that it *did* not matter. However, when probed, black youth also revealed that race shaped the friendships they were able to maintain and their negotiation of school and extracurricular activities.

White adults and children alike shared this yearning for a colorblind world. White parents were excited by the prospect of raising their children in a racially diverse world and overestimated the degree of closeness within their children's friendship networks. The presence of students of color at Cherry and River Elementary Schools suggested that the racial project of school desegregation, which began during many of their childhoods, had reached its fruition. However, demographic profiles provided an opposite picture, with only a few racial minority families having equal access to the spoils of suburbia. Residential segregation continued, placing those of similar race and class standing in the same neighborhoods and subdivisions.

White children inherited a sense of racial worry and racial hope from their parents. With the goal of a colorblind world, white children suggested that race did not influence their everyday lives, but readily admitted that some students practiced racial discrimination. Rolling Acres' children, having been baptized in post–Civil Rights and multicultural rhetoric by the age of 10, downplayed racial issues and wanted to be identified as non-racist and inclusive. Because both white children and adults viewed being labeled racist as a huge taboo, neither group earnestly engaged in discussions of race's pervasive role in everyday life. Instead they framed race as situationally relevant yet not systematically influential, in much the same way that Annette Lareau and others have framed its relevance.

However, my research has revealed race to be situationally relevant for black families in classroom treatment and institutional reception, but race also mattered in the advantages that white families had access to and hoarded. Race was not simply a reality for racial minorities; it also shaped the opportunities that white families leveraged in their daily educational negotiations.

The diversity present in a district like Rolling Acres provides an ideal space in which to launch intercultural dialogues, but these dialogues must be crafted and intentionally designed to discuss race, not just as a trait in a multicultural world, but as a trait that is tied to power and resources. Since the 1990s, conversations about race were often watered down in multicultural town hall meeting formats. In these spaces, celebrating racial diversity was the goal, and recognition of the complexity of racial histories and hierarchies was often absent. These approaches hold some value for acknowledging the diversity of people in the room, but if Rolling Acres is going to move beyond celebrating diversity it has to have challenging conversations about race that acknowledge history, power, and inequality. One model of the possible types of conversations is the intergroup dialogue model pioneered at the University of Michigan. David Louis Schoem and Sylvia Hurtado describe it as follows:

> Although intergroup dialogues can be arranged to address problems that must be resolved across groups, unlike a town hall meeting, there is no assumption of homogeneity or common goals among different group members. In fact, the assumption is that members who come together in dialogue likely will have sociohistorical legacies steeped in intergroup antagonisms due to unequal social relations, hold stereotypical views of each other's behaviors and values, and question whether they are members of the same community.[6]

Beginning conversations about race with the acknowledgement of past differences and the potential for present differences in worldviews and goals is crucial. The intergroup dialogue model works to surface social identities like race, gender, and sexuality in a structured format; in this way, participants can share their different experiences and locate them within larger social systems and broader experiences.

Within Rolling Acres, whiteness was pervasive yet unacknowledged by most white residents with whom I spoke. Whiteness shaped who got what; and it also allowed white families to seldom question why they received the benefit of suburban schooling but their black counterparts did not. This led to an asymmetrical understanding of race's role in the present. Although black parents had experienced racial discrimination and were socializing their children to avoid it, white parents and children were espousing colorblind rhetoric yet living in racially inflected worlds. By talking earnestly about race, privilege, and power, both children and parents would be able to uncover the "invisible hand" that molded unequal worlds and begin to find local solutions to race- and class-based injustices.

NOT FULLY SEPARATE, BUT STILL UNEQUAL

The problems that black families faced in Rolling Acres Public Schools often left them underserved and under-respected. Across class categories, black families received less favorable reception and treatment by schools. Negotiating schooling was not impossible for black families, but the barriers they faced made their schooling experiences markedly different from those of whites within the system. The ways that schools received them served to usher black families into the role of beneficiary. In this role, black families came to see the school as the arbiter of their children's fate and viewed schools as resources for producing educational and social mobility. In contrast, most white families were ushered into the role of consumer. As consumers, white parents were able to customize their children's school experience with little resistance. This was likely tied to the ability of affluent white residents to lobby at at the city and building levels for the schools they desired. When they were met with resistance, the threat of exit encouraged school staff to cave in to their demands.

While previous scholarship has suggested that the differences in home-school relations are attributable to social class and disposition (e.g., concerted cultivation and natural growth), I found that dispositions interacted with institutional reception and then ushered families into learned roles. School staff, in ways that were conscious and beneath the level of consciousness, triaged parents, ensuring uneven schooling experiences. Consistently, the resulting divides left black families fighting for their children's scholastic and social well-being while white children feasted on the district's educational opportunities. For black families with financial resources, the consistent battle between home and school led them to exit RAPS and opt for schools of choice.

Most of the black families that attended schools of choice—private, religious, and charter—were middle income or above. They were, on average, happier with the education that their children received in schools of choice because of their ability to have some influence on their children's educational trajectories. Whether the schools were private, religious, or charter, these black parents felt they had greater control over the schooling experiences of their children. The new schools they attended were not racial utopias, particularly because these schools of choice were demographically even more white than RAPS, but as parents they believed that their concerns, grievances, and suggestions were met with respect, not hostility. A number of these families mentioned that their ability to un-enroll, which would cause the school to lose money, or withdraw other resources from the schools defined them as consumers, rather than beneficiaries. Although the move to schools of choice was helpful to individual families, it served to further bankrupt the social capital of blacks throughout the city, particularly in the public schools. In sum, the role of class was influential in home-school relations, and the role of race was equally pernicious in shaping educational experiences.

CONCLUDING THOUGHTS

In 1903, W. E. B. Du Bois wrote, "To be a poor man is hard, but to be a poor race in a land of dollars is the very bottom of hardships."[7] Du Bois understood that class and race were unceremoniously tied in shaping life opportunities. Though his words were written over a hundred years ago, they prophetically reflect the ways that black families in Rolling Acres were dealt a double blow to mobility by virtue of their skin color and their financial resources. Despite their presence in a city and school district with ample resources, their ability to engage them was circumscribed by white families, who were better able to negotiate access to Rolling Acres' ample amenities.

Decades of educational research have demonstrated that family background is the greatest contributor to student achievement, but in Rolling Acres we see that family background is not simply a static list of demographic indicators. Family background dynamically interacts with school staff and social networks to stratify resources and subsequently opportunity. This book's analysis of these relationships suggests that, long before we consider repairing achievement disparities, we must carefully understand the processes at play. Fixating on educational inputs and achievement outcomes often neglects the fabric of inequality that is woven through daily interactions and opportunity hoarding.

Previous educational ethnographies have oversimplified the interplay of race and class, giving one primacy over the other. In Rolling Acres, we see that race and class are conjoined twins in a process of inequality production. At any given moment race may appear to be more influential in an interaction, yet class still operates to produce that moment of racial reckoning. Equally, class-related differences were duly inflicted with racialized meanings.

Across the class spectrum, I observed black parents and children with a strong desire to perform well academically and, consistently, they were engaged with academics. Black parents were not simply looking at the grades that their children brought home; they were also stressing the importance of their children surpassing their own educational and social accomplishments. This healthy push for a steeper educational trajectory was, however, not enough to ensure idyllic schooling for black children. Instead, black parents were routinely burdened with fighting school systems to get the results they desired for their children. Over time, even the most vigilant parental advocates became weary of engaging in bureaucratic battles. This heavy advocacy burden was unique to black families in Rolling Acres Public Schools and was present across the class continuum.

The inequalities that we observe in school are often an extension of the inequalities that exist in the larger social world. Too often schools are thought of as "great equalizers" when in reality they often recreate or reinscribe the differences that exist outside of school. The suburban ideal of high-performing schools is partially a myth. While students in suburban schools continue to outperform their urban counterparts, not all students in these schools enjoy the spoils of suburban schooling. Black families in the RAPS public schools and poor families, some of whom were white, saw that a high-quality education was desirable but not easily attainable. The disconnect between aspirations and realities was shaped by racial and economic fault lines that too few teachers, families, and scholars have been willing to address. There are no simple solutions to increasing equality, but there is considerable evidence that suggests leaving these differences untended to and ignoring opportunity hoarding does a disservice to all within the schools.

If the United States' education policy continues to trend in the direction of greater accountability, and if suburban areas continue to diversify racially and economically, the dilemmas of Rolling Acres will be increasingly common. Each district and school must discern its own path for creating greater equity. They must look carefully at the institutional and relational processes to have any hope of remediating these differences. Truncated discussions of race and an overemphasis on class have delivered little traction and a misspecification of the dilemmas in well-resourced areas. Schools and communities must expand their perspectives on resources beyond their simple provision and measuring of outcomes. In the time between provision and outcomes, resources are engaged, hoarded, and deflected, and these processes embed inequality beneath the sight of most analyses. If we move our gaze to the day-to-day relations between groups and families, with careful attention to roles of race and class and how they affect the distribution of and access to resources, we will be able to identify not just what makes lives unequal, but how to make them more equal.

Appendix A: Methodological Reflections

The section serves as a reflection on how the research process for this book evolved and why it now appears in this form. This book project began as a doctoral dissertation but evolved far beyond my initial designs and over time expanded my views on educational inequality and our ability to affect it.

Schools

When I decided to study the city of Rolling Acres, I began the process of identifying the schools to observe. Because I was interested in educational inequality and the achievement gap, it was important I locate schools that were diverse both economically and racially. Despite decades of battle over desegregation and educational equity, a number of Rolling Acres schools were eliminated from my pool because they were overwhelmingly white and affluent. Based on the most recent available demographic reports for the district at that time, the 2005 reports, I identified four schools that contained a sizable black population and a population that received free or reduced lunch.[1]

After identifying these schools I contacted the Rolling Acres School District central office. That office informed me that I would have to get approval from each school's principal before Rolling Acres Public Schools would give its final approval. Once the principals agreed, I would then need to contact the individual teachers of fourth-grade classrooms. Neither the district office nor the principals dictated or recommended classrooms for the study. Among the RAPS schools, I had carte blanche at the classroom level. This is important because numerous educational ethnographies are based on schools and classrooms that have been pre-approved or are most easily accessible. In my selection process, I attempted to approach target schools and classrooms with the same vigor so that my observations would reduce any selection effects.[2] Of the initial four schools I approached, I received positive responses from three.

In the three remaining schools, I contacted multiple classrooms within each school and received positive responses from more classrooms than my study could accommodate. Based on preliminary conversations with teachers, I selected three classrooms, one in each school. Unfortunately, one of the classrooms that I chose was undergoing a change in staffing as I began my observations. When the teacher who had approved my presence said that she would be doing very little teaching during my in-class observation time frame, I declined her invitation to study her classroom.

From the remaining two schools I selected two classrooms in River Elementary (those of Mr. Marks and Ms. Reno) and one classroom in Cherry Elementary (Ms. Jackson's). Mr. Marks, Ms. Reno, and Ms. Jackson welcomed me into their classrooms, all of them assured me that their goal was to teach and conduct business as usual. They requested that I create as little disturbance as possible. Each teacher said that he or she did not wish to be the subject of the study. While I could not assure them that they would not be a part of the overall analysis and story of Rolling Acres, I did assure them that their actions would be placed in context and in relation to others in the school community, as well as in the context of the social scientific literature on education and opportunity. This assuaged their concerns, and over time, they came to worry less about my presence and more about the ongoing operations of their classrooms.

Sample

After the arduous process of getting approved by the district, my university, and the principals and teachers, I was excited to recruit family participants into the study. My excitement waned when I received very limited responses to my initial mailings. From each set of classroom parents I received no more than a handful of affirmative responses to my first mailing, which announced the study and its purpose. I repeated the mailing and then began to attend school-wide events such as school carnivals and open houses, and used other opportunities to meet school community members face-to-face. These methods were helpful in increasing my sample in each classroom, but still I was struggling to get black and low-income families to participate. As I began to interview families, I increased my effort to locate minority families by visiting locations they frequented, or I made sure to be present when they picked up their children from activities.

I think that my racial identity as an African-American put some of the black families who did not respond initially at greater ease with me and gave them some assurance that the study was worth participating in. Once I secured a few interviews with families of color and low-income families, I asked them to name other families of color in the classroom who they thought would be willing to participate. Many families agreed to inquire whether their peer families had received my mailings about participation. It was with this form of structured snowball sampling that I rounded out my sample of thirty-one families, which allowed for adequate diversity in the sample.

It was important to me that the sample be composed of families from the same classrooms because relationships between families and within schools were a central focus of the project. If I opted simply to select on demographics such as middle-class blacks or poor whites, without regard to the classrooms the informants were nested in, I would be ignoring significant dimensions of interpersonal relationship as well as systematic variation between classrooms. While in quantitative research it has become increasingly popular to look at nested relationships to produce an ecological analysis, within qualitative education research—particularly interview-based studies—this is not particularly common.[3] School-based ethnographies are valuable for locating patterns within a school, but within classrooms, where pedagogies are different and interaction schemas vary, these differences produce classroom cultures and shared experiences that are crucial for schooling.

In thinking about my own educational career, particularly in the elementary grades, I am most drawn to my classroom-based memories. Classrooms are incubators of shared experiences and, to many families, a school is only as good or bad as their own child's classroom. Parents must negotiate both classroom and school dynamics, but most of the race-related battles that my family had to engage in began at the classroom level and trickled up to the school level. Issues such as race and social class may be presented in aggregated data, but it is the individual negotiation of these categories that shapes the aggregate. Overlooking the classroom's significance in an educational ethnography could lead to the omission of critical information. For example, in the classrooms I studied, many of the black children lived near each other and were in the same classroom, but strained inter-familial relationships kept their parents from sharing important information about their children's educational development with each other. At the same time, these families felt alienated because of the few black families in their classroom and often felt that school staff (particularly teachers) and non-black families were overly critical of them because they were in the minority. These families' negotiation of race-related dilemmas and white families' responses to them can only be understood in a naturally occurring sample.

By basing my sample on classrooms, I was able to triangulate specific events from multiple perspectives. These multiple accounts helped me make sense, for example, of the petition to remove Ms. Baker (chapter 4) as well as class- and race-based student–teacher pedagogical issues (chapter 6). For these reasons, I paid careful attention to the relationships within the classroom and over time often interacted with children and families who were not official study participants but were willing to share their experiences and perspectives with me.

Social-Class Definitions

The class distinctions that I use throughout the text are tied to socioeconomic status, but not exclusively so. In the tradition of previous analysts of class status, I rely on parental educational attainment and/or income. Families in which a parent has a college degree I label "middle class." If a family's household income exceeded $40,000, I considered them middle class.[4] Families whose income exceeded $100,000 I labeled "affluent." I made this distinction because this level of earning was nearly double the median white household income in 2007. While income was a telling measure, I was just as interested in the social relationships between groups and the forms of cultural and social capital they employed to differentiate among themselves and in which they embedded their educational and social experiences.

Interviews

Each student and parent in the sample was interviewed multiple times. The initial interview was typically my first meeting with parents, if they had agreed to participate via mail. The student interviews were often not my first encounter with the children in the study. Because I began observing classrooms as soon as the study was approved, the children were introduced to me by their classroom teachers and were already familiar with me. My sometimes comical attempts to squeeze into elementary school-sized chairs and squatting in reading groups gave them a degree of comfort with me that made the interviews less awkward. All of the formal interviews were audio recorded. They were conducted at a site of the interviewee's choosing. Parents typically requested that their interviews be conducted in their homes in the evening or on weekends. Children's interviews occurred at school or in their homes. For the overwhelming majority of interviews with the children, parents were not present. In the few instances that parents were present, they tended to be present at the beginning of the interview to make sure their child was comfortable and after a few minutes floated away to tend to other tasks in the house.

Parents were interviewed separately from their children. Overwhelmingly, mothers and female household occupants were easier to obtain interviews with than fathers and male household occupants. Mothers and other female guardians often stewarded everyday educational functioning and had the greatest information about school-related processes. Fathers and male guardians, when present, tended to have less information about educational happenings, deferred to their partners, and seemed somewhat bewildered by my consistent desire to talk to them about their children's education.

Each interview with the children and parents lasted approximately one hour. I used a semi-structured set of questions to gather standard information around demographics, schooling experiences, and core areas of study. I worked diligently to inquire about other issues or themes that were of concern or value to my informants, and in some cases these topics were added later the interview protocol. The bulk of first interviews were conducted during the winter and early spring of 2006. From these interviews, I learned about some of the school-related concerns and issues that faced children and parents.

In addition to conducting school-year interviews, I approached families during the summer for interviews designed to capture out-of-school time and the summer months. Unlike the school-year interviews, summer interviews did not include both parents and guardians, but only the primary caregiver.

In addition to students and parents, I interviewed school staff, ranging from teachers to district officials. The interviews with educators and staff were some of the most illuminating because they provided both short- and long-range perspectives on educational issues within Rolling Acres. Whether it was a teacher like Mr. Marks, who had endured multiple generations of policy changes and remained steadfast in the classroom, or a new staff member like Ms. Jackson, who was faced with meeting the demands of a new school culture, principal, and parents, Rolling Acres' school staff helped shape my view on the production of educational inequality. While teachers are the street-level bureaucrats of education, they are also dedicated foot soldiers and developmental catalysts for hundreds of young people.

Interviews with staff often exceeded one hour and touched on district-wide concerns; the concerns of parents were more localized. I interviewed teachers two times formally and multiple times informally during my time in the field. The autonomy of teachers in classrooms was not severely compromised as it is in some schools, but still I sensed their desire for greater freedom and a greater ability to contribute to the educational direction of Rolling Acres. I also conducted a formal interview with each principal. Teachers and principals sometimes referred me to building staff such as special education teachers and literacy coaches; they were not officially targets of my study but could speak to a variety of educational issues in their schools. I used all of these interviews to discern how the relationships within schools and between classrooms functioned and how school and district-wide demands affected building staff.

Observations

In addition to the classroom-based interviews, I selected a subset of male students to observe outside of school. Using traditional participant observation methods and field notes. I shadowed six boys. Each boy was selected based on the basis of his class status and racial identity as gleaned from their first in-depth interviews. All of the boys' families approved of my presence. Importantly, I spent little time in at-home observation; instead I targeted their out-of-school and away-from-home lives. This meant that I spent hours observing the boys at Little League games, in neighborhoods as they milled around and played pick-up games, and at libraries. Most of their away-from-home activities included some form of sports, both adult-organized and child-organized. In hindsight, this may mean that non-athletically oriented youth were overlooked in my shadowing. The youth in this subset were valuable interlocutors in describing their friendship networks and how they understood the role their out-of-school lives played in school, and in providing me access to spaces where families outside the center of my sample interacted.

I also conducted observations in the classroom, both qualitative and quantitative. Specifically, I chose to observe Language Arts classes because of the mixture of group work and whole-class instruction. However, I was more concerned with in-class dynamics than with the curriculum per se. Across three classrooms, Language Arts was the subject that all three classroom teachers routinely taught. For these reasons, I utilized traditional ethnographic observation methods but also undertook systematic in-class observations using the Brophy-Good Dyadic Interaction System.[5] In each classroom, I observed a minimum of ten class sessions.[6] I analyzed these observations following prescribed methodology and demonstrated patterns of uneven interaction. These uneven student–teacher interactions were initially not captured in my ethnographic observations. I thus used the findings from the quantitative observations to supplement my ethnographic observation as well as my interview questions on teaching strategies and approaches to diversity and equality. The mélange of data that I collected consistently led me to ask different questions of participants and challenged my own ideas about the processes that embedded inequality.

Nearly a year after I completed observing and interviewing families in the Rolling Acres Public Schools, I became concerned about the results of my study. While

I believed I had captured the racial and class dynamics within RAPS and in the lives of the students' families, I felt that a significant perspective was missing: that of middle-class to affluent black families. While RAPS was filled with students from working-class families, which constitute the core of the black middle class, there were few middle-class and upper-middle-class black students from families who had achieved their status through formal education and had greater financial assets. In my travels around Rolling Acres, I met middle-class and affluent blacks but rarely found them in the schools I observed. As I spoke to these black middle-class and affluent parents, I learned that many had purposefully opted not to send their children to Rolling Acres Public Schools. The portrait of Rolling Acres as endowed with a sizable black middle-class population did not accurately portray their absence in public schools.

I therefore began to immerse myself in networks of middle-class and affluent black families by contacting associates in black fraternities, sororities, local churches, and universities, as well as posting notices in local coffee shops and bookstores. I reopened my field research with an eye to families with fourth- and fifth-grade children who had decided to send them to schools of choice. I could only conduct these research interviews during the summer months, so the interviews concentrated on general themes around education, not specific classroom cultures. Through these interviews, I was able to capture differences in perceived school cultures and the institutional responses they offered to middle-class and affluent black families.[7] The introduction of these new data helped me understand the collective condition of schooling in the city, particularly its class and racial fault lines.

Documents

This book also draws on a great deal of archival information about schools in Rolling Acres. Early on in my research I made a choice to limit the number of publications I consulted, in part because I stumbled on a trove of archival work that had already been done. Years earlier, a scholar had begun to collect archival information about the achievement gap in Rolling Acres, such as clippings from local newspapers. After I announced my intention to study the Rolling Acres school district, a mutual acquaintance donated this collection of articles to me. Although that other scholar's archival project on the achievement gap never came to fruition (its focus was different from mine), I utilized these clippings to begin my scouring of local documents on race and achievement and supplemented it with other local publications. Ultimately I concentrated my archival work (chapter 2) on four events, but I read widely about the district's dealings with the schools.

In presenting a reconstructed history, I have intentionally obscured some information or changed details to prevent identification of the site of study. Even with these alterations, I have worked to maintain the spirit of the political environment and policy proposals. In addition to newspaper articles, I had access to district memorandums and reports to complement newspaper reports. I then followed up these sources with informal interviews with school staff current and past to help me better understand watershed moments in policymaking in Rolling Acres. These diverse data deepened the nuance of my analysis and reshaped my thoughts on the possible responses to changing demographics and school achievement, as well as race and class issues.

Identity Reflections

As an African-American male, my race and gender undoubtedly influenced the ways that informants saw me and likely what they told me. When I entered the field I had dreadlocks that stretched down to the middle of my shoulder blades. Although typically I would have dressed in a T-shirt and jeans in my daily life, I consciously changed my dress for the observations and interviews, as well as when I traveled around town. I routinely dressed in khakis and a button-down shirt in the event that I ran into families in the study, which ended up being a regular occurrence. My "professional" presentation came up in several interviews with white families, who made comments about me being "well put together." My decision to present myself in this way assisted in developing a professional rapport with the school staff and families and at the same time signaled my class status to families. Despite these superficial intentional alterations, families no doubt noticed my skin color, gender, and hair. How they interpreted these things I will never fully know.

Given my limited budget as a graduate student, I was unable to hire research assistants to conduct interviews and match interviewers to the race of the family. Race-of-interviewer effects have been found to be important in quantitative research, but are less often discussed in qualitative research. My apprehension around cross-race effects was partially allayed by a review of my field notes and interview transcripts. My field notes reveal only a mild discomfort on the part of my interviewees around some race-related questions, such as questions about racial and ethnic identity among white adults. I expected that questions about differences in racial experience would be the most "politically correct" and produce the least in-depth responses; to my surprise, however, white adults' first impulse was not necessarily toward political correctness. One demonstration of this can be found in my interviews with white fathers about discrimination. The fathers in the sample were very open in their responses about their children's future opportunities, and they expressed concern that their children's whiteness would be used against them in college admissions, hiring, and promotion. They related stories of being passed over for promotion by "unqualified minorities" and about ways in which the country was becoming less fair. These men were generally not circumspect in expressing their belief that being white was a hazard.

In subtle contrast, white mothers were less bold in their presentation of race as a barrier for whites in general and for their children in particular. Mothers often began by praising the diversity of Rolling Acres, but on further probing they expressed the opinion that black families were culturally not oriented toward academic success and often the belief that the black children in their children's classes slowed the pace of classroom learning.

The tension between what these white mothers espoused and what they believed came to a head as I interviewed a mother about her child's views on diversity. She told me that her child was colorblind and that she, the mother, had been raised in a white community with little racial diversity. As she talked, she revealed that her son was aware of race and that she too saw race mattering. As she explicated these sentiments she shared a myriad of anti-black stereotypes that she "realized" she had not excised from her life. In talking about her own childhood and her child's life story she began to cry, and her words melted into uncontrollable sobbing. Her realization of racism's bite and embeddedness disturbed her in ways she did not anticipate. It was equally odd for me, a stranger—a black stranger at that—because I could not intervene in her racial "breakdown." As a researcher and an individual, I could offer no reconciliation for her dissonant racial beliefs and rhetoric.

Not all families shared these perspectives or incidents in my interviews, but complicated sentiments around race emerged often enough to make me feel some comfort that my data were reaching beyond rhetoric and into the territory of ideology. I do not offer these anecdotes as evidence of non-bias; rather I offer them to suggest that, even with race-related barriers in place, the information my interviewees shared was rich and likely more authentic than primary narratives of "postracial" worlds that may be offered in less in-depth inquiries.

Among black families, I was able to observe clear patterns of affinity. Many families welcomed me and the study into their lives and stressed the need for "something to be done." While many did not necessarily think the achievement gap would be closed, they were willing to share their experiences in the hope that others would learn about negotiating the racial hazards of Rolling Acres. At the close of my interview with many black parents they asked questions along the lines of, "So you've been doing all this research? What do *you* think it is?" I was always measured in my response, recognizing that I would likely encounter them again before closing out my field research, but shared that I thought a host of factors were shaping the academic realities that faced black families. Black parents tended to agree with statements I made about schools, particularly when I mentioned that the Rolling Acres Public Schools were not as well equipped to deal with student diversity as they thought they were. Some black families would then offer cultural explanations for the underperformance of other black families, such as that they did not value education. The allure of cultural deficit arguments crossed racial and class lines.

One family actively recruited me to mentor their son. Given my background—I am a graduate of a historically black college and relatively accomplished—and because I had a good rapport with her son, this mother told me her son needed "more positive black male role models in his life." At first I was hesitant to accept such a request, but after weighing the benefits to her child and the potential costs to the research project I decided to take him on as a mentee. This turned out to be an extremely valuable choice; it gave me greater insight his and his family's life, and I was able to offer guidance to her son, who was making sense of being a black male and coming of age in a predominantly white environment. The real-life dilemmas that children faced daily were part of my research, but research is not equipped to intervene to address their immediate needs.

The tension between research and intervention were front and center for me in this project because, in many families, I could see my own life's educational experience reflected. The structure of research often means that those who are part of a study do not immediately reap its benefits. Although I intervened in only one case in an official capacity, it is my hope that this work contributes to future interventions and furthers the erosion of educational inequality in spaces like Rolling Acres and beyond.

Appendix B:
Making Resources Work for All

Resources related to schooling come in many forms, but some of the most difficult to gain access to are those provided in schools.[1] The ideas presented here can be used as tools to find the location(s) on the "resource pipeline" where resources that are available may leak before they reach their intended targets. There are three dimensions to understanding the resource pipeline: resource provision, resource value, and resource utilization. I describe some common features and dilemmas of each dimension.

Resource Provision: This is the beginning of the pipeline and often occurs behind the scenes. Many schools, both urban and suburban, offer supplemental educational services such as tutoring, enrichment clubs, connections to off-campus resources.

What usually happens: Families that are closely connected to schools and are perceived as "involved" get notified about these resources, while other families remain "out of the loop." Also, often resources are provided at times when participation is difficult for some families, or there are strict participation guidelines that not all students or families can meet.

What can be done: Families should request a list of school-related and extracurricular activities at their school. If a list is not available, volunteer to assist in creating one that can be distributed to all families. This list should be publicly posted, not just distributed via the usual channels (e.g., PTA newsletters and phone trees).

Resource Value: This is one of the most important steps in ensuring that a provided resource reaches its intended audience. In many cases, when resources are available, their value and utility are not made clear to the targeted population. The school and its staff must make efforts to bring down the barriers to these resources, which often means explaining the goals and value of each resource to the target audience.

What usually happens: When families are made aware of a resource, such as a club or a service, they may not immediately understand why or how it can be useful to them. Thus families view the resource as optional and weigh it against competing activities and responsibilities. As a result, families that already understand the value of the resources participate, while others do not.

What can be done: Education advocates can convey the importance of resources to families that historically have not participated. To convey the value of these resources, it can be helpful to hold an open house for families or to encourage those who have not participated in the past to attend culminating presentations, such as graduation ceremonies and portfolio days.

Resource Utilization: This is the final step in the pipeline, it involves ensuring the resource is "taken up" by its target population.

What usually happens: There are often gaps between the resource that is provided and the necessary support to gain access to it. Even when families are ready to utilize a resource, small-scale logistical issues can affect participation and regular attendance. For example, providing an after-school reading program is helpful, but if school buses are not available to take the children home, the children who need it most may not be able to attend.

What can be done: Educational advocates need to develop a clear sense of the barriers that have kept families from participating. These may include information, transportation, and familial support. They should use this information to talk to program directors and school administrators about funding and providing the missing support.

10 Questions for Educational Equity Advocates to Ask

1. What programs does your school offer and who is responsible for each one?
2. Are there programs that have been discontinued? If so, why were they discontinued?
3. Are the goals of the program clearly stated in a way that all families will understand?
4. Are there deadlines for families to enroll in programs?
5. Are families adequately apprised of the requirements to maintain "good standing" within the program?
6. How does information about educational resources get to parents?

7. What new ways of communicating can be used to reach families that have not participated in the past?
8. Are there ways for children to get to and from the activities?
9. Are there multiple ways to contact the participants in the event of program changes?
10. Are there alternative activities on-site that families with children of different ages can participate in?

Notes

Preface

1. I use the terms black and African-American interchangeably throughout the text.

2. Claude Brown, *Manchild in the Promised Land* (New York: Penguin, 1965).

3. Jeffrey Timberlake, Aaron Howell, and Amanda Staight, "Trends in Suburbanization of Racial/Ethnic Groups in U.S. Metropolitan Areas, 1970 to 2000," *Urban Affairs Review* 47 (2011): 218–255; Thomas Sugrue, *Origins of Urban Crisis: Race and Inequality in Postwar Detroit* (Princeton, N.J.: Princeton University Press, 1996).

4. Mary Pattillo, *Black Picket Fences* (Chicago: University of Chicago, 2013).

5. Lincoln Quillian, "Migration Patterns and the Growth of High Poverty Neighborhoods, 1970–1990," *American Journal of Sociology* 105 (1999): 1–37.

6. Erica Frankenberg, "Understanding Suburban School District Transformation: A Typology of Suburban Districts," *The Resegregation of Suburban Schools: A Hidden Crisis in American Education*, ed. Erica Frankenberg and Gary Orfield (Cambridge, Mass.: Harvard Education Press, 2012), 27–44.

7. Rolling Acres Public Schools' demographic profile and changes are consistent with the majority of suburban school districts that have experienced increased enrollment and slow racial change. See Frankenberg *The Resegregation of Suburban Schools*, 31.

8. Interview subjects were all given the option to choose a pseudonym. Most participants chose their own alias. Among the students interviewed, many chose names of musicians, pop stars, and athletes.

Chapter 1

1. All names used in the text related to the city of study, its schools, and persons within them are pseudonyms.

2. Pedro Noguera, *City Schools and the American Dream: Reclaiming the Promise of Education* (New York: Teachers College Press, 2003); Jonathan Kozol, *Savage Inequalities: Children in America's Schools* (New York: Harper Perennial, 1992).

3. Eric Hanushek brings together a wide body of research on the assumed, but not necessarily demonstrated association between school resources and student achievement. His work suggests that once students' family characteristics have been taken into account, school resources matter little. See Eric Hanushek, "Assessing the Effects of School Resources on Student Performance: An Update," *Educational Evaluation and Policy Analysis* 19 (1997): 141–64.

4. It is important to note that there are a variety of social-class-based as well as race-based explanations of educational inequality. In particular, I am interested in theories that explain processes rather than outcomes. For this reason, both Annette Lareau and John Ogbu's works represent seminal and some of the most influential theories of social process related to unequal schooling. Annette Lareau, *Home Advantage: Social Class and Parental Intervention in Elementary Education* (Lanham, Md.: Rowman & Littlefield, 2000); Annette Lareau, *Unequal Childhoods: Class, Race, and Family Life* (Berkeley: University of California Press, 2011); John Ogbu, *Black American Students in an Affluent Suburb: A Study of Academic Disengagement* (Mahwah, N.J.: L. Erlbaum, 2003).

5. Lareau, *Home Advantage*.

6. Lareau suggests there is "dark side" to concerted cultivation but does not explicate the consequences beyond individual families. This book extends this acknowledgement but also looks at the collateral consequences of concerted cultivation on families, which are enrolled in the same schools. See Lareau, *Unequal Childhoods*.

7. Charles Tilly, *Identities, Boundaries, and Social Ties* (Boulder: Paradigm Publishers, 2005), 14.

8. Lareau, *Unequal Childhoods*, 262.

9. Annette Lareau and Erin McNamara Horvat, "Moments of Social Inclusion and Exclusion Race, Class, and Cultural Capital in Family-School Relationships", *Sociology of Education* 72 (1999): 37–53; Annette Lareau and Elliot Weininger, "Cultural capital in educational research: A critical assessment", *Theory and Society* 32 (2003): 567–606; Elliot Weininger and Annette Lareau, "Translating Bourdieu into the American context: the question of social class and family-school relations", *Poetics* 31 (2003) 375–402.

10. For more on the role of race among whites, see Paula Rothenberg, *White Privilege: A Reader* (New York: Worth Publishers, 2012); Matthew Hughey, *White Bound: Nationalists, Antiracists, and the Shared Meanings of Race* (Stanford, Calif.: Stanford University Press, 2012).

11. Ogbu, *Black American Students*.

12. Signithia Fordham and John Ogbu, "Black Students' School Success: Coping with the Burden of "Acting white," *The Urban Review* 18 (1986): 176–206.

13. For a discussion of the emergence of the contemporary black middle class, see Mary Pattillo, "Black Middle-Class Neighborhoods," *Annual Review of Sociology* 31 (2005): 305–29.

14. Charles Tilly, *Durable Inequality* (Berkeley: University of California Press, 1999), 21.

15. Tilly, *Durable Inequality*, 15.

16. Tilly theorizes multiple mechanisms for producing durable inequality such as exploitation, emulation and adaption. In the case of this study, I found opportunity hoarding to be the most prevalent and observable, given my methodology. While I do not explicitly invoke the other mechanisms, my non-naming should not connote that they are not operating. See Tilly, *Durable Inequality*, 10.

17. For more discussion on the role of socioeconomic status and economic resources, see Tiffani Chin and Meredith Phillips, "Social Reproduction and Child Rearing Practices: Social Class, Children's Agency, and the Summer Activity Gap," *Sociology of Education* 77 (2004): 185–210 as well as Jacob Cheadle and Paul Amato, "A Quantitative Assessment of Lareau's Qualitative Conclusions about Class, Race, and Parenting," *Journal of Family Issues* 32 (2011): 679–706.

18. James Coleman, *Equality of Educational Opportunity* (Washington, D.C.: U.S. Department of Health, Education and Welfare, 1966); Christopher Jencks, *Inequality: A Reassessment of the Effect of Family and Schooling in America* (New York: Basic Books, 1972).

19. Gary Orfield, Susan Eaton, and the Harvard Project on School Desegregation, *Dismantling Desegregation: The Quiet Reversal of Brown v. Board of Education* (New York: New Press, 1996).

20. Estimates of income are derived from the American Community Survey and drawn from Julia Isaacs, Isabel Sawhill, and Ron Haskins, *Getting Ahead or Losing Ground: Economic Mobility in America* (Washington, D.C.: Brookings Institution, 2008).

21. Amy Orr, "Black-White Differences in Achievement: The Importance of Wealth," *Sociology of Education* 76 (2003): 281–304.

22. Mary Pattillo, *Black Picket Fences: Privilege and Peril among the Black Middle Class* (Chicago: University of Chicago Press, 2013).

23. Readers will also note that I have identified a category known as "affluent." This references families whose combined resources exceeded $100,000. This was a category occupied by many white families who attended Rolling Acres Public Schools but not black families. Chapter 7 examines the experiences of black families that opted out of the local public schools; these families were disproportionately affluent. In the tradition of black middle-class scholarship, the bulk of the black families in Rolling Acres Public Schools were the core black middle class, while those who attended private schools were "blue-chip" black, as Karyn Lacy would call them. See Karyn Lacy, *Blue-Chip Black: Race, Class, and Status in the New Black Middle Class* (Berkeley: University of California Press, 2007).

24. John Jackson, *Harlemworld: Doing Race and Class in Contemporary Black America* (Chicago: University of Chicago Press, 2001), 63.

Chapter 2

1. Estimating the black population of the Rolling Acres and within schools at this time was a difficult task given the limitations of the Census—the populations

of smaller municipalities were not enumerated in ways that allowed for disaggregation of data along race and ethnic lines—due to Rolling Acres' population size. Unofficial estimates place the black population at 3–5 percent.

2. Rolling Acres' citywide black population in the 1970s was approximately 6 percent, and when I observed schools, the citywide black population was around 9 percent of the total population. Importantly, as the black population grew modestly over more than thirty years, during the 1980s the white population was approximately 86 percent and by the 2000s had dropped to roughly 75 percent. As is the case in many public school systems, black families were overrepresented in the public schools.

3. Lareau, *Unequal Childhoods*, 308.

4. This figure is designed to show how education policy around equity is influenced. Although it may explain other education policies in the same district, the data that I have only allow me to discuss equity policy.

5. See Albert O. Hirschman, *Exit, Voice, and Loyalty: Responses to Decline in Firms, Organizations, and States* (Cambridge, Mass.: Harvard University Press, 1970), for a discussion of how consumers respond to decline in firms.

6. Assumptions about middle-class and affluent white families' positive influence on schools were pervasive. While in part based on empirical evidence, the specter of racial demographic change often operated to expedite white school exit. Kimberley Goyette and colleagues found that, as school demographics changed, white adults perceived that school quality dropped; Kirabo Jackson found that changing demographics influenced experienced teachers to leave racially diversifying districts. See Kimberly Goyette, Danielle Farris, and Joshua Freely, "This School's Gone Downhill: Racial Change and Perceived School Quality among Whites," *Social Problems* 59 (2012): 155–76; Kirabo Jackson, "Match Quality, Worker Productivity, and Worker Mobility: Direct Evidence from Teachers," *The Review of Economics and Statistics* 95 (2013): 1096–16.

7. It is difficult to assess the race and class status of historical participants in the desegregation of 1985 and 1997 from archives and interview accounts. Despite this, I am confident in my characterization of race and class dynamics because of the consistency of my respondents' comments. Families that lived in the district, as well as district staff, verified that most public pressure was created by a particular group of affluent white parents. Respondents tended to refer to "wealthy" or "rich" families who objected to district-level changes and organized against them. Although their race was not always mentioned, given the race-related economic distribution, it is logical to assume that most of those they referred to were white.

8. Residents exhibited attitudes that fell neatly into the new orthodoxy, which suggested that the maintenance and durability of inequality were based on the individual failings and choices of black residents. For more, see Michael Brown and David Wellman, "Embedding the Color Line: The Accumulation and the Disaccumulation of Opportunity in Post–Civil Rights America," *Du Bois Review* 2 (2005): 187–207.

9. These types of policies are sometimes called "equality" policies because all students receive the same treatment. Equality policies stress equality of opportunity, whereas equity policies stress equality of outcome.

10. Bonilla-Silva suggests that whites participate in colorblind racism and often use the rhetorical approach of abstract liberalism. Abstract liberalism argues that equal treatment mandates that no one group should get additional attention. As a result, support for race-based policies is painted as unequal. Bobo, Kluegel, and Smith argue that whites support policies targeted at equality in the abstract, but not in their implementation. See Eduardo Bonilla-Silva, *Racism without Racists: Color-blind Racism and the Persistence of Racial Inequality in the United States* (Lanham, Md.: Rowman & Littlefield, 2003); Lawrence Bobo, James Kluegel, and Ryan Smith, "Laissez-Faire Racism: The Crystallization of a Kinder, Gentler, Anti-Black Ideology," *Racial Attitudes in the 1990s: Continuity and Change*, ed. Steven Tuch and Jack Martin (Westport, Conn.: Praeger).

11. Amy Stuart Wells, *Both Sides Now: The Story of School Desegregation's Graduates* (Berkeley: University of California Press, 2009).

12. Wells, *Both Sides Now*, 34.

13. The assumption that all students were in the same classroom was particularly problematic. In one classroom that I observed, 50 percent of the African-American children received special education instruction (e.g., pull-out instruction). In addition, within the district's middle and high schools where there was greater curriculum differentiation, there were also known gaps in rates of suspension and expulsion, which again suggested that students were not in the same classrooms. For more on this phenomenon, see Karolyn Tyson, *Integration Interrupted: Tracking, Black Students, and Acting white after Brown* (New York: Oxford University Press, 2011); and Carla O'Connor, Jennifer Mueller, R. L'Heureux Lewis [Lewis-McCoy], Deborah Rivas-Drake, and Seneca Rosenberg, "'Being' Black and Strategizing for Excellence in a Racially Stratified Academic Hierarchy," *American Educational Research Journal* 48 (2011): 1232–57.

14. A number of anti-redistricting advocates were not parents of current students in Rolling Acres Public Schools. Despite this point, many narratives used language like "our schools" and "our children." Though they did not have an immediate stake in RAPS schools, they were able to argue they had been participants in the past or might participate in the future. These voices were given legitimacy through their frequent coverage in local news media and in the responses of the school district.

15. The data used for proposed redistricting were not the most current. The company was quickly provided with the most current data, but the narrative about outsider planning changes with out-of-date data did not vanish.

16. Dionne Danns, "Racial Ideology and the Sanctity of the Neighborhood School in Chicago," *Urban Review* 40 (2008): 64–75.

17. Though there were no major disturbances, there were small protests. One notable protest was conducted at a local middle school where students, predominantly white, walked out of classes and demanded that their school not be

dismantled. The protest received attention in a local newspaper, but had little or no influence on derailing the policy's implementation.

18. Lee Corkorinos, *The Assault on Diversity: An Organized Challenge to Racial and Gender Justice* (Lanham, Md.: Rowman & Littlefield, 2003).

19. Bell's interest convergence theory suggests that meaningful transformations in race-related policies occur only when there is significant benefit for those with power in race relations and the minority groups involved. Importantly, Bell argued that the *Brown* decision was not guided by an ethical crisis around domestic race relations, but rather, that international public relations issues for the U.S. government drove it. In this way, interest convergence must not necessarily be based on the benefit of the outcome, but more on the benefit of actors on both sides of the divide. See Derrick Bell, "Brown v. Board of Education and the Interest-Convergence Dilemma," *Harvard Law Review* 93 (1980): 518–33.

20. By identifying the superintendent's race and gender I do not mean to insinuate that he was the reason the achievement gap initiatives were abandoned. Rather, I think public perception of him, as a white male, made his concentration on achievement for all students less controversial than if the previous superintendent, a black woman, had attempted such a shift.

Chapter 3

1. The theory of segmented assimilation spawned a great deal of literature and challenges to its original formulation. In my analysis, I do not desire to dive into this debate; rather my goal is to draw from some conceptual dimensions to aid understanding of the cases I present. For more on the segmented assimilation literature and its nuances, see Alejandro Portes and Min Zhou, "The New Second Generation: Segmented Assimilation and Its Variants," *Annals of American Academy of Political Social Science* 530 (1993): 74–96; and Alex Stepick and Carol Dutton Stepick, "The Complexities and Confusions of Segmented Assimilation," *Ethnic and Racial Studies* 33 (2010): 114–1167.

2. Peggy Levitt and Mary Waters, *The Changing Face of Home: The Transnational Lives of the Second Generation* (New York: Russell Sage Foundation, 2002).

3. Vivian Louie, "Second Generation Pessimism and Optimism: How Chinese and Dominicans Understand Education and Mobility through Ethnic and Transnational Orientations," *International Migration Review* 40 (2006): 537–72.

4. W. E. B. Du Bois, *Souls of Black Folk* (New York: Dover, 1994[1903]), 9.

5. James Collins, "Social Reproduction in Classrooms and Schools," *Annual Review of Anthropology* 38 (2009): 33–48.

6. Samuel Bowles and Herbert Gintis, *Schooling in Capitalist America: Educational Reform and the Contradictions of Economic Life* (New York: Basic Books, 1976); Paul Willis, *Learning to Labor: How Working Class Kids Get Working Class Jobs* (New York: Columbia University Press, 1981).

7. Prudence Carter, *Keepin' It Real: School Success beyond Black and White* (Oxford, U.K.: Oxford University Press, 2005); Amanda Lewis, *Race in the*

Schoolyard: Negotiating the Color Line in Classrooms and Communities (New Brunswick, N.J.: Rutgers University Press, 2003).

8. MacLeod's ethnography has been very influential in the social reproduction literature because it vividly draws from youth voices and negotiations of opportunity structures. My study is about younger youth, so unsupervised time, barriers encountered, and active planning of future paths were less frequent domains of discussion and concern than in MacLeod's study. Jay MacLeod, *Ain't No Makin' It: Aspiration and Attainment in a Low-Income Neighborhood* (Boulder, Colo.: Westview Press, 1995).

9. MacLeod, *Ain't No Makin' It*, 61.

10. Alford Young, "Black Men Rising: A Cultural Sociological Perspective on Engaging Upward Mobility while Confronting Race," lecture, Columbia University, New York, N.Y., October 25, 2006.

11. John Diamond, "Still Separate and Unequal: Examining Race, Opportunity, and School Achievement in "Integrated" Suburbs, *Journal of Negro Education* 75 (2006): 495–505.

12. Travel teams were elite sporting teams that one had to be invited to participate in or try out for. Typically they were composed of the best players in an age group and competed against teams in other cities and states. The monetary cost of participation was hefty.

13. Lareau, *Unequal Childhoods*.

14. Tiffani Chin and Meredith Phillips argue that the enrollment in extracurricular and the engagement of concerted cultivation is likely more a resource-based phenomenon; this view is also, in part, supported by Jacob Cheadle and Paul Amato. See Tiffani Chin and Meredith Phillips, "Social Reproduction and Child Rearing Practices: Social Class, Children's Agency, and the Summer Activity Gap," *Sociology of Education* 77 (2004): 185–210; Jacob Cheadle and Paul Amato, "A Quantitative Assessment of Lareau's Qualitative Conclusions about Class, Race, and Parenting," *Journal of Family Issues* 32 (2011): 679–706.

15. In contrast, among the black non-public school attenders, their attitudes toward pursuing education were more similar to those of the white middle class of Rolling Acres. In large part, this can likely be attributed to their educational attainment, given that the majority of them had completed college or above.

16. Eunyoung Kim and Jeanette Diaz, *Immigrant Students and Higher Education* (Hoboken, N.J.: Association for the Study of Higher Education, 2013).

17. It is conceivable that the utility-focused approach to education is more class-based than race-based. However, in the bulk of my sample, there was very little evidence that black families applied an abstract approach, except among black public school exiters (see chapter 7).

18. Status attainment models have continued to demonstrate the importance of ascribed characteristics such as father's employment as an indicator of children's future outcomes. See Robert Bozick, Karl Alexander, Doris Entwisle, Susan Dauber, and Kerri Kerr, "Framing the Future: Revisiting the Place of Educational Expectations in Status Attainment," *Social Forces* 88 (2010): 2027–52.

19. Odis Johnson, "Ecology in Educational Theory: Thoughts on Stratification, Social Mobility and Proximal Capital," *Urban Review* 40 (2008): 227–46.

20. Erin McNamara Horvat, Elliot Weininger, and Annette Lareau, "From Social Ties to Social Capital: Class Differences in the Relations between Schools and Parent Networks," *American Educational Research Journal* 40 (2003): 319–51.

21. James Coleman, "Social Capital in the Creation of Human Capital," *American Journal of Sociology* 94 (1988): S95–S120.

22. In Rolling Acres, the high school with the highest concentration of black students was one of the special needs high schools. Students who were diagnosed with behavioral issues were sent to the school to finish out their high school tenure. Consistent with national evidence, in Rolling Acres, black students were disproportionately diagnosed with behavioral issues. For more on disproportionality and diagnosis, see Russell Skiba, Ada Simmons, Shana Ritter, Kristin Kholer, Michelle Henderson, and Tony Wu, "The Context of Minority Disproportionality: Practitioner Perspectives on Special Education Referral," *Teachers College Record* 108 (2006): 1424–59; and Russell Skiba, Ada Simmons, Shana Ritter, Ashley Gibb, M. Karega Raush, Jason Cuadrado, and Choong-Geun Chung, "Achieving Equity in Special Education: History, Status, and Current Challenges," *Exceptional Children* 74 (2008): 264–88.

23. Horvat, Weininger, and Lareau, "From Social Ties," 341–42.

Chapter 4

1. Joyce Epstein, *School, Family, and Community Partnerships: Preparing Educators and Improving Schools* (Boulder, Colo.: Westview Press, 2001).

2. Horvat, Weininger, and Lareau, "From Social Ties."

3. Amanda Lewis and Tyrone Foreman, "Contestation or Collaboration? A Comparative Study of Home-School Relations," *Anthropology of Education Quarterly* 33 (2002): 60–89.

4. This distinction is derived from the work of Lewis and Foreman, "Contestation and Collaboration" and a similar one is made by Epstein in *School, Family, and Community*.

5. Eliot Weininger and Annette Lareau, "Translating Bourdieu into the American Context: The Question of Social Class and Family-School Relations," *Poetics* 31 (2003): 588.

6. Lareau, *Home Advantage*; Lareau, *Unequal Childhoods*.

7. Since Lareau is one of the co-authors of the study by Horvat, Weininger, and Lareau (2003), it is logical to assume that her individual scholarship supports the belief that social networks are class-based and that race has only marginal influence.

8. Lareau, *Unequal Childhoods*, 262.

9. See Tilly, *Durable Inequality*, 21. I draw from Tilly's notion of relational analysis, though not fully embracing Tilly's more idiosyncratic insistence on using this metatheoretical framework. See Erik Olin, "Metatheoretical Foundations of

Charles Tilly's Durable Inequality," *Comparative Studies in Society and History* 42 (2000): 458–74. For the purposes of my projects, relational analyses should consider that multiple actors and "race problems" exist between groups, not within an individual or a single group. In order for this to be empirically observed, a researcher must capture the experiences of both groups and their relationships, not make inferences from a single group or substitute demographically similar cases that are relationally exogenous. See Ogbu, *Black American Students*; and Lareau, *Unequal Childhoods*.

10. Admittedly, a similar dilemma occurred in my own research, where I encountered low numbers of poor white students in the district and schools I studied. Rather than observe low-income white students in another environment, I opted to maintain the integrity of the naturally occurring sample (see discussion in Appendix A).

11. In the main sample, 81 percent of white parents had earned a bachelor's degree or greater; 36 percent of black parents had done so.

12. It is important to note that while RAPS in the early grades did not have separate gifted classes or programs, they did have pull-out special education instruction as well as self-contained special education classrooms. Within classrooms it was up to the teachers' discretion whether to use ability grouping for instruction in different subjects, such as mathematics and language arts.

13. Bourdieu has defined habitus multiple times but I draw from his definition in *The Logic of Practice*: "a system of durable transposable dispositions, structured structures predisposed to function as structuring structures, that is, as principles which generate and organize practices and representations that can be objectively adapted to their outcomes without presupposing a conscious aiming at ends or an express mastery of the operations necessary in order to attain them." Pierre Bourdieu, *The Logic of Practice* (Stanford, Calif.: Stanford University Press), 53.

14. Although Martin suggested that her manager told her she could not read the Bible at all during her break or shift, I suspect that Martin brought the Bible out from the break room and to the counter at work. Unfortunately, I have no way of verifying which dimensions of the situation that led to Martin's suspension were fully and accurately related to me.

15. In RAPS, principals were tasked with producing student racial balance between classrooms. This typically meant spreading students of color into different classrooms, which was a source of tension that black parents mentioned with sending children to Rolling Acres.

16. Principal Bell and Ms. Jackson, both African-American women, discussed their concern that black families were not involved at Cherry Elementary. Principal Bell lamented that parents from Mulberry Houses tended to miss appointments and were disorganized. Ms. Jackson expressed a desire to have positive relationships with her black students, who mainly came from Mulberry Houses, but she acknowledged that she did not take extra steps to strengthen home-school ties. When I discussed Bell with Ms. Newton, an African-American mother in Mulberry Houses, she said she suspected other black families felt camaraderie with Bell because she was a black woman but felt that she "looked down" on them.

17. It is noteworthy that Principal Bell during our interview asked that the audiotape be stopped. This often happened when she began discussing tension with district officials or racial issues. She did not want a traceable record of her comments on the building, staff, or families. Thus, unlike most others, the quotes from Principal Bell were produced from field note jottings rather than recorded interviews.

18. Granovetter argued that weak social ties served to connect multiple networks. In Rolling Acres, all families who participated in organizing were not necessarily close with each other. However, their connections based on things like subdivisions and sports teams allowed the organizing to reach beyond a small circle of families. This did not necessarily mean that all families had equal access to information; rather it means that select families who were not necessarily close to each other had access to information about teachers and other school-related matters. Mark Granovetter, "The Strength of Weak Ties," *American Journal of Sociology* 78 (1973): 1360–80.

19. Hirschman speaks to a variety of different firms and organizations, but his ideas all hinge on decline in quality, be it perceived or real. In the case of RAPS, the decline was much more perceived than real for white parents; nonetheless, they worked tirelessly to be heard and responded to by the RAPS administration. Hirschman, *Exit, Voice, and Loyalty*.

20. Other affluent white families who were not in the Beaver subdivision that I interviewed, such as the Stone family, did have knowledge of the issues and organizing surrounding Ms. Baker.

Chapter 5

1. Lewis, *Race in the Schoolyard*; Mica Pollock, *Colormute: Race Talk Dilemmas in an American School* (Princeton, N.J.: Princeton University Press, 2004); Erin Winkler, *Learning Race, Learning Place: Shaping Racial Identities and Ideas in African American Childhoods* (New Brunswick, N.J.: Rutgers University Press, 2012).

2. Fordham and Ogbu, "Fear of Acting White"; Ogbu, *Black American Students*.

3. Diane Hughes, James Rodrigues, Emilie Smith, Deborah Johnson, Howard Stevenson, and Paul Spicer, "Parents' Ethnic-Racial Socialization Practices: A Review of Research and Directions for Future Study," *Developmental Psychology* 42 (2006): 747–70.

4. Lacy, *Blue-Chip Blacks*.

5. The bulk of my research was conducted before the election of Barack Obama, but the research that was conducted after his election makes me confident that black parents did not subscribe to the idea that a postracial United States had arrived with his election. For an in-depth discussion of the meaning of race in the election and post-election, and of questions of racial progress in the United States, see Michael Jeffries, *Paint the White House Black: Barack Obama and the Meaning of Race in America* (Stanford, Calif.: Stanford University Press, 2013); and Imani

Perry, *More Beautiful and More Terrible: The Embrace and Transcendence of Racial Inequality in the United States* (New York: New York University Press, 2011).

6. Waters argues that third- and fourth-generation children of European immigrants employ symbolic ethnicity. These symbolic ethnicities stress Americanness and are employed selectively to convey cultural relevance, which stands in contrast to the racial identities that blacks and other ethnic minorities do not have the option of ignoring. Mary Waters, *Ethnic Options: Choosing Identities in America* (Berkeley: University of California Press, 1990).

7. I intentionally asked about their racial and ethnic identities because it is rare that laypeople understand the distinction between the two. I asked the same question of black and white respondents; whites usually responded by referring to ethnic identity, while blacks responded using a mixture of language about racial and ethnic membership.

8. Michelle Fine, "Witnessing Whiteness/Gathering Intelligence," *Off White: Readings on Power, Privilege and Resistance*, ed. Michelle Fine, Lois Pruitt, and Linda Powell (New York: Routledge, 2004), 245–56; Rothenberg, *White Privilege*; Beverly Tatum, *Why Are All the Black Kids Sitting Together in the Cafeteria? And Other Conversations about Race* (New York: Basic Books, 1997).

9. As an interviewer, the longer I spent with families the more "comfortable" they became. In this case the casual conversation after an interview allowed this father to "open up" about race, but he was chagrined that he had shared this sentiment publicly and requested that his name not be used.

10. David Harris and Jeremiah Sim suggest that racial identification among multiracial populations is often multilayered, with parents choosing racial identifications that do not necessarily match the identification of the children or the other parent. Lewis and Bell argue that multiracial individuals may choose to identify in different ways in different situations. David Harris and Jeremiah Sim, "Who Is Multiracial? Assessing the Complexity of Lived Race," *American Sociological Review* 67 (2002): 614–27; R. L'Heureux Lewis [Lewis-McCoy] and Kanika Bell, "Negotiating Racial Identity in Social Interactions," *Mixed Messages: Multiracial Identities in the "Colorblind" Era*, ed. David Brunsma (Boulder, Colo.: Lynne Rienner, 2006), 249–65.

11. Robert was the exception to this pattern. He was a black-white biracial child but was phenotypically very light skinned with straight blond hair, which he kept in a crew cut. During my time in the field, when adults listed students of color in their classroom, he was not mentioned. Despite being identified as biracial by his mother, he identified as Caucasian. This highlights the complexity of racial identity and membership.

12. While it is not possible to pinpoint the source of the perception of whiteness, there are a number of factors that could have led to this classification. For a more nuanced discussion on the labeling of blacks as white or acting white, see Carter, *Keeping It Real*.

13. Scott Brooks argues that although black men are often portrayed as being naturally drawn to basketball and as natural athletes, this is not the case. Brooks

follows basketball culture in Philadelphia and found that, through sets of complex networks, negotiations, and patronage, pathways to basketball opportunities were maintained or dismantled. Brooks, *Black Men Can't Shoot* (Chicago: University of Chicago Press, 2009).

14. For a further discussion of how race is understood and engaged by contemporary white Americans, see John Jackson, *Racial Paranoia: The Unexpected Consequences of Political Correctness* (New York: Basic Civitas, 2008); Glenn Loury, *The Anatomy of Racial Inequality* (Cambridge, Mass.: Harvard University Press, 2002); and Shelby Steele, *White Guilt: How Blacks and Whites Together Destroyed the Promise of the Civil Rights Era* (New York: HarperCollins, 2006); Shelby Steele, *The Content of Our Character: A New Vision of Race in America* (New York: Harper Perennial, 1991).

15. Bonilla-Silva, *Racism without Racists*; Joe Feagin, *Racist America: Roots, Current Realities and Future Reparations* (New York: Routledge, 2000).

16. Jackson, *Racial Paranoia*.

17. Bonilla-Silva, *Racism without Racists*.

18. Eduardo Bonilla-Silva, *White Supremacy and Racism in the Post–Civil Rights Era* (Boulder, Colo.: Lynne Rienner, 2001); Feagin, *Racist America*.

Chapter 6

1. Ann Swidler, "Culture in Action: Symbols and Strategies," *American Sociological Review* 51 (1986): 272–86.

2. For a discussion of the multiple perspectives on Pygmalion research, see Robert Rosenthal and Lenore Jacobson, *Pygmalion in the Classroom: Teacher Expectations and Pupils' Intellectual Development* (New York: Holt, Rinehart and Winston 1968); and Clark McKown, Anne Gregory, and Rhona Weinstein, "Expectations, Stereotypes, and Self-Fulfilling Prophecies in Classroom and School Life," *Handbook of Research on Schools, Schooling and Human Development*, ed. Judith Meece and Jacquelynne Eccles (New York: Routledge, 2010), 256–74.

3. For more insight into how legal definitions of discrimination have influenced social science and everyday thinking, see Samuel Lucas, *Theorizing Discrimination in an Era of Contested Prejudice: Discrimination in the United States* (Philadelphia: Temple University Press, 2008).

4. Miles Hewstone, Mark Rubin, and Hazel Willis, "Intergroup Bias," *Annual Review of Psychology* 53 (2002): 576.

5. Mary Jackman, *The Velvet Glove: Paternalism and Conflict in Gender, Class, and Race Relations* (Berkeley: University of California Press, 1996).

6. Jackman, *The Velvet Glove*, 10.

7. Lucas, *Theorizing Discrimination*.

8. Ann Ferguson's analysis of school disciplinary practices uncovered some of the mechanisms that contributed to the disproportional punishment that black boys received in a Bay Area California school. Julie Bettie, in a study of young adult

women, found they formed identities that were centered on issues of class and race simultaneously. Ann Ferguson, *Bad Boys: Public School in the Making of Black Masculinity* (Ann Arbor: University of Michigan Press 2000); Julie Bettie, *Women without Class: Girls, Race, and Identity* (Berkeley: University of California Press 2003).

9. Maureen Hallinan, "Sociological Perspectives on Black-White Inequalities in American Schooling," *Sociology of Education* 74 (2001): 56.

10. Gloria Ladson-Billings, "Toward a Theory of Culturally Relevant Pedagogy," *American Education Research Journal* 32 (1995): 465–91; Gloria Ladson-Billings, "But That's Just Good Teaching! The Case for Culturally Relevant Pedagogy," *Theory into Practice* 34 (1995): 159–65.

11. Mica Pollock finds a similar culture of silence around race in a California high school among staff and students. Pollock, *Colormute*.

12. Steele, *White Guilt.*

13. For more on culturally relevant pedagogy and cross-cultural issues within the classroom, see Ladson-Billings, "But That's Just Good Teaching"; Ladson-Billings, "Toward a Theory"; Lisa Delpit, *Other People's Children: Cultural Conflict in the Classroom* (New York: New Press, 1996).

14. For more on disproportionate school discipline, see Russell Skiba, Robert Michael, Abra Carroll Nardo, and Reece Peterson, "The Color of Discipline: Sources of Racial and Gender Disproportionality in School Punishment," *Urban Review* 34 (2002): 317–42.

15. For a more detailed discussion, see Meredith Phillips, "Family Background, Parenting Practices, and the Black-White Test Score Gap," in *The Black-White Test Score Gap*, ed. Christopher Jencks and Meredith Phillips (Washington: Brookings Institution Press, 1998), 103–45.

16. Behavioral issues were more common among boys than girls. Girls did have conflicts, but they seemed to occur more often during recess. Teachers' in-class corrections were frequently directives such as "Girls, stop talking!" Boys' disciplinary issues occurred in and outside of class and typically involved milling around the room, throwing materials such as pencils and books, and occasionally fighting. Teachers met these behaviors with more strict responses.

17. Ronald Ferguson, "Teachers' Perceptions and Expectations on the Black-White Test Score Gap," in *The Black-White Test Score Gap*, ed. Christopher Jencks and Meredith Phillips (Washington: Brookings Institution Press, 1998), 273–317; Rowan Pigott and Emory Cowen, "Teacher Race, Child Race, Racial Congruence, and Teacher Ratings of Children's School Adjustment," *Journal of School Psychology* 38 (2000): 177–95.

18. Ferguson, *Bad Boys.*

19. Anthony Greenwald and Linda Hamilton Krieger, "Implicit Bias: Scientific Foundations," *California Law Review* 94 (2006): 945–67.

20. Lincoln Quillian, "New Approaches to Understanding Racial Prejudice and Discrimination," *Annual Review of Sociology* 32 (2006): 319.

21. Leslie Ashburn-Nardo, Megan Knowles, and Margo Monteith, "Black American's Implicit Racial Associations and Their Implications for Intergroup

Judgment," *Social Cognition* 21 (2003): 61–87; Andrew Baron and Mahzarin Bajani, "The Development of Implicit Attitudes: Evidence of Race Evaluations from Ages 6 and 10 and Adulthood," *Psychological Science* 17 (2006): 53–58.

Chapter 7

1. Seventy-seven percent of the black households in this chapter's sample earned upwards of $125,000 annually, in contrast to 35 percent of the black families in the RAPS sample.

2. Jack and Jill is a social and service group for African-American mothers and their children founded in 1938. Its members are traditionally middle-income black families, and membership is by invitation only. Karyn Lacy, "Black Spaces, Black Places: Strategic Assimilation and Identity Construction in Middle-Class Suburbia," *Ethnic and Racial Studies* 27 (2004): 908–30.

3. Amy Orr and Dalton Conley find that wealth, though less commonly measured than income, can be better at predicting differences in student achievement and a host of social outcomes. Amy Orr, "Black-White Differences in Achievement: The Importance of Wealth," *Sociology of Education* 76 (2003): 281–304; Dalton Conley, *Being Black, Living in the Red: Race, Wealth and Social Policy in America* (Berkeley: University of California Press 1999).

4. It is important to note that public knowledge was not even or necessarily accurate. Often when I queried informants on the date of newspaper articles, facts, or more specific dimensions of these public artifacts, they struggled to provide accurate details.

5. For more discussion of the multiple functions of the Black Church beyond religious indoctrination, see Eric Lincoln and Lawrence Mamiya, *The Black Church in the African-American Experience* (Durham, N.C.: Duke University Press, 2003).

6. Diane Ravitch, *The Death and Life of the Great American School System: How Testing and Choice Are Undermining Education* (New York: Basic Books, 2011).

7. I interviewed several families who sent their children to religious schools. Among those schools there was no requirement to be a member of the sponsoring congregation or to profess agreement with the school's faith. However, the schools did offer church services and religion classes.

8. Like many charter schools that use a lottery system, certain community members, such as siblings, were given preference for enrollment in a school.

9. Richard Majors and Janet Billson, *Cool Pose: The Dilemmas of Black Manhood in America* (New York: Lexington Books, 1992), 4.

10. While hip-hop culture was commonly read by adults as oppositional to ideals of mobility and often detrimental to black masculinity, this view is a short-sighted and reductionist view of hip-hop, which has rich and diverse origins. Imani Perry and Michael Jeffries offer complex considerations of the cultural terrain of hip-hop culture, particularly as it relates to mobility, masculinity, race, and

opportunity. See Imani Perry, *Prophets of the Hood: Politics and Poetics in Hip Hop* (Durham, N.C.: Duke University Press, 2004); Michael Jeffries, *Thug Life: Race, Gender and the Meaning of Hip-Hop* (Chicago: University of Chicago, 2011).

11. In particular, hip-hop was read as anti-intellectual, which has become a popular trope among authors across the political spectrum. See Thomas Chatterton Williams, *Losing My Cool: How a Father's Love and 15,000 Books Beat Hip-hop Culture* (New York: Penguin, 2010); and John McWhorter, "All about the Beat: Why Hip-Hop Can't Save Black America (New York: Gotham Books, 2008). However, there is a emergent field of hip-hop education studies that suggests hip-hop can play an active role in educational engagement across the subject matter spectrum; see Marc Lamont Hill and Emery Petchauer, eds., *Schooling Hip-Hop: Expanding Hip-Hop Based Education across the Curriculum* (New York: Teachers College Press, 2013).

12. Respectability has long been a strategic emphasis among African-Americans seeking social acceptance and/or integration. Higginbotham offers a detailed discussion of the relationship among respectability, race, gender, and civil rights. Evelyn Brooks Higginbotham, *Righteous Discontent: The Women's Movement in the Black Baptist Church, 1880–1920* (Cambridge, Mass.: Harvard University Press, 1993).

13. Lacy argues that black middle-class families did not simply code-switch; instead they script-switched to negotiate racially hostile environments, which served to signify their class statuses and make their social passage easier. Lacy, *Blue-Chip Blacks*.

14. The suggestion that hip-hop contributes to anti-intellectualism has been proffered by several scholars; see Ronald Ferguson, "Test-Score Trends along Racial Lines, 1971 to 1996: Popular Culture and Community Academic Standards," in *America Becoming: Racial Trends and Their Consequences*, ed. Neil Smelser, William J. Wilson, and Faith Mitchell (Washington: National Academy Press, 2001), 348–90; John McWhorter, *Losing the Race: Self-Sabotage in America* (New York: Free Press, 2000); and Orlando Patterson, "A Poverty of the Mind," *New York Times*, March 26, 2006. For a more nuanced exploration of the role of culture on academic engagement, including hip-hop culture, see Prudence Carter, *Keepin' It Real*; Marc Lamont Hill, *Beats, Rhymes, and Classroom Life: Hip-Hop Pedagogy and the Politics of Identity* (New York: Teachers College Press, 2009).

15. National Research Council, ed., *Minority Students in Gifted and Special Education* (Washington: National Academy Press, 2001).

16. For years, Rolling Acres had black parent advocacy groups at the middle-school level, which were designed to make sure the needs of black families were advocated for school-wide. However, during my time in the field they were largely dormant. There were multiple reasons for this, according to residents. The advocacy group meetings were attended mainly by middle-income blacks. This is consistent with evidence presented in chapter 2 and this chapter on the class divides in the RAPS schools. The advocacy groups were organized by volunteers, and if no one stepped up to call meetings, there were no meetings held. Although white

families often utilized ad hoc advocacy groups, they did so most often in response to a perceived threat. While black families found education unequal in Rolling Acres, they felt little sense of either urgency or hope about rectifying educational inequality.

Chapter 8

1. Frederick Hess, "Our Achievement-Gap Mania," *National Affairs* 9 (2011), 113–39.

2. Tilly, *Changing Forms of Inequality*, 34.

3. In Appendix B, I provide a list of ten questions that education advocates should ask of their schools and districts.

4. For more on trust, see James Comer, Norris Haynes, Edward Joyner, and Michael Ben-Avie, *Rallying the Whole Village* (New York: Teachers College Press, 1996); and Anthony Bryk and Barbara Schneider, *Trust in Schools: A Core Resource for Improvement* (New York: Russell Sage Foundation, 2002).

5. "Improving Media Coverage and Public Perceptions of African-American Men and Boys," The Opportunity Agenda, September 20, 2013 (http://opportunityagenda.org/files/field_file/Black_Male_Messaging_0.pdf).

6. David Louis Schoem and Sylvia Hurtado, *Intergroup Dialogue: Deliberative Democracy in School, College, Community, and Workplace*. Ann Arbor: University of Michigan Press, 2001), 5.

7. Du Bois, *Souls of Black Folk*, 5.

Appendix A

1. Free and reduced lunch is a very crude indicator, but it was useful for understanding the overall poverty distribution among RAPS.

2. Because each school and teacher could opt in or out, it is not possible to be completely unbiased; however, my goal was to minimize the influence of this bias. Within classrooms I had the same dilemma, but a naturally occurring sample ultimately consists of those who desire to participate more than others. Throughout my time in the field, my goal was to hear as many different voices as possible, particularly the voices and experiences of racial and economic minorities.

3. Bronfenbrenner proposed a model of development that is ecologically based and stresses the importance of individuals nested within groups and institutions. Uri Bronfenbrenner, *The Ecology of Human Development: Experiments by Nature and Design* (Cambridge, Mass.: Harvard University Press, 1979).

4. This cutoff was chosen because in 2007 the poverty line for a family of four was $20,650. In collecting income information, I requested categorical, not continuous answers. As a result, $40,000 is the closest cutoff to the doubling of the poverty line.

5. For more on the system of student–teacher interaction that was used in the classroom observations, see Thomas Good and Jere Brophy, "Teacher-Child Dyadic Interactions: A New Method of Classroom Observation," *Journal of School Psychology* 8 (1970): 131–38.

6. I was not able to complete observations in Ms. Jackson's Language Arts classroom. Partway through my observation period she informed me that she felt her students were falling behind in other subjects and that she would be instructing in Language Arts only intermittently. In addition, the Language Arts classes would be offered at a different time, but only as she deemed necessary. With limited time and the need to observe my other two classrooms, I opted to concentrate on them.

7. Of the ten families interviewed, only one would have fallen into the working-class or black-middle-class core group.

Appendix B

1. A previous version of this appendix was prepared as a handout for the Centennial Convention of the National Association for the Advancement of Colored People (NAACP) in 2009.

Index

CPSIA information can be obtained
at www.ICGtesting.com
Printed in the USA
LVOW12s1829110118
562712LV00005B/973/P